An introduction to

the religion

of the Limba

# of Sierra Leone

With Love to Ian Crossland

7 November, 2007

Prince Sorie Conteh

An introduction to

the religion

of the Limba

# of Sierra Leone

University of South Africa
Pretoria

© 2007 University of South Africa
First edition, first impression

**ISBN 978186 888432-2**

Published by Unisa Press
University of South Africa
P O Box 392, 0003 UNISA

Editor: Gail Malcolmson
Cover and layout design: Elsabé Viljoen
Electronic origination: Compleat
Printed by Jakaranda Printers, Pretoria

*I dedicate this work in gratitude to:*

*The Late Madam Yealie Koroma – my aunt*

*and to all the Limba people of Sierra Leone,*

*especially the clergy, elders, and members of*

*the National Pentecostal Limba Church*

*who have always supported me*

*in all my endeavours*

# Contents

# Foreword

The title of the book, *An introduction to the religion of the Limba of Sierra Leone*, states explicitly the aim of the book and whets the reader's appetite regarding what Dr Conteh has described as 'An introductory systematic study of the fundamental tenets of Limba indigenous religion'.

Of all the existing literature on the Limbas of Sierra Leone, this study is the first that will provide readers, especially non-Limbas, with the knowledge that is lacking about the religion of this ethnic group.

This work is of fundamental importance and gives credit to the writer for undertaking such an insightful work. In a country of over 15 ethnic groups, only a few groups have received adequate scholarly attention. The author has no doubt opened the way for studies to be undertaken by other Sierra Leonean scholars in the religion of their own ethnic groups.

This study will prove authentic and authoritative as Dr Conteh is writing about the group of people into which he was born, with whom he lived, and whose religious beliefs he experienced. The writing therefore reveals his passion and love for that which he knows and is a part of him.

*An introduction to the religion of the Limba of Sierra Leone* is written in simple language for all to understand. It is written with the authority that only a Limba theologian can command, yet the knowledge is passed on effortlessly to readers. By the end of the book much has been taught about the religion of these people and especially about 'Kanu Masala', their supreme God, and his role among the people.

Dr Conteh is a true Limba and a lover of God. Little wonder then that he undertook this study. May we be able to see the work of God in our lives as we read about Kanu and his work among his people.

Rev. Olivia A. Wesley, Principal

Sierra Leone Theological College and Church Training Centre

Freetown, Sierra Leone

# Acknowledgements

There are many people whose help and support were vital in writing this book. I would like to recognise them and I hope I do not forget anyone. I am grateful to the members of the United Church of Canada Tamarack Presbytery and the Saskatchewan United Church Women for their financial support which made my fieldwork in Sierra Leone possible.

My thanks go to the boards and members of the Bridging Waters Pastoral Charges for their financial support of part of my fieldwork and local research, and for supporting me in pursuing my studies while ministering with them.

I am indebted to Prof. Tinyiko Maluleke for his academic guidance and for inspiring me to work hard. My thanks go to Prof. Simon Ottenberg and Prof. Ruth Finnegan for offering advice and materials on Limba research.

Thanks to all the incredible people I interviewed and consulted: Kabba Bangura, co-author: Limba Textbook and Reader for Secondary Schools, series 1—3, member: Limba Literacy Committee (LLC), Freetown; Rev. Dantheke Kanu, Pastor: National Pentecostal Limba Church (NPLC); Translator: LLC; Rev. David B. Kallon, Pastor: NPLC; Supervisor: LLC; Momodu Kamara; Pa Dauda Kamara, Diviner/Herbalist; Rev. MacFoday Kamara, co-author: Source Book for Sierra Leonean Languages, Freetown; Hamusa Kargbo, Member: LLC; Madam Kumba Koroma; Rev. Samuel G. Koroma, Pastor: NPLC; Rev. T. A. Koroma, General Superintendent: NPLC; Alimamy Mansaray; Hamidu Mansaray, Seattle, Washington: Former Research Assistant to Prof. Simon Ottenberg; Paul Mansaray; Santigie Nyankuthɛbɛ, Diviner/Herbalist; Rev. S. S. Pahlor, Pastor: NPLC; Alie M. Sesay, Member: LLC; Pa Alimamy Sesay, Section Chief: Freetown West; Santigie Sesay, student: Limba Studies; Alex Turay, co-author: Limba Textbook and Reader for Secondary Schools, series 1—3; Sinneh Thoronka; Officials of The Ministry of Local Government and Community Development, Freetown, Sierra Leone.

Thank you to 'Aunties' Esther Epp, Joan Jamieson, and Marilyn Ens for their personal attention and encouragement, and Rev. Heather Anderson, 'Aunty' Diane Berg, and Richard Manley-Tannis for their interest and morale support.

I am very grateful to my wife, Peggy Conteh Wallace for sparing me many hours at my computer and for giving me feedback on each draft of the manuscript. Last but not least, my thanks go to the officers and members of my present congregation, Carleton United Church, for their valuable support.

Portions of this work are derived from my doctoral thesis, 'Fundamental Concepts of Limba Traditional Religion and its Effects on Limba Christianity and Vice Versa in Sierra Leone in the Past Three Decades' (D.Th. thesis, University of South Africa, 2004). Details of the 2002 fieldwork are contained in this thesis.

# Introduction

This book is a study of an African indigenous religion. Its subject is the Limba people of Sierra Leone, who account for approximately 500 000 people, making them the third largest ethnic group in the country, smaller than the Mende and the Temne.[1] It seeks to provide for the first time a broader understanding of the fundamental concepts of Limba indigenous religion (LIR) for students, teachers, religious leaders, and those interested in the culture and religious landscape of Africa, particularly Sierra Leone. It is hoped that this work will significantly contribute to the field of African religious studies, concerning Limba religious beliefs, practices and teachings, and will foster further research on Limba socio-religious culture.

Like most ethnic groups in Sierra Leone, the indigenous religion of the Limba people is African Traditional Religion (ATR). In that regard, it could be said that LIR, like most African religions, emanated from the 'sustaining faith held by the forebears of the present generation'[2] and is 'being practised today in various forms and intensities'[3] in the Limba homeland and settlements. Although it is not prominent as before, LIR continues to play a vital role in influencing and shaping the Limba people and societies. Yet, like other African religious systems, it 'continues to suffer from lack of acceptance and inadequate understanding of its central tenets and essence'[4] in the hands of non-practitioners. Among the ethnic groups of Sierra Leone, the Limba are viewed as more involved in traditional religious practices 'than any other ethnic group in the country'.[5]

While the religious beliefs of certain Sierra Leonean ethnic groups[6] and many other African groups[7] have received significant amounts of attention from anthropologists, ethnologists and theologians, no one has written much about LIR.[8]

This book then, is a product of library and field research. In order to update the very few extant publications and provide a comprehensive study of LIR, fieldwork was required to interview and experience contemporary Limba religio-cultural practice; this was carried out in Sierra Leone in 2002 just after the civil war, and later in 2005. In both instances my pool of interviewees was selected from among members of the five main Limba dialects: Biriwa, Safuroko, Sela, Thonko and Warawara. They came from different generations, and walks of life. All the Limba words used are the generally accepted words used by all the five Limba dialects. Where there is more than one accepted word, all accepted terms appear, separated by forward slashes.

This book will take the following form. Chapter 1 outlines the socio-history and is followed by Chapter 2, 'Influences on Limba culture and Limba indigenous religion', which looks at the external and internal effects on the Limba. Chapter 3, 'Components of Limba indigenous religion', provides elements from which the framework for chapters 4 through 11 is built. Chapter 4, entitled 'The Supreme Being' focuses on Limba belief in, teachings about and worship of God. Chapter 5, 'Angels' provides an understanding of the position, nature and role of angels. In Chapter 6, 'Ancestral spirits/ancestors', the position, role and veneration of the ancestors is discussed. Chapter 7, 'Non-ancestral spirits' describes the categories of spirits, their roles and how they are venerated. Chapter 8 presents Limba beliefs about 'Humankind'. It discusses humankind's origins, relationship with the supernatural and the universe. Chapter 9, 'Lifecycle' discusses how religion permeates the lifecycle of the Limba and Chapter 10 addresses 'Sin and salvation'. It focuses on the different categories of sins and crimes, their consequences, the procedures for forgiveness and absolution, the importance of salvation and the attainment of salvation. Chapter 11, 'Sacred specialists' presents the different categories of these human intermediaries, and describes their roles. The book concludes with Chapter 12, 'Concluding remarks' which provides a recapitulation of the contents, and concludes with a few recommendations for a positive dialogue and understanding among traditionalists, Limba Christians, and the church.

# 1

## Socio-history of the Limba

### Introduction

Compared to other major ethnic groups in Sierra Leone,[1] very little has yet been written about Limba history and culture. Ruth Finnegan[2] has attributed the cause of this problem to the spite shown by other ethnic groups towards the Limba which resulted in lessened interest in the Limba from European writers and researchers. While this spite may have been a valid reason for the paucity of Limba research forty years ago, it does not explain the continued lack of research since the disappearance of this stigma brought on by Limba ethnopoliticisation.[3]

There are, of course certain exceptions. Finnegan has written extensively on Limba socio-culture.[4] Simon Ottenberg has written several works on the Bafodea Warawara Limba people.[5] Richard Fanthorpe,[6] W. A. Hart,[7] Magbaily Fyle,[8] Joe Alie,[9] M. McCulloch,[10] and Christopher Fyfe,[11] have all written about the Limba. However, there is still much of their cultural life which is unexamined and/or unpublished. This study makes use of all these available works and provides a broader picture of LIR.

In what follows, I will provide a general overview of the Limba within the Sierra Leonean context and discuss historically their origin, traditional homeland and outside settlements, language, political and administrative structures, economy, and other social and cultural characteristics.

### Sierra Leone and the Limba

The Limba are one of 17 ethnic groups[12] within Sierra Leone. The country is located in West Africa; and is bounded on the Northwest and the Northeast by the republic of Guinea, on the South by Liberia, and on the West and Southwest by the Atlantic Ocean (see figure 1 below for a map of Sierra Leone in its setting in West Africa). Sierra Leone occupies a total area 27 925 square miles (73 326 km)[13] and is fairly circular in shape: the distance from north to south is 210 miles (332 km), and from west to east is approximately 204 miles (328 km).[14]

There are two main seasons in the country, the Wet, from May to early November, and the Dry from mid November to April. Sierra Leone became an independent state within the British Commonwealth on 27 April 1961, and subsequently attained republican status on 19 April 1971. The capital city is Freetown and there are four administrative divisions: the Eastern, Northern, and Southern Provinces, and the Western Area. As a former British colony, Sierra Leone retains English as the official language, although it is used primarily by the literate minority, while Krio is the lingua franca. According to figures from the Central Statistics Office, the estimated population of Sierra Leone as of July 2005 is 6 017 643.

## Origin of the Limba

After several decades of research, the issue of the Limba's origin and traditional immigration into Sierra Leone is still a mystery.[15] Although other peoples of Sierra Leone have traditions about their origins,[16] the Limba have no such tradition. While there are some traditions pertaining to the origins of specific ruling families, these usually only go back four or five generations.[17] Due to the lack of evidence from the Limba's own tradition, scholars have attempted to construct an early history out of the few extant stories about the Limba found in the traditions of other tribes. However, even these attempts have been largely unsuccessful, as they are admittedly conjectural and based on very little evidence. The earliest verifiable account of the Limba in their current position is on the map of a sixteenth century navigator.[18] However, little else is known about Limba history until the nineteenth century.

Tracing the earliest societies in Sierra Leone, Cecil Fyle[19] offers proof that the Limba may have been the first group in the Sierra Leone hinterland. He states that some stone tools believed to have been left by the Limba and dating to the eighth century were found in Warawara Limba country near Kekoia in the Northern Province.[20] Thus, while it is not currently possible to determine an exact date for the Limba migration to Sierra Leone, it is known that they have been in their current location since at least the sixteenth century and may have been there as early as the eighth century CE.

## Traditional homeland and outside settlements

Although, for economic and social reasons,[21] pocket settlements of Limba can today be found throughout the country, the historical homeland of the Limba is in the Northern Province of Sierra Leone. According to the Ministry of Local Government and Community Development (MLGCD), Limba settlements in their homeland are now found in 5 districts[22] namely: Bombali, Kambia, Koinadugu, Tonkolili and Port Loko. The Limba share common borders with the Soso on the northwest, the Yalunka and Fula on the northeast, the Kuranko on the east, the Loko on the southwest, and the Temne on the south and southwest.[23] Limba country extends over about 2 000 square miles (5 180 km), which begins east of Tonkolili extending to the Guinea borders north of Bafodea, and in the extreme southwest reaches a point just north of Kambia (see figure 2 on p.17 for a map of Limba current traditional homeland in Sierra Leone).[24]

The Limba homeland comprises mainly savannah, with occasional areas of farm bush and grass. Two large rivers, the Little Scarcies and the Rokel, bound it on the north. Small rivers and streams flow through the area. In the northern and eastern areas there are hills between 300 and 2 000 ft (100 and 667 m) high, 'interspersed with low plateaus of savannah and grass land, with some inland swamps. With the exception of the flood plains along the Little Scarcies in Thonko Limba in the west, most of Limba country is over 400 ft (133 m) above sea level'.[25]

Outside the Limba homeland, the second largest population of Limbas is found in the Western Area (this is the area that includes Freetown). There most Limba settlements are found in mountainous areas, for example: Dwarzak Farm, Tengbeh Town, Malamah/Kaniko, Red Pump, Sorie Town, Sumaila Town, Kuntolo, Malimba Town, and on the shores of Congo Town, Ascension Town, and Kingtom. An interviewee told me that the Limba in Freetown deliberately settle in mountainous areas because it reminds them of home. These isolated and bushy areas bring a sense of belonging because the Limba do not like to mingle with other groups. One suggested reason for the Limba preference for keeping to themselves is that they do not wish to upset others with the offensive smell of *poyo*.[26]

Like other ethnic groups in the hinterland, migration by Limba people to Freetown in the past three decades can be attributed to economic, political, educational, social, and religious factors. The largest migration was necessitated by the rebel incursion into Sierra Leone, via the hinterland in 1991. Thousands of people were forced to flee from their homeland to Freetown, which was presumed heavily protected by military personnel and civil defence units.

## Language and nomenclature

The Limba speak a 'prefix language',[27] which is classified as part of the West Atlantic family of languages.[28] The generally accepted term *Limba* comes from the root 'Limba', which may refer to anything about the ethnic group depending on the prefix added to it.[29] The Limba language contains five regional dialects.[30] Biriwa Limba is spoken mainly in the Biriwa and Kasonko chiefdoms in the districts of Bombali and Koinadugu. Safuroko Limba is the dialect of the Safuroko and Paki Massabong chiefdoms of the Bombali District, and the Kafe Simiria and Kalansonkoya chiefdoms of the Tonkolili District. In the Sela chiefdom of the Bombali District, the dialect is Sela Limba. Thonko Limba is spoken in the Kambia District and in the Sanda Magboloton chiefdom of Port Loko District. Finally, in the Koinadugu district, in the chiefdoms of Bafodea and Yagala, Warawara Limba is spoken. Because many Limba from all over have migrated to the Western Area, all of the Limba dialects are found there. All five Limba dialects are very similar with only slight differences between them.[31] Social conventions often have religious significance. For this reason, some of the topics in the following segments will be discussed again under Chapter 9 'Lifecycle'.

## Ethnic politics and administrative structures

Limba country is divided into 11 chiefdoms:[32] Biriwa, Safuroko, Sela, Thonko, Kasonko, Warawara Bafodea, Warawara Yagala, Kafe Simira, Kalansonkoya, Paki Massabong and Sanda Magboloton. Although ethnic divisions existed in Limba country before colonisation, the current borders are a British invention intended to harness local politics to colonial rule and facilitate tax collection[33] through a clear re-definition of ethnic borders, which codified chiefdoms with well-defined ethnic boundaries.[34]

Since 1946, each Limba chiefdom has been ruled by a Chiefdom Council, a system inherited from the 1937 British 'Native Administration' scheme.[35] This administrative structure was an attempt by the British to modify and transfer the considerable economic and judicial powers that were vested in the Paramount Chief to a Tribal Authority,[36] which was later renamed the Chiefdom Council.[37] This body is charged with responsibility for the welfare and oversight of the chiefdom.[38]

The first in the chain of command in the Chiefdom Council system of an independent Limba chiefdom, is the Paramount Chief (*Bathanpi*),[39] whose position is mostly supervisory, as the head of his people. In this regard he should be informed of occurrences and developments in his chiefdom or jurisdiction as the case may be.[40] His approval and blessing must be sought before certain things may happen. In Limba practice, the role of a Paramount Chief or Head Chief is reserved exclusively for men. However, in the 1970s, government sanction reinforced the participation of women in ethnic politics[41] and today in most Limba chiefdoms and settlements there is a female chief called 'Ya Almamy' who works under a male counterpart called 'Pa Almamy'. 'Almamy' is an Islamic term meaning 'headman'.[42] The Ya Almamy is responsible for settling certain disputes among females and arranging for the feeding of visitors as well as certain other duties.[43] Before the government sanction, the chief's head wife carried out these duties. Unfortunately, the Ya Almamies are still not as powerful as the male leaders.

A government provision, made in the mid 1950s and still effective to date, dictates that 12 Paramount Chiefs, each representing one of the 12 districts in Sierra Leone, are elected on a non-partisan basis through an electoral college, comprising Councillors and other Paramount Chiefs, to sit in parliament.[44] This system enables the representation and participation of ethnic groups in national policy making. The downside of this system is that it takes away the relationship and bond between the elected parliamentary Paramount Chiefs and their people, because they are required to leave their respective chiefdoms and stay in Freetown during parliamentary sessions.

The list of Limba Paramount Chiefs in Sierra Leone in 2005 is:

| Paramount | Chiefdom/ Jurisdiction | Chiefdom/ Jurisdiction Headquarters | District/ Area |
|-----------|------------------------|-------------------------------------|----------------|
| Alimamy Kawala II | Biriwa | Kamabai | Bombali |
| Alimamy Dura II | Safuroko | Binkolo | Bombali |
| Kandeh Luseni II | Sela | Kamakwie | Bombali |
| Amadu Augustine Conteh | Paki Massabong | Mapaki | Bombali |
| Alfred Momoh Bangura | Thonko | Madina | Kambia |
| Alimamy Hamidu I | Warawara Bafodea | Bafodea | Koinadugu |
| Alimamy Y. Mansaray III | Warawara Yagala | Gbawuria | Koinadugu |
| Alfred B. S. Kamara | Kasunko | Fadugu | Koinadugu |
| Brima Sanda Sori | Sanda Mabolontor | Sendugu | Port Loko |
| Alimamy Bangura | Kafe Simiria | Mabonto | Tonkolili |
| Bockarie Koroma | Kalansongoia | Bumbuna | Tonkolili |

Second in the administrative line-up is the Chiefdom Speaker (*Bagboŋkoli wo*). As the name implies, he acts as spokesman both to and on behalf of the chiefdom and is the Paramount Chief's confidant. Because the Paramount Chief is no longer required to participate in the judicial system, the Chiefdom Speaker represents him at court sittings and later reports to him.

Next in line is the Court Chairman (*Bagbʲdʲ wo*) who is a government employee and the official representative at chiefdom level, and presides over chiefdom court proceedings. With the assistance of other appointed court officials (*kʲt mɛmbɛŋ*), the Court Chairman presides over several kinds of cases including, land disputes, theft, witchcraft, adultery, some divorce cases, loans of money or other goods and treachery. These matters are judged according to chiefdom bylaws and customary laws.[45] A person who has a complaint or wants a redress takes the matter to the chiefdom court clerk and pays the required fees. A court summons is then sent to the defendant stating the complaint and the scheduled date for the court hearing.

Then comes the Court Clerk (*Bagbali wo*) also a government employee, who records proceedings and performs all court clerical and secretarial duties. Each chiefdom also has a chiefdom police force to keep the peace and enforce the law.[46]

The British further divided the chiefdoms into section towns and villages.[47] The section towns are ruled by Section Chiefs (*Bathagba ben*) and the villages by Village Headmen (*Bamɛthiŋ/ Bayahɛŋ*).[48] The positions of Section and Village Chiefs are analogous to that of the Paramount Chief. Unlike the Paramount Chief, however, the Section and Village Chiefs still preside over cases similar to those handled by the chiefdom courts. At village level, the complainant goes to the village headman with a small token gift to open a case. After questioning by the headman, a writ of summon stating the complaint and the date for the hearing is then sent through a court messenger to the other party.

At chiefdom/section and village levels, in most cases the guilty party pays a very heavy fine and in some instances restitution is required (e.g., theft, destruction of farm and cattle). Most often, a person convicted of witchcraft is flogged publicly, and banished.[49] The Paramount Chief, Chiefdom Speaker, Section and Village Chiefs form the Chiefdom Council and are responsible for electing chiefdom leaders.[50]

In the Western Area, where there is no chiefdom policy, all of the ethnic groups settled there are ruled by the Tribal Administration Act which was legislated in 1905.[51] The equivalent of a Limba Paramount Chief in Freetown is the Limba Tribal Headman. B. S. Bangura is the current Limba Tribal Headman for the Western Area. His administrative headquarters are in Wellington, Freetown. Tribal Headmen for the individual hinterland ethnic groups living in Freetown first appeared in the late nineteenth century. These government officials functioned in an unofficial capacity until they were given legal recognition in 1905.[52] As an elected official, the Limba Tribal Headman, like any other Tribal Headman, is the official liaison between the provincial chiefs and their people in Freetown and often provides direct assistance to the central government. He provides the initiative for many of the ethnic group's activities and provides a bridge for the newcomer in Freetown to his former life the Provinces.[53] At the Tribal Headman's administrative headquarters, the arrival is assisted by the Court Chairman, who with the assistance of Court Elders (a group made up of between five and seven members), presides over cases in the central court. The court handles most socially-based cases as well as certain criminal cases.[54] Non-literate Limba in the Western Area take their cases to either the Tribal Head's Court in Freetown, or the closest local Limba head. Most literate Limba likewise, often begin with the tribal heads, but sometimes prefer the Westernised legal system. The Court Clerk's job is analogous to that of his chiefdom counterpart. Apart from the aforementioned officials who work in his administrative headquarters, Section/Area Chiefs called Pa Almamy, and sub chiefs called Pa Alikali also assist the Tribal Headman.[55] The Section Chiefs and sub-chiefs fill a socio-political role which is part chief, part judge.[56]

## Economy

### Agriculture

Historically, the Limba have primarily been subsistence farmers.[57] Agriculture is the backbone of their economy with rice (*pakala*) as their main crop.[58] Finnegan states that, 'the growing and eating of rice is, in Limba eyes, one of the main characteristics which differentiate them from the other peoples with whom they have come into contact'.[59] This perception cannot be accurate, because neither the growing nor the eating of rice has ever been unique to Limba. Rice is the staple food of Sierra Leone and all ethnic groups in the country grow it.[60]

The Limba practise two systems of growing rice: the more popular upland farming and the less popular swampland farming. For many, the farming season starts in March with brushing (*mahi*) of the bush.[61] Brushing is the cutting and clearing of smaller trees, undergrowth, shrubs and branches from the spot where the farm is to be made.[62] The felled trees, branches and shrubs are then piled up into a big heap and burnt.

Because the brushing is very hard and time consuming work, and is difficult for any given family to complete alone, a group of hard working men known as Kunɛko[63] will come and help in exchange for food and drink. This group is made up of young men from local households. Any household that does not have a member in the group pays to compensate the group for the day they worked. *Kunɛko* is divided into several units, each of which is responsible for one stage of farming. *Kunɛko katha mahaɛŋ* does the brushing. *Kunɛko katha kariya* clears and burns the material that has been brushed out. Hoeing and sowing is the responsibility of *Kunɛko katha yɈla*. *Kunɛko katha puruna* works at weeding time and *Kunɛko katha ŋɈna* brings in the harvest.

As *Kunɛko* and other helpers brush the bush, they are entertained with music, drumming and singing. In some areas, these entertainers are referred to as the *Kalla Band*. In other areas they are called *Bira*. The older men in the *Kalla Band* are called *ŋkali* and the younger men and boys are called *kɈthɈbede*. These two groups are each identifiable by their distinct attire. The music is meant to keep the workers from getting tired until the end of the day.

Rice is sown in May and June just as the rains begin. This is followed by the making of fences (*kuŋku ba/kufiya*) to prevent animals such as grass cutters (*Sumbuŋ*) and other rice-eating animals from destroying the rice when it grows. Usually, each family/household fences their own farm without the help of *Kunɛko*, although some families employ people to help them. Fencing is usually followed by the weeding (*hu puruna haŋ*) of grass with the help of *Kunɛko katha puruna*, assisted by a group of women called *Ba gheŋdeŋ/Ba fani gheŋdeŋ* who weed with small hoes.

Children play an important role in the stage that follows: the scaring/driving away of birds (*hu pama haŋ*). To many Limba, this is the most important part of the farming process. If the birds are not driven away they will eat the rice, and there will be hardly a grain of rice left to harvest. This task is not exclusively reserved for children. Wives as well as any young men or women in the household and under the care of the husband or head of the house also participate. A farm hut (*Ku wera*) about 10 ft (3,3 m) high with a podium is erected for the bird scarers to stand on as they work. The height of this structure gives the worker an advantage in seeing the destructive birds. Slings (*Lathi/Lathu*) are used to throw objects at the birds and scare them away. At harvest, the *Kunɛko* unit called *Kunɛko katha ŋɈna* will come to work and musicians will also be around to entertain them. Millet, groundnuts (peanuts), cassava, sweet potatoes, and some maize are also grown as secondary crops for food and cash along with various garden crops such as onions and fruits. Rice is also grown on a very small scale on the outskirts of Freetown.

Palm trees (*hɔtala*) grow wild all over Limba country. Red palm oil is made from fruit for cooking, and palm wine (*poyo*) is extracted from the trunk for drinking. The Limba are known all over the country for the fondness for palm wine and their skill in tapping it. At home and away the Limba are sought after as professional palm wine tappers.[64] Palm tree products are also sold for cash, including wood, fibre, broom, and material for making shoes, soap, rope, and leaves for roofing huts. Chiefs and affluent people often have a few cattle. Some sheep, goats and poultry can be found in all villages.

## Micro-business

Craftspeople also contribute greatly to the economy providing the livelihood of some families.[65] Blacksmiths provide and repair most of the important farming implements, such as hoes, axes and cutlasses, as well as various kinds of knives for harvesting and cooking, and guns for hunting. Sculptors make wood carvings and iron sculptures.[66] Leather workers cure and dye skins and use them to make various items. Native cloth (*lankɔnɔ*) making is also popular. Small-scale fishing, hunting and trapping are also common in Limba country, and in the Western Area.

All of the above generate income for individual Limba families as the products are marketed and exchanged at village, town and chiefdom levels. These products are also found in many ethnic communities in the country and are vital to providing their socio-economic needs.[67]

Although community self-help (*mamasiteke*) development projects are carried out through communal labour, the village or chiefdom generates funds through fines and taxes. All adult males in the hinterland are expected to pay an annual local tax at the beginning of every year. In Freetown and urban areas, men and women alike, who receive a salary, pay income tax. Most non-literate Limba men, in Freetown work as house servants, office messengers or sanitation officers, while a few have tailoring or carpentry shops or their own businesses. Women engage in small-scale businesses usually termed as 'petty trading'. Literate men and women work in offices and national establishments.

In the hinterland, some people who do not have families and who due to circumstances beyond their control cannot fend for themselves, are looked after by the chief.[68] In the Western Area relatives and friends help with financial and material contributions.

# Other socio-cultural characteristics
## Household and gender roles

The basic social unit of the Limba is the household (*baŋka*) or family (*Kub]ri*).[69] This unit, as in other ethnic groups of Sierra Leone, comprises a husband, a wife or wives, their children, 'and frequently also blood and affinal relatives – for example, junior brothers and their wives, and unmarried sisters – as well as dependants …'[70]

The household is usually under the charge of the husband or a responsible adult male. Two decades ago the husband, as head of the home, was considered to be the sole breadwinner and everyone in the home depended on him to provide for their needs. In the hinterland, it was in turn, the assumed responsibility of the wife/wives to help on the farm, prepare meals, nurse infants, nurture and instruct the children in the norms of the society.[71] In the absence of capable grownup children, the chores, such as cleaning, gathering firewood, and doing laundry, fall on the wife or if there is more than one wife in the home, on the junior wives. In the Western Area, the wife/wives assume similar responsibilities (with the exception of working on the farm) and women who work outside of the home take maternity leave in order to raise their children.

Today, as a result of social and economic changes, some gender roles have been altered. As well as general living expenses, families now have to pay head and income taxes, and children who show academic promise have to be sent to college or university after secondary school. As these expenses have increased, in many cases, a single salary and/or produce from the farm is often not enough to meet the financial demands of the household. In the hinterland, most married women are involved in petty trading to supplement their husbands' farming income. In the urban areas, non-educated women are also engaged in petty trading while educated women either take jobs in offices or begin their own businesses. Thus, bread-winning has become a responsibility shared between husband and wife, often with the wife managing the finances of the home.

Although bread-winning is now a task shared between husband and wife, traditionally the husband is still seen as the provider. Even if the wife's income is greater than that of the husband, it is still seen as the responsibility of the husband to provide for the family's necessities. For this reason, if the husband requires his wife's assistance in providing for the family, he should be very kind and polite to her, because if the family is not provided for, society will hold only the husband accountable for his failure to provide, regardless of his wife's financial status. This change in gender roles has positively affected the lives of many Limba women and has made a significant impact on the status of women within Limba society. Some women have taken over as much as seventy per cent of the household responsibilities and this has earned them immense respect and appreciation from their families and society.

## The compound and beyond

Family relations are traced through both clanship (*humpo/mpo*) and kinship (*nthela*). 'Kinship differs from clanship in that if people are kin the exact genealogical links between them are actually or potentially known, whereas the relationship between clan co-members is not known in this way even though they are loosely spoken of as all being "brothers"'.[72]

Kinship is primarily traced through the mother and father and is identifiable by household, compound and village. Clanship, on the other hand, is a more ethereal relationship that indicates a common ancestry. Currently there are 15 identifiable Limba clans. Formerly, because Limba society was predominantly chauvinistic, clan membership was solely acquired through patrilineage. Today, the custom varies from dialect to dialect.

Some clans are strictly exogamous,[73] but in others[74] clan descendants as close as first cousins may marry,[75] and in Freetown where clanship is not well recognised clan-based exogamy is not noticeably practised.

## Childbirth (*hukomisine*)

In Limba society, like many African societies,[76] men and children are not permitted to be present for the delivery of a child. When the baby is born, the birth attendant gently spanks the baby, to make it cry, as the cry proves that the baby is alive and healthy.[77] In Freetown, where most births take place in government hospitals, medically trained midwives assist in the delivery, and in most cases boys are circumcised before leaving the hospital. Boys born in the hinterland, where in most cases there is no proximate medical centre, are usually circumcised during their pre-teen or teenage years before their initiation into the secret society. A boy born at home in Freetown, is later taken to a local druggist or nurse for circumcision.[78]

Both mother and baby are required to stay inside the house for several days before coming outside. During this time the husband or another close relative is obligated to prepare meals called *marɛbɛ/masepe* ('to cleanse the stomach') for the new mother. *Marɛbɛ*, is made up of rice and palm oil stew.

## Naming (*athundu keŋ*)

Limba children are usually named on the seventh or eighth day[79] if the umbilical cord has dropped off, otherwise it is delayed until this happens. The naming and out-dooring of a child on the seventh or eighth day, is a custom borrowed from Islam. Before the coming of Islam, the Limba did not have a specific time for the child to be named or taken out of the house, only that a child should not be named until the umbilical cord had fallen off.[80] The umbilical cord is usually buried near the house.[81] As the guests arrive they take turns complimenting the parents and expressing their appreciation for the invitation. The father usually names the child.[82]

In many cultures, names given to children are chosen and formed quite deliberately for their meaning, and a name in Limba worldview is often an indication of a person's character, nature, birth position, rank or of some peculiar quality.[83] For example:

- A name may portray the bearer's position and function in the family: The first son is sometimes called *Sara*, and the first daughter *Sira*, while the second son is sometimes named *Thamba*. The last child, whether a boy or girl, is sometimes called *Manke*. If twin boys are born, the first is named *Yandi*, and the second *Yemmi*.

- A name may portray the child's relationship with the parents or family: *Bude* is the name of a beloved daughter; *Thambo* ('hatred') is the name of a child hated because of birth defects.

- A name may indicate the day on which the bearer is born: *Kathi* is a girl born on Sunday; *Thɛnɛ* is a girl born on Monday; *Thalatha* is a girl born on Tuesday; *Yaraba* is a boy born on Wednesday; *Yalamusa* is a boy born on Thursday; *Yarimɛ* is a boy born on Friday, and *Simithi* is a girl born on Saturday.

- Sometimes, names are given to mark an important occasion, especially if a child is born on such an occasion. For example, a child born during a circumcision or initiation period is often called *Bureyo* ('female') or *Buremaŋ* ('male').

- If a child is born during a memorable or unfortunate event in the life of a family, the parents may give to the child a name that portrays that experience: *Mallo* ('joy and peace'); *Thebota* ('no peace'), or *Baleytʃkʃ* ('do not rejoice').

- A child's name may indicate the situation of its birth. A sickly child that has incurred a lot of expenses is sometimes called *DʃYoo* ('laboured upon'). When the last parent of a child passes away after its birth, the child is called *Peyo* ('orphan/left/forsaken'). A child called *Piiti* ('was forgotten') indicates that its birth was over due. Rarely, if a mother was not aware of her pregnancy, the child is called *Thakʃthʃ* ('did not know'). If a child is born during a journey or by the roadside, it is called *Gboŋa* ('road'). A child who is stillborn or who dies shortly after birth is named *Muruyo* ('no hope').

- If a baby is born deformed or disabled, its appearance is attributed to the work of a witch or evil spirit. Society considers such a child to be a manifestation of the devil (*waali*). The child is often named: *Yɛliyaŋ* ('throw away for me').

- Names may also be given in honour of deceased relatives who have contributed positively to the family and society. In this regard, the bearer is expected to follow the traits of his/her deceased namesake so that the physical memory of the deceased will linger.

In certain aspects, the name of a person,[84] place or event in Limba culture and custom is to a large extent more than a mere personal label or tag and a naming ceremony 'signifies that the transmission of life is completed'.[85] After the child is named, it is taken outside the house to be shown 'the world'.[86]

## Nursing (adinki)

In Limba culture, breast-feeding of infants is the norm. The duration of breastfeeding depends on the health of the mother and the wishes of her husband. The Limba practice both in the hinterland and in urban areas requires a minimum of six months and usually lasts 18 months. During this time the woman should abstain from sexual intercourse.[87] This is why children in a Limba family are typically spaced by a year and a half to two years. A woman who does not follow this norm is scorned. Working women in the Western Area are usually given a year's maternity leave by their employers.

## Engagement (kuliathi/kudethi) and marriage (hud]ŋ]/kuyɛntande)

Girls are sometimes engaged in infancy[88] or even while still in the womb.[89] In the latter case, the prospective husband expresses his intention towards the expected baby in anticipation that the child will be a girl. He starts giving gifts and helping the expectant mother as a sign of beginning the marriage. If a girl is born, the man continues to give gifts and assistance to his future in-laws, and watches as the girl grows.[90] If a boy is born, the man volunteers to become the boy's instructor (soma/sema) during his initiation ceremony, and helps him until this is complete.

When a couple is engaged as teenagers or adults, the procedure is different. Representatives of the man go to see the girl's family with a small amount money to 'lock-the-door' guaranteeing his interest in her so that no other interested man may take the girl before he is ready to marry her. In the hinterland, girls are usually given in marriage between the ages of 13 and 16 after their initiation into the Bondo society.[91] The family of the husband-to-be sends a message to inform the girl's relatives that they will be coming on a certain date. On the appointed date, as soon as the visitors arrive, a small sum of money called kɛmɛ is given to the girl's parents. They respond by giving the leader of the visiting group water to drink from a cup containing some kola nuts.

In spite of the occasional difficulty inherent in having multiple wives, Limba men in the hinterland, traditionally like to marry many wives if at all possible.[92] The reasons given for polygamy are both economic and social.[93] A man's wealth is measured by the number of wives and children that he has. The understanding is that a man with more wives must maintain a larger farm and build more houses than a man with fewer wives. It is also believed that each wife brings added wisdom to the husband. A man with one wife has only one outside source of information and guidance; a man with many wives will have many sources and therefore, a distinct advantage. Polygamy is practiced only rarely in Freetown because the higher cost of living in an urban environment makes it very difficult for a man to support more than one wife.

When a husband dies, a close relative, usually a younger brother, normally inherits any surviving wives, especially if they have children.[94] If the widow does not wish to marry the appointed relative, she is allowed to marry someone outside the family, but the children often remain with the family of her deceased husband.

Divorce is not uncommon among the Limba.[95] If there is a marital dispute it is usually the wife who leaves, returning to her relatives. If the husband wants his wife back, he will approach his in-laws to settle the matter. If the wife refuses his attempts, the matter will be taken to the native court for trial and the husband may demand a refund of the bride price. If, however, the husband has lost interest, and does not make the effort to bring his wife home, her family may also make attempts at reconciliation and the husband stands to lose the bride-price if he refuses several of these attempts. If there are children, they will stay with the father or the mother depending on a number of factors.

The·most common cause of divorce among the Limba is adultery (*abalaŋaŋ*).[96] Adultery is seen as a spiteful challenge to the husband's dignity and manhood. A husband, who suspects his wife of cheating with another man, will force her to confess *kuhiŋ* (lit., 'call-name') to adultery. The husband normally reacts by demanding a fine called *kubali* ('woman damage') through the chief or through the Traditional Court. At times the adulterous wife is returned to her family. On the other hand if a married man commits adultery with an unmarried woman, the wife usually prefers not to confront her husband, because society frowns upon any woman who attempts to humiliate her husband. Illicit sex is not considered a serious offence when committed by a married traditionalist man. For these reasons, a maltreated wife usually only cries and tries to forget about her husband's infidelity, or simply turns a blind eye to her husband's adulterous behaviour. Others may put up a strong fight to show their husbands that the man should not always be in control.

## Respect

In most Sierra Leonean cultures, the elderly are accorded a great deal of respect.[97] Limba culture teaches that, to gain long life; to be wise, and to be blessed and protected, you must respect not only the elders of your own family, but also those of the society. In general, older people are addressed by a title of respect and not by their ordinary names, for example: *yapo, pa, kʃtho, hɛmo* ('old man'), *iŋa, moyo, ma* ('old woman'), at times you may call those of a similar age to your parents 'aunty' or 'uncle'. People older than yourself, but significantly younger than your parents, should be addressed as brother or sister.

The words and counsel of the elderly are held in very high regard.[98] In most Limba homes, as a sign of respect, a child should not sit in the company of visiting adults or older people. When an adult enters a home for a visit, all the children are asked to either go outside and play or go to their rooms until the stranger leaves. A young person kneels down slightly to greet an elderly person. Children and young people are expected to greet their parents, and any other elder around, each morning on rising (hɛri bahure), and each evening when going to bed (masanka).

When eating with an adult, it is considered disrespectful for a younger person to take a piece of meat or fish and eat it without first having the consent of the older person. This type of disrespectful behaviour is called wutebede. In most homes the father will occasionally eat together with his son(s) and the other men in the house, while the mother eats with her daughter(s) and the other women in the house. This is not a hard and fast rule, especially in Freetown, but, the Limba like to eat in this manner so that the adults can teach the children proper table manners. More often, the younger children will eat together, while their parents watch them reprimanding anyone caught doing anything uncustomary.

The traditional Limba prefers to eat with their hand and it is Limba custom not to talk while eating. Outside of the home in general, when there are two or three people of the same gender, the Limba prefer to share a meal of rice and soup from the same dish. Often, at gatherings, a group of women will be in one corner eating, a group of men in another, and a group of youths in their own area all doing the same.

## Social courtesies

Greetings (mande/nsɛkɛ/nsɛ), with appropriate gestures, show respect and good relationship. Thanking (kalaŋaŋ), someone for a good deed shows appreciation for the efforts of others, and makes way for future considerations. A person, who does not 'thank you', is considered an ingrate. Gift-giving is another way to express your appreciation and respect. Travelling guests carry gifts called mutʃŋʃti ('what I brought for you') for friends and hosts/hostesses. Hosts/hostesses and friends also give gifts called mudɛŋ ('what I kept for you') to visitors when they are returning.

Reporting (tʃŋ danthɛkɛ), apologising (theteke) when you are in the wrong or presumed to be in the wrong, story and parable telling (mbʃrʃ/ngbaŋ), riddle telling (nlʃŋ) and making music (mathurʃkʃ/muluŋ/yakali)[99] are also considered essential to Limba culture.[100] Drumming, dancing, singing and story-telling are considered to be cultural inheritances – sometimes referred to as 'Limba things' or 'Limba times' (malimba ma).[101]

# Death

In general, death is regarded as both a natural and inevitable aspect of human life. When death occurs, wailing starts immediately. Acquaintances begin to gather at the house to express their condolences. The women begin to express their sympathy by wailing[102] loudly as they approach the compound where the funeral is being held. This custom expresses the communal bond that exists between families and friends. The laughter of one, as well as the sorrow, belongs not only to the individual, but to the community as well. The women sit on the floor inside the house, while the men sit around a table with a plate to collect money for the funeral expenses. A learned person (if one is available) will record the financial contributions and the names of the donors. This provision also shows the spirit of community. A funeral is the responsibility not solely of the bereaved family, but of the public.[103]

In the Limba homeland where there are no embalmers, the burial of a deceased person takes place on the same day, usually within a few hours of the death. In the Western Area, certain processes have to be followed before burial. First a death certificate must be obtained and registered at the Department of Births and Deaths in the Ministry of Health, and a grave must be purchased and dug. Before burial, the deceased is washed and wrapped in a new piece of white shroud, and laid on a flat board, normally close to the entrance of the house. Generally, if no post-mortem has been performed, cotton wool is placed inside the nostrils, to prevent the deceased from sneezing. This custom comes from the Limba belief that as long as the deceased has his/her internal organs intact, it is possible for the person to come back to life before burial. It is believed that if the corpse sneezes, all those present will die. If a post mortem has been done, the organs have been severed; the cotton wool is therefore not required, unless a particularly superstitious relative wishes to take extraordinary precautions.

In the village, when the time for burial arrives, usually two or more men carry the corpse to the cemetery in the forest. Graves in these cemeteries are less than six feet (2 m) deep. After a brief ceremony, the deceased is buried with the head facing eastward. Since the corpse has not been placed in a box or coffin, a canopy is constructed at the grave's mid point from horizontal sticks and leaves so that the earth used to fill in the grave does not touch the corpse itself. Some branches or flowers are then placed on top of the grave. Most of the people present at the burial ceremony then return to the deceased's home for some food and to visit with the bereaved family. The presence and company of sympathisers is considered a vital source of comfort. The traditionalist believes that if a person does not return to the deceased's house after the burial, the person is inviting a funeral in their own home. In the Western Area the corpse is usually kept for several days in the mortuary or funeral home, while burial arrangements are being made.

## Conclusion

The Limba have been in their current location since at least the late sixteenth century and, although it is impossible to prove or disprove, it is believed that they may have been the first people in the Sierra Leone hinterland. The largest population of Limba outside of the Limba homeland is now in Freetown.

The Limba speak a 'prefix language' which is part of the West Atlantic family of languages, and has 12 dialects which have been categorised into five regional dialects. Politically, the Limba are governed by the Chiefdom Council system in their homeland, and by the Tribal Administration system in Freetown. Both systems were adapted from the British. Judicially, the tribal courts governed by Court Chairmen deal with most basic cases, excepting capital offences and divorce cases. Economically, Limba communities make their living through rice farming, the harvesting of palm tree products, animal husbandry, fishing and hunting, petty trading, craftsmanship, and in Freetown, office employment.

Socially, the household or family is the basic unit. Families are connected to each other through kinship and clanship, the acquisition of which varies from dialect to dialect. Other notable cultural qualities of the Limba are respect for elders, table manners, an appropriate manner of greeting, thankfulness, and the giving of gifts.

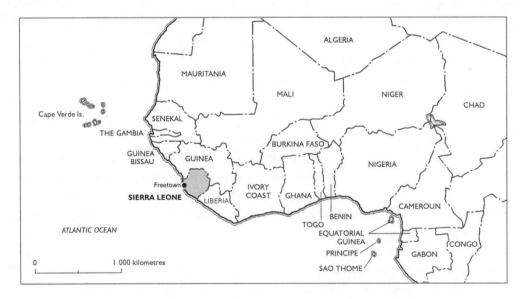

Figure 1:    Sierra Leone in its setting in West Africa    [Modified from Fyle 1981]

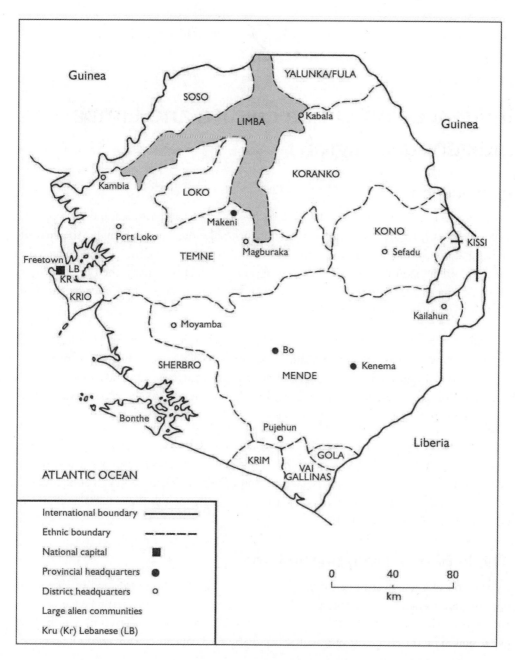

Figure 2:    Limba current traditional homeland in Sierra Leone [Modified from Alie 1990]

# 2

# Influences on Limba culture and Limba indigenous religion

## Introduction

Limba indigenous culture and LIR,[1] like many other African cultures and religions, has undergone many changes due to external[2] and internal influences. Externally, the intrusion of comparatively new religions,[3] and the complexities of modern changes have both affected Limba traditional beliefs. Modernisation in Africa has encroached upon religious societies, affecting their religious worldviews and existence.[4] After three decades the words of Mbiti are still applicable:

> Africa is going through a tremendous and rapid change in every aspect of human life. Many individuals are becoming increasingly detached from the corpus of their tribal and traditional beliefs, concepts and practices. On the other hand, these concepts have not all been abandoned, nor are they likely to be wiped out immediately by these modern changes.[5]

J. O. Awolalu[6] describes the intrusion of Islam, Christianity, Western imperialism and modernisation as militating factors against traditional rites. This is largely because of their dedication to ordered views and fixed ideals, and their criticism and even condemnation of anything different from themselves. Let us now briefly look at the external and internal influences that have affected LIR.

## The impact of Islam on the Limba

By the end of the eleventh century, Islam had become firmly established in the Sudan, north of Sierra Leone, near the Sahara.[7] It has since spread into Sierra Leone as far as the Gulf of Guinea and the Atlantic coast. Very little has been written about the early expansion in Sierra Leone, or of its influence on Sierra Leonean culture and religion.

The familiar account of the infiltration of Islam into Sierra Leone recounts its expansion south from the Sudan through small groups of Fula and Mandingo traders in the eighteenth century.[8] Upon arrival at any place, and during their temporary or permanent stay, the Fula and Mandingo opened schools to teach Arabic and the tenets of Islam.[9] Many of the people and their leaders rallied around these teachers, embraced the Muslim faith and became the patrons of their teachers.[10]

Among the Thonko, Warawara and Biriwa Limba peoples, Mandingo Muslims took Limba wives and had children, forming new clans: the Samura, Kamara and Kargbo clans of the Thonko; the Mansaray clan of the Warawara; and the Conteh clan of the Biriwa.[11] The Mandingo became rulers among the Limba, and fought on the side of the Limba in battles against other ethnic groups. In spite of this seemingly fruitful interaction between the Mandingo and the indigenes, these early Fula and Mandingo invaders did not succeed in establishing Islam among the Limba to any great degree.

A major Islamic breakthrough came about through the 1727 political and economic war between the Fula and the Yalunka. This war, known as the Futa Jallon Jihad, resulted in a strong wave of Muslim migration into Sierra Leone. The Jihad dispersed many peoples over a wide area, and it contributed to the Islaminisation of Sierra Leone in general and of the Northern Province – the traditional home of the Limba – in particular.[12] New Muslim rulers and converts helped spread Islam into many parts of Limba country. Mass conversion to Islam came much later in the late nineteenth century after the conquests of Samori Turay the Mandinka warrior.[13] By the twentieth century a considerably large number of Limba were devoutly Muslim.[14] Islam came into Limba country much as it did into other Sierra Leone cultures, sometimes through war but, more often by peaceful means.

As it did in the other ethnic groups it encountered in Sierra Leone, Islam gained influence among the Limba because it was brought by other Africans who retained many traits and accoutrements of traditional ethnic culture. As such, Islam was able to adapt itself to the culture of the people. It is reasonable to say the brand of Islam which evolved in Sierra Leone was an accommodating one. Muslim leaders approved of, or at least tolerated, traditional practices such as sacrifice and polygamy. This attracted many people to Islam. Less of a demand for change was made with regard to charms and medicines. Islam accepted LIR with an overlay of Muslim belief and practice. Muslim men called *alfa* or *morimen* (because they were powerful in the use of 'medicine') adopted the making of charms from the indigenes.[15] They made charms out of various objects with verses from the Qu'ran written on paper and enclosed in pouches. These charms were used by warriors, farmers and traders, and are believed to bring prosperity or victory and to ward off evil spirits. Many Muslims use these charms. Qu'ranic verses were also written over doors as protection, or written on boards and placed on farms or in trees to prevent stealing.[16] In addition to making charms, Muslim men used prayer, divination, potions, and magic tablets to identify culprits and to protect and cure people. Much of the Islamic worldview was diffused into the indigenous religious thought of the Limba, bringing the two faith traditions together. The fact that Islam in Sierra Leone incorporated aspects of traditional religious practices made it more acceptable and appealing to the indigenes.

However, not all Muslim missionaries were prepared to tolerate the accommodating brand of Islam practised in Sierra Leone. The Ahmadiyah movement, which was established in Sierra Leone in 1937 by missionaries from Pakistan, aimed at purifying West African Islam.[17] With such an approach; Ahmadiyah's success in Sierra Leone has been small. However, there are still strict Muslims in Sierra Leone who consider most traditional religious practices to be Satanic.

The influence of Islam on Limba culture and religion is evident in Limba rites of passage (e.g., the naming ceremony of a new born as noted in Chapter 1), ethnic politics (e.g., 'Almamy', the title of a male chief), and worldview. Another indication of Muslim influence on indigenous culture is the introduction of Arabic loan words like *barika* ('thanks'), *saraka* ('sacrifice') and names like Momodu (Muhammad), Lansana (al-Hasan), Brimah (Ibrahim), and Suliman (Sulaiman).

## The effect of Christianity on the Limba

The beginning of Christian missionary work in Sierra Leone, by the Roman Catholic Jesuits from Portugal, in September 1605,[18] paved the way for many later missionary endeavours,[19] including contemporary efforts. The first Christian missionary efforts in the Limba homeland were made by the Wesleyan Methodist Society (WMS) in 1878, and failed.[20] Undeterred by the setback, the WMS sent the Revds Godman and Jope to the Thonko Limba area in 1879 'to explore the possibility of establishing a mission there'.[21] Positive prospects were discovered and the Rev. James Booth arrived in Fourecaria in March 1880 starting work with the support of the Thonko Limba king and sub-chiefs. By mid 1884 he had translated parts of the Bible into Limba. Although only a small minority of the Thonko Limba people embraced Christianity, 'their influence on the majority' of the population 'was considerable'.[22] For example the Christians succeeded in influencing the authorities to pass a law 'that anyone found working on the Sabbath should be severely punished'.[23] This marked the beginning of the struggle between Limba culture and Christianity in Limba country. Ironically, Rev. Booth later married a Temne woman according to the Temne cultural rites; this led to a falling out with his superiors and his eventual resignation. Nevertheless, WMS missionary work continued in the Thonko Limba area and it was later turned over to the American Wesleyan Methodist Church (AWM) in 1937.[24]

The AWM's first major missionary effort in the Limba homeland was started in 1889.[25] The interest of the AWM in Northern Sierra Leone was motivated by several factors. First, only a few missionary societies had ventured beyond the coast. Second, the tribes in the interior provided better opportunities for missionary work because the effects of the old slave trade and of the liquor trafficking were less, and because the people governed themselves. Third, and perhaps most important, J. A. Cole, an educated Limba and a member of St. John's Church in Freetown, also a relative of a Limba paramount chief, specifically requested the AWM to come to Limba country.

By 1910, 'seven mission stations were opened and staffed by thirteen missionaries' working among the Limba, Temne and Loko ethnic groups.[26] The AWM method of evangelisation included education, medical work and 'wide itineration' and by 1930, '462 people were converted, and 319 of them joined the church'.[27] The Limba people of Kamakwie at first resented Christianity until a missionary doctor in Mobai cured a respected man in their community who was dying. This amazing medical result motivated the people to listen to the gospel. Five years later, the AWM work in Kamakwie closed because of insufficient funds, the paucity of missionary staff and the death of the chief who had been patronising Christianity. The only missionary still stationed there was then moved to the boys' school at Binkolo.[28] The mission in Kamakwie was later resurrected and four main AWM mission stations at Kamakwie, Binkolo, Kamabai, and Bafodea[29] remain today.

One thing that was evident when I visited these areas during my fieldwork is that, although the missions had been established in these Limba areas many years ago, the effects of Christianity on traditional religious worldview are still limited. As Finnegan observed, almost four decades ago, it is not too far from these mission stations that 'old rituals continue'. This proves that still today, 'the results of the Mission teaching, however effective locally, are not very evident on a wider scale in the Limba religious belief and practice'.[30]

On the whole, Christianity did not thrive in the hinterland of Sierra Leone. By the end of the nineteenth century, a majority of the people were still unconverted. Several factors contributed to the lack of Christian missionary success:

(a) Islam was firmly entrenched in many areas in the interior, particularly in the north. And Islam was able to present itself, though also an immigrant religion, as an African religion, whereas Christianity always suffered from being the 'white man's religion'. (b) Christianity was not adapted to African society and it made heavy demands on the convert. For instance, admission into the Christian church involved arduous teaching and spiritual preparation of the catechist, who was required to abandon completely his old religion. (c) In addition to making conversion more difficult, Christianity also attacked the African way of life. For example, polygamy, slavery, magic, use of charms and initiation ceremonies were vehemently condemned. (d) Many people regarded Christianity as a disruptive force; this was largely why many missionaries were killed and their churches destroyed during the hut tax rising of 1898.[31]

The notion of Christianity as a white man's religion, which disrupts society through the condemnation of African religio-cultural practices is a factor still responsible for the ongoing conflicts between the church and Sierra Leonean traditionalists both in the hinterland and the Western Area. Christian missionaries to Africa are still blamed for their cultural insensitivity to African values which resulted in the transplantation of 'an ethnocentric form of Christianity'[32]

Outside of the hinterland, the Assemblies of God (AOG) missionaries from Springfield Missouri, United States of America (US) founded the first Limba congregation in Freetown.[33] This congregation separated from the AOG in March 1965 to form the National Pentecostal Limba Church (NPLC), two years later the Fort Street Church branch (which is now the NPLC headquarters) was built. The NPLC has grown to be the largest Limba Church in Sierra Leone with branches in almost every major town in the country. There are a few predominantly Limba AOG churches which are made up of members and families of those who did not support the breakaway.

Successive AWM and AOG missionaries to the Limba attacked African culture, and required a complete abandonment of African culture and practices. For example, the AOG required monogamy and abstention from alcohol, smoking, secret society membership, (which was considered non-Christian, and non-allegiance to God) and Sunday marketing.[34] The AOG enforced 'a complete break with the past through the burning of medicine and charms … a symbol of complete rejection of the old way and of complete dependence upon God through Christ and the Holy Spirit … members were prohibited from using charms or making sacrifices'.[35]

There are still a few surviving members in most Limba communities in Freetown, who can attest to the insensitivity of AOG missionaries to Limba culture from the late 1940s to the mid 1960s. Christ was 'presented as the answer to the questions a white man would ask, the solution to the needs that a Western man would feel, the Saviour of the world of the European worldview, the object of the adoration and prayer of historic Christendom'.[36]

Insensitivity to African culture and worldview was not unique to Euro-American missionaries. They were not alone in their condemnation of traditional practices as heathenism or Satanism. Although AWM and AOG missionaries have handed leadership to indigenes, and although the NPLC separated from the AOG several decades ago, these churches still painstakingly follow the practices and teachings of the missionaries. Like their forebears, AOG and NPLC leaders continue the tradition of destroying by fire the charms possessed by Limba Christians. Indigenous leaders are still 'espousing the same views and philosophy that the missionaries held'.[37] They stress the 'aspects of discontinuity between Christianity and African cultures and traditional religion' to such an extent that they exclude the aspects of continuity between the two.[38] It appears that the church condemns Limba religious beliefs and practices without proper evaluation, and substitutes 'western cultural and religious practices'. This makes it difficult, if not 'impossible for a person to be a Christian and remain genuinely and authentically an African'.[39]

Some traditionalists/Limba Christians expect to find a prevalence of the western missionaries' stances and ideologies in those autonomous Limba church denominations that still have a western missionary presence, such as the AWM and AOG. An African separatist or independent church, however, should be 'reared on its own indigenous roots, bearing fruit under the stimulus of its own environment and sustained by the proprietary labours of those it served',[40] therefore, they do not expect to find overwhelming elements of missionary Christianity in breakaway or independent Limba churches like the NPLC.

The strongest opposition to the persistence of traditional practices in all the Limba denominations comes from the spiritual leaders and the youths/young adults who strongly believe that traditional religiosity is satanic and must be condemned.

The effects of missionary Christianity and the present church on LIR need not be overemphasised. Positively, traditionalists have given credit to the missionaries for their stance against the Limba traditionalists' inhumane practice of child/human sacrifice. Missionaries condemned this outrageous act long before the government stepped in and banned the practice. Also, some amount of credit is given to the missionary churches for the introduction of the western system of education that has helped and continues to help many Limba attain social prominence, and the introduction of western medicine that provides cures where traditional medicine cannot. The negative effects however, outweigh the positive. There is no doubt that factors such as missionary policies or revolutionary ideologies that are still being espoused in Africa have taken their toll on traditional religions and continue to do so by questioning their basic premises or outlawing certain practices.[41] An interviewee had this to say:

> Here in the Western Area, Christianity has affected traditional practices greatly as it (ATR) is no longer publicly in wide practice. The church insistence that it is ungodly is removing the sense of belonging from our culture to a borrowed one. Some of our people have changed their traditional names to Christian names. They are made to believe that as long as they carry their unchristian traditional names, life will always be difficult for them. When you are a Christian, the old traditional ways must be eradicated for a better life. Young people are saying their parents are lost and are going to hell because they are traditionalists who are refusing to accept Jesus as their saviour. Our cultural heritage of consulting

our ancestors is frowned upon. Many aspects of our language which have to do with our culture are dying out because the church views them as evil influences. Today we have several Limba literacy programmes to help people in the cities who have been swept by force of modernism and Western culture.

Within the church, the primary purpose for the negative attitude towards LIR is to guard against syncretism and nominalism among its membership. A majority of AWM, AOG and NPLC members do not think it is right to mix elements of traditional beliefs into Christianity because LIR is considered 'crude, uncouth and devilish', and any such incorporation would alter the church's spirituality. Therefore, 'anything that would dilute or substantially alter the basic structures of Christianity' is strongly combated.[42] The NPLC continues to 'take a rigid line on the question of any cultural accommodation whatsoever'.[43] This zero tolerance attitude has affected LIR considerably. Homes have been divided as older people stick to their past while younger people embrace Christianity as their new found way of life. The negative attacks on traditional values are destroying the foundation of the culture and the young Limba are being deprived of their cultural heritage.

In spite of the church's vigorous attack on Limba culture and religion, some members are still unwilling to give up their religious heritage in place of an immigrant religion. This issue of African Christians clinging tenaciously to their traditional religious beliefs and customs, combined with their reluctance to give them up in favour of Christianity, and the resulting conflicts between ATR and Christianity, is common to many parts of Africa and is known in Christian circles as the African Christian Problem.

It is, ironically, the persistence of Limba culture and religion into Christianity that has caused the church to blend some traditional beliefs and practices with Christian values. This compromise is more evident in the rite of passages. As already noted in Chapter 1, the church has adopted the traditional child naming and out-dooring ceremony, the engagement ceremony is a mixture of traditional and Christian practices, as is the fortieth day funeral observance. All Limba churches use African instruments in their worship service. This is also the case with the majority of westernised Limba. They have completely thrown away their culture.

## Postmodernism

Another external factor is the Postmodern ideology of the educated elite, who are proud to maintain their traditional practices irrespective of their westernisation. This has promoted the freedom of personal expression of opinions that view religion differently from the long established norms. The expression of personal opinion is common among the young and the educated elite. In similar vein, all modern peoples may hold beliefs very different from those of their forebears.[44] Within this climate, it does not matter how logical or rational the view is, every opinion should be respected and accepted. Long-held traditional positions on sexuality, marriage, pregnancy, and abortion are now being challenged and outlawed by the educated and the westernised. Traditionalists blame the exposure to western education and ideology as the cause for the challenge.

## Internal interaction

Internally, the settlement of other ethnic groups within and around Limba country, and the settlement of Limbas within the Western Area have brought religious, social, political and economic changes to the Limba worldview and language.[45] There is a constant dialogue between the Limba and their neighbours, about issues including culture, behaviour and practice. Words like sɔnkɔsɔnkɔ ('noise'), and *bampi* ('a farm land') are from the Temne language. The Temne, Susu, and Kuranko styles of music, drumming, dancing, and instruments (e.g., the *bubu* dance accompanied by the blowing of cane) have entered Limba culture.

## Dialectal divisions

Another factor that should be taken into consideration is the dialectal divisions, which dictate the adoption and promotion of personal identities. Each dialect within an ethnic group possesses a uniqueness that contributes to the whole and, just as there are minor variants in the dialects, so also in religion.[46] This is true because people 'hold differences of opinion on various subjects; and the myths, rituals and ceremonies may differ from area to area'.[47]

## Conclusion

Like many ethnic groups in Africa, the Limba are aware that their 'traditional ideas are being abandoned, modified or coloured by the changing situation'.[48] LIR 'like all religions has had to accommodate itself to the process of social change and the effects of modernization'.[49] This does not imply that everything traditional has been changed or abandoned so that no traces of it can be found. 'If anything, the changes are generally on the surface, affecting the material side of life, and only beginning to reach the deeper levels of thinking pattern, language content, mental images, emotions, beliefs and response in situations of need'.[50]

Unlike Christianity, Islam shares a strong affinity with Limba culture and religion. As such, many more traditionalists are attracted to Islam than Christianity. The effects of Christianity and modernity in particular on traditional culture and religion are stronger in the Western Area than in the Limba homeland, the seat of Limba culture and religion, where Christianity and westernisation are still struggling to survive. In both the hinterland and the Western Area, diehard traditionalists continue to put up strong resistance to keep their cultural heritage intact. To completely give up their God-given heritage in favour of a foreign culture, as the church requires, seems a very difficult task, and is tantamount to losing their entire heritage, identity, and place, both spiritually and physically within their religio-cultural community. This is why African traditionalists, even after conversion to Christianity, 'do not always adhere to religious and ritual demands that are formulated and expressed by the leaders of their churches'.[51] This situation has created tension between Christianity and ATR, which has attracted the attention of scholars and religionists.

Postmodernism has affected and continues to affect Limba traditionalists by challenging and reforming long-held cultural and religious worldviews. Traditionalists are blaming the exposure to western education and civilisation as the factor responsible for the challenge on their culture. Interaction with other ethnic groups, and the dialectal divisions of the Limba, have also brought changes to Limba culture and religion.

# 3

## Components of Limba indigenous religion

### Introduction

Chapter 2 discussed the influences that have impacted and continue to impact on Limba culture and religion. Before these changes progress any deeper, beyond the material side of life, it is necessary to document the traditional beliefs of the Limba while it is still possible to do so – especially because there has not been a previous comprehensive documentation of LIR.[1] It is hoped through this analysis of LIR to equip the reader to evaluate those elements that constitute LIR, and to map it out for the study of its function within the ethnic group.[2]

### The elements of Limba indigenous religion

In general, ATR consists of a belief in the supernatural and the practices by which the African relates to the supernatural. There is a hierarchy of supernatural forces which comprises a Supreme Being, ancestral and non-ancestral spirits, as well as deities or divinities. The practices employed by ATR include both those showing reverence to these beings (e.g., sacrifice) and those intended to control supernatural forces (e.g., magic and medicines). While the various African cultures, and resultant various scholars, hold differing views on the interrelationship of these elements,[3] they form an identifiable core. By this core, it is possible to define ATR as the institutionalised beliefs, teachings, practices and behaviours of various African societies in relation to the Supernatural, in the context of their respective societies and experiences. This definition addresses both the sacred and functional aspects of religion.

In particular, LIR is a way of life that is expressed both personally and corporately through, belief (*kulaniya*) in a Supreme God (*Kanu Masala*), angels (*malekɛŋ*), ancestral spirits (*fureni be*) and non-ancestral spirits (*mbaalin*), religious objects (*sɛbɛ, kudori*), sacred places (*ŋkaniyki*), social institutions (*kahu*), religious officials and leaders, the observance of ceremonies and festivals (*kahuin*), and in the teaching and practice of morals and ethical values. In a nutshell, LIR is a way of life based on beliefs, practices and teachings.[4] It is pertinent now to look at these three components of LIR:

## Beliefs

There are four types of spirits in Limba worldview: the Supreme Being, angels, the ancestors, and non-ancestral spirits.[5] The majority of the Limba have categorised these spirits according to a scale of preference.[6] At the top of the scale is the Supreme Being. Next are the angels, and the ancestors. Most Limba place the angels just above the ancestors, but a few reverse this order.[7] Non-ancestral spirits are ranked fourth.[8] Outside of this ranking, the Limba also believe in certain other powers of a spiritual nature. These include artefacts/objects for protective purposes like amulets, objects on farms and on door posts; objects used for ordeals like 'swears', traditional clothes and medicines; and sacred places, like shrines, caves and trees where the supernatural could be present and venerated. These powers are also manifest in the secret societies of *Ghangba* and *Bondo*. Limba religiosity is not limited to a belief in supernatural entities and abstract powers. There is also a strong belief in sacred specialists/officials[9] because they are gifted with spiritual abilities for the good of individuals and of the community. Sacred specialists are believed to have a special relationship with humans and the supernatural of all levels. Although sacred officials are not worshipped, they are trusted and respected as intermediaries and as people gifted with spiritual prowess to maintain harmony between the community and the supernatural.

## Practices

The belief in the supernatural is expressed through practices including sacrifice, offering, prayer, libation and cleansing rites,[10] all of which are seen as a means to stay connected to the Supernatural. God is worshipped through sacrifice and prayer. The ancestors are venerated, through the same means as God, for their interest in the living as mediator between the individual, the community and God, and for the guidance and instruction they provide for better living, both physical and spiritual. Offerings are made to both malevolent spirits and benevolent spirits. The practice of participating in the annual priestly celebrations is an expression of the belief that the Limba have in the work and office of the priesthood. At the centre of all these religious phenomena is humankind. The Limba believe that humankind is created with a spiritual entity which enables humans to relate to a higher power or powers as a means of keeping in balance the supernatural, self, family, clan and the society. Humankind then is a spiritual agent that makes the sacred functional by transmitting what is on the heart and mind into words, actions and practices.

## Teachings

Religious and ethical teachings are primarily a result of the belief in the supernatural. Apart from their teachings concerning the components of the supernatural, worship and veneration, Limba traditionalists teach about evil and its consequences.[11] They teach that sin is both anti-spiritual and anti-social, and includes offences against God, spiritual agents, humankind, animate things and inanimate things. These offences may take the form of witchcraft, or any other anti-social deed or intention. Because sin, of any kind, offends the Supernatural, it forms an important part of Limba teaching and must be dealt with in order to restore a healthy relationship with the supernatural and with society. The process of eradicating evil and restoring harmony through the courts, or through 'swears', ordeals and curses is seen as justice. God is believed to be behind all the moral and ethical values held by the Limba. These values play an important role in their worldview. Moral and ethical teaching is done at home and in secret society bushes, and is accomplished through story telling and discussion.[12] Everything that exists (animals, birds, reptiles, plants, rocks, the land, the sea, the sun, the moon, the stars, and people) possesses spiritual qualities. We all share the same origins; therefore, all of God's creation should be treated with appropriate reverence and attention.

In their descriptions of all these beliefs, practices and teachings, the Limba explain and interpret the world around them and the place of humankind in society. As Charles Nyamiti points out: 'African religious behaviour is centred mainly on man's life in this world, with the consequence that religion is chiefly functional, or a means to serve people to acquire earthly goods ... and to maintain social cohesion and order'.[13]

## Conclusion

External and internal influences continue to affect LIR, but in spite of these changes and challenges, LIR continues to thrive.[14] This is due to its organic nature as a way of life that is deeply rooted in the hearts and minds of its believers and is expressed through their words, actions and symbols as a way to maintain a cordial and healthy relationship with the supernatural, the community, and the self. The fundamental concepts of LIR are vested in their belief in the Supreme Being, angels, ancestral and non-ancestral spirits; in religious objects, sacred places and social institutions, and in religious officials and leaders. LIR is also vested in their practice/observance of ceremonies and festivals, and in their teaching and practice of morals and ethical values.

The expression of belief through practice and teaching makes LIR both sacred and functional. Religion can, of course include a wide range of beliefs, practices, and cultural behaviours, and each religion, whether organised or organic consists of different qualities of each of these elements.

With the analysis of the components of LIR in place, it is now necessary to look in depth at each of these components. Because, among the influences discussed above, Christianity has had the most significant impact on ATR, the introduction to each topic in Chapters 4 through 11 (the heart of the book) will be followed by a brief general view of the opinions and positions of Christian Limbas on the subject based on scripture and missionary Christianity. The deeper study now begins with a look at the Supreme Being.

# 4

## The Supreme Being

### Introduction

As an integral part of their worldview, the Limba hold a belief[1] in a Supreme Being called *Kanu Masala*. The existence[2] of this being is not a point of contention among the Limba. 'God is no stranger',[3] and he looms large in the consciousness of the people. Their prayers, worship, and most of their speeches, stories and proverbs, manifest an awareness of God.[4] Attempts to prove God's existence[5] are rare in Limba society. The existence of God is, to Limba traditionalists, unquestionable[6] and should not be debated.[7] As with other African peoples, the Limba take the existence of God as a matter of course.[8]

The Limba church does not dispute the fact that Limba traditionalists have a belief in a God: the church's contention is that the traditionalists do not serve the one true God. The God who has revealed himself as the eternally self-existent 'I AM', the Creator of heaven and earth and the Redeemer of humanity, and who has further revealed himself as embodying the principles of relationship and association as Father, Son, and Holy Ghost. In that regard, the Christian Limbas do not equate the traditional God with their own.

Who is this God in whom the Limba traditionalists believe? What is this God's role in the life of the Limba traditionalist?[9] I will attempt to answer these questions by studying Limba notions about God as they are expressed in his names, his attributes, his works, and his relationships as well as through the worship he receives.

### The names of God

As already noted, like other Sierra Leonean cultural groups, the Limba attach great importance to names. In most African cultures, names function not merely as 'identification marks' applied to people,[10] but they 'often express qualities for which the owners are conspicuous'.[11] Usually a name either portrays or denotes a defining characteristic of its bearer. In other words, a name, in Limba worldview, is often an indication of a person's character, nature, or rank, or an expression of some peculiar quality. A name denotes essence, identity and power. It is upon these premises that the Limba traditionalists base their understanding of God. I will now discuss the names[12] of the Limba Supreme Being to discover what light they shed on their concept of God.

## Kanu Masala

The origin and meaning of any name in Limba culture is crucial.[13] The personal name of the Limba Supreme Being is *Kanu Masala*. The first word, '*Kanu*' is believed to have come from the Biriwa and Safroko Limba peoples.[14] Two theories exist about the origin and meaning of the name *Kanu*. The first theory takes the form of a story about a caring king (God) who was living side by side with humankind, and who fled because of the increasing demands of his people. An interviewee told the following story:

> There once lived a king who had a few subjects. He one day called to assure them that they could come with whatever problems they had and he would help to solve them. The king indeed kept his word by solving all degrees of problems that were brought to him. He used to meet with his subjects in person to fulfil their requests. As the people began to increase in number, their problems also increased. The king, who lived in a place where he could be easily reached, then said to himself: 'Now that my subjects are increasing rapidly and their problems and requests continue to rise immensely, they have left me with no time and privacy of my own. If things continue this way, these people will send me to my grave before my appointed time'. So one evening when most of his subjects had gone to bed, the king moved from his usual place to an unknown location. The following day, some of his subjects went, as usual, to meet him with their problems. Unfortunately this time, their king was not there to help them as usual. As they were returning home disappointedly, they came across other subjects who were also going to see the king with their problems. Likewise the second group could not find the king. Later, when both groups were together in the town, they all said, '*Kanu niŋka dethiya*' ('let us go and find him'). Then the search for the lost king began. The people looked on treetops, caves, deep streams, thick bushes and forests. Occasionally, offerings and sacrifices were made to plead with the king to return. All their efforts went in vain. The king never returned. Therefore, the subjects called the invisible king '*Kanu*' ('the one we all continue to search for'). The Limba believe that God is hidden in some place where he cannot be easily seen or reached.

The second theory is etymological and theological and begins with the etymology of the word 'Kanu'.[15] It is a lengthened form of the word 'Kan' which means 'sun'. As everyone feels the sun during the day, so also is the presence of God felt in every life. Whether you like it or not, the sun shines during the day on good and bad people alike, likewise God's goodness is shown to all people, to believers as well as unbelievers. As the sun is bright and clear, so also, is God's magnificence and glory. Nothing is hidden from the sun, and this is also true of God who sees and knows all. God is likened to the sun which shines above.[16]

Like the sun, God 'beams into the entire universe'.[17] The Limba are careful to specify that they do not worship the sun as a deity.[18] It is not just a matter of comparison between God and the sun. This is rather a way of explaining their perception of the nature and activity of God using a familiar human experience. If then, the sun is not a manifestation of *Kanu*; it is rather used as a type. Some of the attributes of *Kanu* are found in these comparisons. Just as the existence of the sun is not disputed, the same is true of God's existence.

Further, the Limba sees the indiscriminate attribute of the sun as a portrait of God's character.[19] The sun does not discriminate. It shines on everyone irrespective of his/her status or beliefs. In the Limba view, God gives his blessing and grace impartially. Finally, as the light of the sun makes it possible for people to distinguish things, so God shows the Limba how to discern between right and wrong. *Kanu* is the light that guides the Limba on the right path. Discerning between right and wrong is important for the harmony and continuation of the community.

The second half of the Limba name for the Supreme Being is '*Masala*'.[20] This part of the name is believed to have come from the Thonko and the Sela Limba peoples. There are three theories about the origin of the word 'Masala'. One theory is that *Masala* is a Limbanised form of the word 'Allah' (the name of the Muslim God). Another theory is that *Masala* is borrowed from the Kuranko[21] word 'Mansa' ('Chief'). The final theory is that *Masala* is a Limbanised form of the Temne word 'Masaba' ('Supreme').[22] This is perhaps the most probable origin; the generally accepted meaning of *Masala* is 'Supreme'. Therefore, *Kanu Masala* means 'God Supreme'.[23]

## Kanu Kabekede/Wobekede/Kathinthi

*Kanu Masala* ('God supreme') is believed to live above the sky[24] just as the sun, and in that regard he is also called *Kanu kabekede/wobekede/kathinthi* ('God above'). There is a story about 'Why Kanu is now up above in the sky'[25] that is still told. In the old days *Kanu*, humans and animals lived together on earth. Because the animals and the elements, (such as fire and water), kept quarrelling and involving God in their disputes, and because they refused to heed his advice to stop, *Kanu* became angry and went to live above.[26] This is how the story goes:

> The deer and python were in search of food in the forest when they bumped into each other. The python asked the deer 'What are you looking for?' The deer replied that it was looking for food and the python said: you will be to me the food that you have come to look for. The deer pleaded for its life – to no avail. Then it ran to Kanu for help. The python went after it and they both presented their cases to Kanu. Kanu accused the python of starting trouble and advised the

python to let the deer go free. The python refused to listen to Kanu and seized the deer and swallowed it. Some time later the python disturbed an army of ants and the ants followed it to eat it up. Like the deer the python ran to Kanu – again Kanu could not prevent the ants from eating the python. In like manner, the fire claimed that the ants disturbed it and it licked them all up. The water claimed that fire disturbed it and it ate up the fire. Because of this unending fighting Kanu became upset and went to live above the sky.[27]

The belief that God lives above in the sky, out of reach of humankind suggests, 'He is obviously a transcendent Being'.[28] The transcendence of *Kanu* portrays his supremacy over any other spiritual being.[29] *Kanu* is not only transcendent in terms of time and space, but he also transcends human understanding. He is thought of as being incomprehensible.

The Limba believe that God's transcendence is appropriate and necessary so that he can effectively watch over his creation and seek the interests of his people. It is also necessary so that his people might, in turn, focus on him. *Kanu* lives far above in the sky overseeing the everyday activities of every individual on the earth below. He is in the sky so that Limba can focus on him and not be distracted by the troubles of the world around them.

It is a generally accepted concept that although *Kanu* lives in the sky, his spirit is present everywhere to influence the activity of his creation, especially the activities of the Limba. His transcendence is not a concern to Limba traditionalists because they maintain a strong belief that God takes part in everyday human affairs. In other words, although God is conceived as being physically out of reach, he is accessible through worship, natural manifestations and his establishment of and participation in human activities. Thus, *Kanu* is both transcendent and immanent.[30] God's transcendence 'is a difficult attribute to grasp and one which must be balanced with God's immanence. The two attributes are paradoxically complimentary: God is 'far' (transcendent), and men cannot reach him; but God is also 'near' (immanent), and he comes close to man'.[31] However, the association of God with the sky and the fact that although God is far away from humankind, he is still reachable are two vital components of the African concept of God.[32]

## Kanu Wopothi

It is no longer a fact that all Limba traditionalists believe only in a single high God that lives in the sky. Some juxtapose their belief in *Kanu Wobekede* with a belief in a God below, whom they call *Kanu Wopothi* ('God below').[33] *Kanu Wopothi* is not perceived of as a personal being, but is used as a general category to describe any evil spirit.[34] In other words, there is a Supreme God who lives in the sky and is considered to be the good God, and there is a God who resides on earth, who is held responsible for all the evil and mischievous occurrences in the universe. Stories are told that make references to both *Kanu* above and

*Kanu* below,[35] for example, 'Kanu gave food to the Limba',[36] and 'Kanu above and Kanu below'.[37] While the majority of Limba will bring gifts to *Kanu Wopothi*, these are not sacrifices, but acts motivated, admittedly, by paranoia.

## Kanu Masaraka

Another name for *Kanu* that is used somewhat less frequently is *Kanu Masaraka*[38] ('God of sacrifice' or 'God who accepts sacrifice').[39] This name is probably derived from the word *saraka* ('sacrifice'), and is often used to distinguish between *Kanu* above and *Kanu* below. *Kanu Wobekede* is *Kanu Masaraka* who accepts sacrifice (*saraka*) while *Kanu Wopothi* does not deserve sacrifice.[40] Sacrifice[41] is the primary means through which the Limba stay connected with *Kanu*. An in-depth discussion of this issue is found below under the topic 'Worshipping *Kanu*'.

# Attributes of *Kanu*

An attribute is a quality regarded as a natural or typical part of someone or something. The attributes of God then are the qualities which constitute his nature and are characteristic of who he is. These attributes comprise his intrinsic, eternal and moral characteristics,[42] and should not be confused with his activities.[43] God's attributes are not humankind's conceptions projected upon him, but are eternal and cannot be separated from his being and essence. The attributes of transcendence and immanence have already been dealt with – what follows is a discussion of the rest of *Kanu*'s attributes.

## Omnipotence

The Limba use two ascriptions to describe the omnipotence of God: *Basɛmbɛ wo* ('The Powerful One')[44] and *Womandi wo* ('The Great One/The Almighty').[45] God is the one to whom absolute power and might are attributed.[46] *Kanu* is who he is, and can do what he chooses because of his omnipotence.[47] Ultimate responsibility for everything that happens from birth until death is attributed to God. *Kanu* is considered the ultimate cause of a person's fortunes or misfortunes in life and death, the determiner[48] of the number of children born in a household, of all events and even of the existence of the world. Therefore, the Limba depend on *Kanu* for every aspect of their daily endeavours and their welfare.

In the Limba worldview, every plan is made and every human achievement is reached '*th]k] ba Kanu*' ('by the grace of God'). Humankind lives and exists by the grace of *Kanu*.[49] No human effort will ever succeed *mɛmɛ Kanu tha mɛ* ('if *Kanu* does not agree'). His stamp of approval is indispensable to make any activity effective. Even when all necessary actions have been taken to have a good farming season, to hunt animals, and to rise to positions of prominence, if *Kanu* is not consulted for his approval and blessing, human efforts are in vain.[50]

Anything that happens in a person's life is attributed to the will of God – that is why the Limba say, *'mani moka Kanu'* ('it is God's doing').[51] This does not imply that God is held responsible for evil or for unfortunate happenings – it simply infers that God has allowed these situations to happen. Therefore during times of serious problems or disappointments the Limba say *'yaŋ piy] mafeŋ ma ka Kanu'* ('I will leave everything in the hands of God'). There is a cause behind every problem or disaster that befalls humankind. When a plight befalls someone, the Limba often say *bagbontɛ* ('not for nothing'), which means that there is something responsible for the problem. God's overriding power surpasses that of any being. He has no equal. He knows what is right for the Limba. *Kanu* is ultimately responsible for each person's life and status, and for everything in creation.[52] He is 'the ultimate cause and justification of all things'.[53] The Limba traditionalist sees the omnipotence of God as the source of all his other attributes. God's omnipotence is the basis upon which his other attributes are discussed.

## Omnipresence

The Limba say *Kanu kin kamɛ kamɛ* ('God is everywhere').[54] *Kanu* is believed to manifest himself during times of worship and religious gatherings. His presence is strongly assumed at all sacrifices. He is there with them. The omnipresence of *Kanu* is also seen in connection with natural occurrences such as thunder and lightening. The Limba, like many other Sierra Leonean people are especially afraid of curses/'swears' relating to thunder and lightening.

## Omniscience

Because *Kanu* is omnipotent, he is also omniscient. He is *Wo k]thɛ wo/Wo hakiyando* ('The one who knows all').[55] He knows and understands the thoughts of everyone on earth, and he knows what is right for us. God's omniscience means that his wisdom and knowledge are limitless and that even if humans may know 'some things, it is only God who knows all. No one else is worthy of, or is given, the attribute of omniscience'.[56] Often it is because of humankind's imperfect and incomplete knowledge that people affirm God's omniscience. There is a common view in West Africa which originated from Nigeria that says: 'No one knows tomorrow'. A person plans ahead but from a human point of view he/she cannot tell exactly how things will turn out; in the final analysis only God knows. As a result of this limitation of imperfect and incomplete human knowledge, the Limba are accustomed to making decisions and plans 'by the grace of God' (*th]k] ba Kanu*). Because of God's omniscience, he knows what is right and suitable for us. *Kanu* not only knows, he also sees, for nothing is hidden from the sun, this is also true with God who sees and knows all. Everything is under God's observation. 'God sees whatever we do'.[57] The Limba, like the Kono and Yoruba, believe that 'wrong-doers cannot escape the judgment of God'.[58] In this regard, if the Limba have been wronged and are unable to discover the person who has wronged them, they say '*Kanu kJtena yi koni penki*' (God sees you, you will meet him). Idiomatically this means, 'I did not see you doing the act but God saw you and you will meet him in judgment'.

# Activities of *Kanu*

## *Kanu* the Creator

Like most Africans, the Limba 'attribute the creation of the universe to God'.[59] In that respect *Kanu* is known as, *Wolehine Kafay wo* ('The one who made the universe'). To the Limba there is no one with such power to have created the world except *Kanu*.[60] The Limba word '*lehinia*' ('creation') means not so much 'creation from nothing' as 'fixing or ordering'.[61] Apart from the belief that they are created by God, for which reason they refer to him as *Wolehine wo/wameti/ mina* ('The one who made humankind/Us'), the Limba in the hinterland still maintain that the ethnic group was God's primary creation, followed by the different cultural groups in the country.[62] God not only created the Limba, but he owns them. In that respect *Kanu* is further referred to as *Wobile mina* ('Our owner').[63]

*Kanu*, as creator, is the ultimate cause and justification of all things: animate and inanimate things, everything seen and unseen. He is the source of all life. In some prayers God is thanked for the creation of the river, forest, mountains and trees, and for the benefits which come from them. In such prayers, God is thanked for the fish in the river, for wild food and medicine in the forest, for the awesomeness of mountains and hills. The Limba see nature as representing God's creative power and provision for their needs. The belief that God is the creator implies that God exists and that he is 'the fount and apex of all existence'.[64]

## *Kanu* the Chief and Judge

Because of his outstanding power and his ability to rule well and to dispense justice without prejudice,[65] *Kanu* is referred to as *Gbaku* ('Chief'),[66] *Gbaku wunthe* ('The Only Chief')[67] and *Gbaku Womandi* ('The Great Chief').[68] Chieftaincy is the greatest institution and 'most Limba would find it difficult to conceive of social life' without it.[69] It is by the chief's authority that the people in his jurisdiction are able to carry on their day-to-day affairs or maintain their respective positions. As in the case of the human chieftaincy, the Limba would find it very difficult to conceive of social life and maintain their daily living without God's rule and provision. As a chief, *Kanu* is always thought of as a political head who performs the functions of a judge, and maintains justice and equity. Among other things, a Limba chief[70] must be able to 'cool people's hearts', 'know everything that happens in the country' and should be kind, 'generous and continually helping people' by looking 'after orphans and those with no relations and help those who are poor.' It is implied in one story that the purpose of the chieftaincy is to look after orphans and the sick.[71] For this reason God has been referred to as *Kanu Wolɔ hoy* ('God is good'). *Kanu* not only does good to the poor and needy, he is also the one to whom the marginalised and the victims of injustice turn in times of distress. When taken advantage of, the Limba are quick to say *Yaŋ pɛnɛni ka Kanu* ('I leave my case with God'). God as a chief fits this profile. Most Limba chiefs I have met, are not shy to tell you that the ability to rule well is a task that only God can handle perfectly. The village/town and section chiefs who, as well as ruling, also judge cases will tell you that interpreting the traditional by-laws and giving right judgements is not easy without a conscious dependence on God's wisdom.

## Kanu the Teacher and Adviser

The Limba believe that the skills and abilities they possess and by which they make their livelihood or perform religious requirements are learnt from God, *Bathanani iŋ Bamaŋ wo* (The Teacher and Adviser). Traditionalists believe that God gave their forebears all the trade skills that they passed on to them as well as the present skills and abilities that they possess. In stories,[72] it was *Kanu* who 'showed the Limba how to grow rice, tap palm wine, make sacrifice, exercise their strength, and cook their food'.[73]

# Anthropomorphic attributes of *Kanu*

The concept of *Kanu* as father is currently popular among the Limba. It appears that this may be a recent development, as Finnegan earlier observed, '*Kanu* is never addressed as "father"'.[74] *Kanu* is seen as a male figure and is now often referred to as 'Our Father' (*Fandantu/Handantu*). The Limba understanding of God's fatherhood is influenced by the role of the father in their family structure. The father is looked upon as the ultimate authority and there are several ideal qualities that belong to him, for instance, the giving of life, love, faithfulness, continued care, and protection, and the wisdom that guides and instructs.[75] The notion of God's fatherhood indicates an intimacy that can be compared to that which exists between a parent and child.[76] The Limba strongly believe that God has parental compassion for his creatures, and if they as disobedient children, make the appropriate ceremonial sacrifice for restoration, pardon and forgiveness, no doubt, God will have pity and restore them. In that regard God is known as *Kanu wo pɛnɛni biya* ('God who forgives people') and *Kanu kin kinikini* ('God who has pity'). Because Limba society is still dominated by male chauvinistic ideals, the consideration of God as a female figure has not yet reached most Limba traditionalists. *Kanu* as a male or father figure is comfortably accepted without reservation in Limba communities.

# Worshipping *Kanu*

Worship is the way in which the traditionalists stay connected with the supernatural and continue their intimate relationship with God. The Limba also worship to achieve *hu/ kutheben lima* ('a peaceful heart')[77] because living at peace with the Supernatural and the world around you, requires inner peace. A mind that is divorced of greed, envy, hate and bitterness of any kind is considered peaceful. Outward peace and health come as a result of inner peace and a cool spirit. In particular, God is worshipped for whom he is and for what he continues to do for humankind.

The primary method through which the Limba worship God is by offering sacrifices (*Saraka*). Pouring libations (*Agbumandi*), invocations (*Kama-gbonkilitande*), prayer (*Kuramine*) and singing *(Kamaluŋa)* are all part of the sacrifice liturgy and ritual.

It should be noted that although libation usually takes place as part of a complete sacrifice, it can stand alone as worship in a few instances, such as at the ground-breaking for the construction of a new building, when dedicating a house/building, at state functions, and in most cases when welcoming a newly wedded person into a family. These ceremonies provide continuity for the survival of the community. Also, through these ceremonies, believers are reminded that they all share a common heritage.

The items offered as sacrifices to *Kanu* vary according to the level and purpose of the sacrifice, the social and financial status of the bearer, and the advice of the sacred specialist. If the ceremony requires the offering of an animal, it may be a cow, a sheep, a goat, or a chicken. An animal sacrifice may be either a blood sacrifice or a bloodless sacrifice. In the former, the animal is slaughtered. Some of the meat is cooked and eaten by the worshippers, while the remaining uncooked meat is distributed to households.

When the animal is not killed (in the case of a bloodless sacrifice), the animal is set free after the ceremony and it should be left for the remainder of its life to die a natural death. Because it is God's living sacrifice-property belonging to God, it is sacrilegious to kill and eat such an animal. The offering of plants and fruits to God is also considered a bloodless sacrifice. Bananas, oranges and kola nuts, are the most common choices for fruit offerings. Rice can also be used as an offering.

In every case, three items must be present to make a Limba sacrifice complete: water, kola nut and moulded rice flour mixed with sugar. Often there is also wine, charcoal and a prepared meal. These items are all symbolic:

- Water (*mandi*) has several symbolic meanings;[78] it stands for peace and harmony, and life. It cools and refreshes, and 'it is also the simplest and most acceptable manifestation of hospitality'.[79]

- Rice-flour (*hudɛgɛ*), because of its whiteness, symbolises purity and cleanliness.

- Kola nut (*huthugeŋ*) is a means of communicating with the supernatural and is used to determine the willingness or readiness of *Kanu* and or the ancestors to accept the advances of the living. This is accomplished through throwing the two halves of kola nut on the floor. If both the inside halves of the kola nut land turned upright, it is an indication of acceptance and the ceremony may continue.

- If wine (*maŋpa*) and charcoal (*tɛrɛ*) are included in the ceremony, the wine is for happiness/merriment, and the charcoal is to prevent misfortune.

- A prepared meal (*kutuŋ*) stands for joy and satisfaction.

Sacrifices for forgiveness, cleansing, protection, health, well-being, fortune and averting misfortune, thanksgiving, the various degrees of sin, politics, victory and as required by the worshipper, are all offered on five levels. Acquiring the items for sacrificial purposes does not present a challenge for the Limba. The main concern is the ability of the worship leader to 'speak well' (*gboŋkoli/thenlika*) in order to achieve a positive result.

Sacrifices for thanksgiving are less stressful than those made for liberation from sin, averting plagues, protection and welfare, because they are not for the removal of sin or misfortune (although a brief intercession for the forgiveness of sin is made at the start of the occasion in order to stand blameless).

In thanksgiving, the worshipper comes with the assurance that he/she is fulfilling God's purpose by being grateful in return for his goodness to them. Because the Limba are grateful by nature, the skills for expressing appreciation and thanks are known by the majority of the people.

Penitentiary and petitionary worship are a different matter. The ability to speak well to the supernatural is not treated lightly. The leader's duty could rightly be compared to the role of a solicitor/advocate, in a judicial matter, as he/she pleads for clemency on behalf of a convicted client. A defence lawyer who wants a more lenient punishment, or perhaps no punishment, for a guilty client(s) must mount a strong appeal in order to win the mind of the judge or jury. In Limba thought, a lawyer who succeeds in liberating a guilty client is a person who 'speaks well'.

Penitentiary worship is a pleading for forgiveness and salvation. Therefore, 'speaking well' to the supernatural is of vital importance to attain this end. Speaking is a key component of Limba philosophy and society and plays a prominent role in the entire Limba cosmology. A comment made frequently in Limba circles is: 'If humans know how to talk to one another with respect and with the proper use of words, what about talking to God who owns us with far more honour'?

## Levels of worship

There are several levels and forms of sacrifice offered to God in different places and at different times of the year. Five levels are prominent:

### Chiefdom level

Of all the levels, chiefdom sacrifice is the most elaborate because it involves participants from all the villages and sections within the chiefdom. The most common occasions which call for a chiefdom sacrifice are natural disasters (such as floods, droughts, and sickness) or accidents.[80] Less common occasions, on which chiefdom sacrifices may be offered include the installation of a new chief, the death of a chief or a notable chiefdom official, as well as the ceremonies held on the fortieth day after and on the first anniversary of the death of such an individual. Chapter 9 will deal with the sacrificial rites pertaining to the installation or death of a chief made both in the Limba homeland and in the Western Area.

### Section, village or town level

Sacrifices at the section and village levels are less elaborate and deal with issues that do not affect the entire chiefdom. The purposes are often the same as those of the chiefdom level sacrifices.

### Compound or clan level

Sacrifices made at the compound level are offered mostly for the welfare of the compound's members, to return thanks for their prosperity, and to make requests for the various needs of the members. Weekly sacrifices are also made in some compounds.

### Household level

Sacrifices made at the household level are usually bloodless. Kola nuts, rice flour, fruits and cooked rice are common items for household level sacrifices. The oldest active member of the family leads the worship. This may be done at the grave site of a family ancestor or in the house. In many homes, for the first forty days after the death of a relative, white rice and any of the palm oil sauces are cooked daily without salt and pepper (*kulemeti nuth]ŋ*) and placed near the head of what used to be the deceased person's bed. In some homes, simple sacrifices and prayers are offered daily.

## Personal level

Personal sacrifices are essentially the same as those made at the household level. The difference is that at the personal level as the name implies, the ceremony can be done by an individual, or in some cases, an uncomfortable individual may seek the help and guidance of a sacred specialist to perform the rite on his/her behalf. For instance, if an ancestor gives an instruction to be carried out by an individual (such as to offer a sacrifice), the person may inform a sacred specialist about his/her experience. He/she relays the full message or received instruction to the sacred specialist who, in turn, performs the ceremony.

## Acts of worship

Sacrifices at the chiefdom, section, village and household levels all involve groups of people, share similar communal characteristics and contain numerous rituals. Because of the degree of similarity between these levels, this study will only consider rituals at the chiefdom and personal levels.

## Chiefdom level

### (a)    Prelude

When a disaster of large proportion occurs within a chiefdom, people come together to try to make sense of what has happened and to give support to those who are directly affected. The diviner is called upon to find out the cause of the calamity. Most often, when the tragedy is natural, a sacrifice for propitiation is recommended. A date for the sacrifice will be fixed and a message sent to all the villages and sections of the chiefdom to participate in the arrangements and the ceremony.

The main components for the sacrifice are cows (the number depends on the crowd expected), which are usually provided by the Paramount Chief. The ceremony may take place at the Paramount Chief's compound or at the source or location of the disaster. For example, in the case of flooding, the ceremony may take place on the banks of a river, or in the case of a mudslide, it may take place on a mountaintop.

Representatives from all the villages and sections of the chiefdom (mostly chiefs or dignified officials) are expected to travel to the Paramount Chief's compound a day or two before the event to present their gifts and contributions, and to give support where it may be required. Upon arrival, the local arrangements team, which is normally made up of important personnel, welcomes the visitors as they arrive, further explains the rationale behind the sacrifice and concludes with the customary way of expressing thanks and appreciation for the gifts and contributions through a well-spoken oratory.

On the day of the sacrifice, the occasion may begin with dancing, led by several musical groups within the chiefdom, at different spots around the compound. A traditional meal is served after the dance or at the end of the sacrifice. In some communities, the cooking of food for the occasion is the sole responsibility of the men, and women are not allowed to enter the cooking area.

When the sacrifice is ready to be made, the cow (*manaŋ*) and the other items prescribed by the diviner are brought and placed at the centre of the compound. Because of the deference given to old age, and the belief that older people are closer to the ancestors and posses the experience needed to 'speak well', the oldest active male in the community (or the one appointed) is called upon to officiate. Where there is a community priest, he takes charge instead. Men who are wearing hats immediately remove them. Women are expected to cover/veil their heads and stay behind the men. All participants are obligated to sit or kneel on the floor and stretch their right hands over or towards (depending on proximity) the gifts to be offered.

## (b)    Invocation

Once the consent and readiness to accept worship has been sought through the use of kola nut, the leader then moves on to invoke the presence and attention of God:

| | |
|---|---|
| *Ka bari bena ye, l]ŋthaŋ* (three times) | Excuse us, let it be so … |
| *Ya mandi ye - manɛnitɛ* (three times) | Here is water – it is not tears |
| *Te beŋ/be foma nabgeleku:* | All of you/to you all as you go around: |
| *Yi yapoŋ …,* | You old men … (here the names of the outstanding ancestors are called) |
| *iŋ yapoŋ …* | with the other old men (their names are also called) |
| *Yi ndo komisa w] bohitɛ mina* | You as our parents and guide |
| *Beŋ kay na nde kay;* | You went to your place |
| *Beŋ pey mina dondo* | You left us here |
| *Miŋ ndo thɛbinɛ lima na-pɛthɛ* | helping us so that we may have perfect peace |

After every completed phrase, the participants respond with the word *amin/amina* (a Muslim word for 'Amen'). Because the Limba have enormous respect for age and position, no one casually approaches an elder with a request. For this reason, it is customary to seek permission when approaching the supernatural. It shows deference, and it ensures that the worshippers will not disturb God or the ancestors. The Limba concept is that if humans can give respect and reverence to elders, greater respect should be given to God. The word *bena* ('us') is commonly used when addressing God and the ancestors. The usual word for 'us' is *mina* which is used later in the prayer. If God is the focus, the second person singular pronoun *yi* or *yina* ('you') is used. References to non-ancestral spirits are clearly stated.

Water is poured out as libation to God or the ancestors in order to 'cool' their minds. In Limba culture, one way a victim expresses forgiveness to an offender is to accept water from the latter and drink it as an indication that his/her anger or bad feelings have been cooled down or washed away. Water is both qualitatively and quantitatively better and greater than tears which are not adequate to fulfill this requirement. That is why worshippers offer water, and specify that it is not tears.

After water has been poured out three times as libation the focus of the sacrifice is then identified. 'All of you/to you all', is a reference to God and the ancestors who are believed to be 'moving around' as spirits. This is one of the many times that God and the ancestors are jointly referenced. In most cases, God is addressed, in prayer, through the ancestors. This action buttresses Finnegan's earlier findings that *Kanu* is worshipped in prayers and sacrifices both through the ancestors, and at times concurrently.[81]

The word *yapoŋ* ('old men') used here to refer to the ancestors is the common word of respect for old men who are alive. This is the part in the prayer where the names of the community ancestors as many as the worship leader can remember are then called. The relationship between the living and the ancestors is like that of a parent and child. The ancestors are in the 'abode of the dead' manifesting great interest in the living.

The above invocation is common in sacrifices performed at all five levels. In invocations, the supernatural is approached in reverence with water and invoked to be present and pay attention to the worship and needs of the people. This enables the worshippers to then express the purpose of their worship.

### (c)    Purpose of worship

A statement of the purpose of the worship follows the invocation. Here the leader states the reason for which the sacrifice is being offered. If the nature of the sacrifice is for propitiation, the leader may say:

| | |
|---|---|
| *Kɛrɛ nthonani na kunthe mina* | But sickness has overcome us |
| *Awa miŋ luwe na miŋ thake bena* | So we heard that we offended you |

| | |
|---|---|
| *Bɛŋ na se mina thetiyeke* | That is why we have come to apologise |
| *Iŋ miŋ bena pɛnkita yiki bambaŋ* | And to present you this respect |
| *saraka sathamɛ bali ye* | Sacrifice is capable of handling any problem |

In this case, the sacrifice is necessitated by an epidemic. Although God/the ancestors are helping the living, sickness/disaster has struck. The cause of the epidemic might be that the supernatural has been offended. In that case, the people have come to apologise and make amends to God/ancestors. As already discovered, apologising is a prominent characteristic of Limba culture. The worship is both an expression of apology and an offering of respect through sacrifice which is the highest respectable means of relating to God and to the ancestors. It is also the most capable means of handling problems. Literally, the prayer 'Saraka sathamɔ bali ye' means, 'Sacrifice does not get tired in handling problem'. This expresses the confidence and belief that the Limba have in the power of sacrifice.

Or the following will be said:

| | |
|---|---|
| *Yi k]thɛn nambara/nampara* | You know what has |
| *ba pɛnka kub]ri ko* | befallen our community |
| *Mina npati nda/be kɛnda* | We are your children |
| *Miŋ se iŋ huberina do* | We have come with our crying to you |
| *Ba masitay mina* | So that you can help us |
| *ka nambara/nampara ba kantu ba* | with our problem/suffering |
| *Na yɛr]koy yi ba miŋ sa hɛ/fɛ* | As you have allowed us to come to you today |
| *N]ŋ yibe yɛr]koy thanaŋ tha* | May you accept the gifts |
| *sise miŋ than* | we bring |

Because God is 'All-knowing' and he is considered a parent, in some prayers, as in this case, the situation that necessitated the sacrifice is not given. As their God and parent par excellence, *Kanu* already knows their predicament. The word 'cry' may mean real tears, sorrow, problems or needs. God as their parent is the only Being to whom they can cry for help. He is the only one who is more than capable of wiping away their tears, soothing their sorrow, taking away their problems and providing for their needs. The strength and ability to stand before God in worship is a privilege that comes through God's grace. God should further allow them to present their gifts of sacrifice and to accept them in the spirit in which they are presented.

## (d)    Presentation of gifts

The purpose of worship is followed by the presentation of the items to be offered for the sacrifice. The size of the gifts for the sacrifice depends on the number of worshippers and the chiefdom's financial capability. One by one, the items brought for the sacrifice as the case may be, are called out to God and their significance is stated.[82] For example:

| | |
|---|---|
| *Ya manaŋ kɛndaŋ* | here is your cow(s) |
| *Ya manpaŋ kɛndaŋ* | here is your wine |

## (e)    Intercessory prayers

After the presentation, the main prayers are said to the ancestors for God's approval (*yɛr]k]y*) and blessing (*thaduba*) for the sacrifice about to be offered. The leader may pray:

| | |
|---|---|
| *N]ŋ miŋ be tha th]m] bali* | May we have power to confront any problem |
| *Ba thankaha tha kantu* | And to protect our lives |
| *Hɛɛrɛ kobekede, hɛɛrɛ kapothi;* | Peace above, peace on earth; |
| *N]ŋ mu be niy] mu kantu* | May it be ours |
| *Ho, masala!* | O God! |
| *Miŋ be d]ŋ] iŋ kub]ri ko* | May we have peace in our families |
| *N]ŋ nthonay be mina gbarih],* | May sickness escape us, |
| *ho, Masala* | O God |
| *Ka piriŋine miŋ,* | Where we wronged you, |
| *beŋ be mina pɛniyɛ- ho Masala* | forgive us, O God |
| *N]ŋ miŋ be bariŋande* | May we stay away |
| *iŋ gboroho-baliŋ ba gbarahɛŋ* | from evil matters and problems, |
| *ho Masala* | O God, |
| *Te beŋ kay,* | The day you will go, |

| | |
|---|---|
| *tɛŋ tuma do* | that is the time we will come |
| *Na wuŋ pate mina* | As we end it |
| *ka barika- woo-lʃnthaŋ* | in peace Amen |
| *Mawumaŋ, sɛkinthaŋ ko kandeŋ* | Right now, take yours |
| *e mina dununa ko kantu* | and give us ours |

In life's journey and struggles, *Kanu* is the source of empowerment who can confront the known and unknown challenges that threaten people's harmony and success. The people also need the protection of God as the battle rages. As peace is vital for individuals and for keeping society together, the worshippers need the peace that comes from God for themselves and their families on earth. The sickness which has caused the sacrifice is not a sign of peace and well-being; therefore God's healing is required. Suffering is believed to be a measure from God for wrong doing. If the epidemic is due to a wrong deed, the people are seeking God's forgiveness so that they will be healed. They need a heart that is divorced from all evil and that will guard against destructive motives and actions. If, on account of their supposed wrong doing, God does not listen to them this time, they will come again even if he is not there. Assuming that all has gone well, it is fitting to end the prayers with an assurance that peace has been made with God. God's immediate response to their worship is then sought by the throwing of kola nuts to know God's mind. The effectiveness or ineffectiveness of a sacrifice is determined by the response of the supernatural.

Alternately the following prayer may be used:

| | |
|---|---|
| *Miŋ thʃnthʃn nʃŋ tha duba abekede* | We ask that blessing from above |
| *be mina penki ka kɛkɛŋ do* | be granted to us below |
| *Miŋ kiŋ ka berina kɛnda* | We are here to pour out our cry to you |
| *Masala* | the Mighty One; |
| *Yi wuntheŋ ko sɛkiti namparɛŋ* | You alone can take away |
| *ba kɛntu* | our plight |
| *iŋ dunkuna mina ma thɛbɛ* | and restore peace |
| *iŋ malʃholima* | and happiness to us |

| | |
|---|---|
| *Dunkuna mina malʃholima* | Grant us peace (within and without); |
| *NʃŋJŋ nampara be tha mina pɛnki* | May we not experience trouble anymore |
| *Miŋ se iŋ sarakabaŋ* | We come with this sacrifice |
| *ba malʃholima* | so that we can have happiness. |
| *Gbaku wo sise manaŋ* | The chief has brought a cow |
| *ka hɛra ba dunku yi ninbaŋ* | out of what you have given him |
| *Ba yina miŋ be kutu malɔlima* | So that we can give it to you and find peace. |

The worship leader may start by asking God to bless them with blessing from above and proceeds to tell God the reason they came to Worship. As in other cases, the worshippers are pouring out their cry to God Almighty. He is the only one that is capable of taking away their troubles and giving them peace and harmony. Therefore, he is implored for the absence of disaster through sacrifice which is the most vital means of worshipping and reconciling with God. The prayer concludes with a statement expressing the chief's effort in providing the sacrificial animal to be offered for the attainment of peace.

### (f)    Offering and sharing of gifts (saraka baŋ)

The items are then offered to God. Cows are bound and thrown down by the young men before they proceed to cut the animals' necks. The cows are then skinned and the meat is shared amongst the participants. The one who kills the animal always gets the neck, the Paramount Chief gets the breast portion and the fore legs and portions are given to the village and section representatives. The rest of the meat is shared amongst the elders and participants.

### (g)    Conclusion

At the end, the leader concludes with the words *lɔŋtha na wuŋ pate mina, kabarika oo lɔŋthaŋ* ('we have finished, excuse us, Amen') indicating an end to the ceremony. Then the cultural dance resumes.

## Personal level

The invocation ritual at the chiefdom and personal levels are virtually the same. Words in the plural used at the chiefdom level are changed to the singular at the personal level. If the worship is done without the assistance of a sacred specialist, the individual may say the following:

| | |
|---|---|
| *Kanu yina leyinɛ mina kafaido* | God you created us in this earth |
| *Hati wo kɛnda se iŋ huberina do* | Your child has come crying to you |
| *Ba masitay yan ma ka bali yan* | so that you can help me solve my matter |
| *Yi kʃthɛn wo kin yan* | You know mine |
| *NʃŋŊ yi yɛrʃkʊy yiki baŋ* | May you accept the honour |
| *yan sise bena* | I bring to you |

God who is solely responsible for the creation of Limba knows the situation and solution to the worshipper's predicament that is why he/she has brought sacrifice not only to him (*Kanu*) but to the ancestors (*bena* 'you') as well.

Or the following alternate prayer may be said:

| | |
|---|---|
| *Kanu yan Kʃtɛ yan thake bena* | God I know I have offended you |
| *Awa bɛna se yan* | So, that is why I have come |
| *ba thetiyeke bena* | to apologise/beg you |
| *Iŋ yan bena sisa yiki* | And to bring you respect |
| *Ba bena duŋkun yan* | In order that you will give me |
| *ma malɔholima* | rest and happiness. |

Misfortunes are believed to be the result of wrong doing; it is therefore not uncommon for a worshipper at the outset to acknowledge that his/her actions have offended God (*Kanu*) and the ancestors (*bena*). The only way to be at peace with the supernatural is to beg (*thetiyeke*) for forgiveness in order to attain rest and happiness. The achievement of rest and happiness which is true peace is, in a sense, salvation for the Limba.

If a sacred specialist performs the ceremony, when the items for the sacrifice are required, the individual takes them to the officiating person who will say the following on behalf of the worshipper:

| | |
|---|---|
| *Yan sise hati/pati wó kɛnda* | I have brought your child (the name of the worshipper) |
| *Wundɛ tepe yan ma ni* | He/she told me to tell you |

| | |
|---|---|
| *ba tepe bena na be mase* | to help him/her |
| *Nambara/nampara na kunthe ni* | Problem/trouble has overwhelmed him/her |
| *Yi* wunthe pe na bilɛ sɛmbɛ | You alone have the power |
| ba mase ni | to help him/her |
| *Wundɛ sise saraka* | He/she has brought sacrifice |
| *ba bena mase ni* | so that you can help him/her |

As the worshipper stands and watches, the sacred specialist introduces him/her by name to God and the ancestors, and proceeds to relate the cause and purpose of the sacrifice on behalf of the worshipper with the understanding that God and the ancestors are the only ones able to help. The following intercessory prayers may be said personally. If a specialist assists the worshipper, the same words are used in the third person.

| | |
|---|---|
| *Yan se ba niya yina thubu* | I come to worship you |
| *NJŋ malekeŋ beŋ saŋ ba mase yama* | May the angels come and help me |
| *Fandaŋ wo kinyan yan dunku yina* | My father I give to you |
| *dayina yah* | my entire being |
| *KJtJ ko iŋ siɛba;* | My body and my spirit; |
| *yan thon dunku dayina yan dan mu* | I give to you, look at them |
| *Sa punku ba tJta* | I am unable to carry |
| *doni ba kiyan woŋ…* | my burden… |
| *Sarakaŋ baŋ iŋ wuŋ raminɛ* | The sacrifice and prayer |
| *kon mase yama* | will help me |
| *Nambara kabanka ba sɛkiti* | Take away the trouble at home |
| *Nambara ka bonshJ sɛkiti* | Take away the problem in our family |
| *yan pe bali wo bali kɛnda* | I leave every matter with you |
| *Yina kJtɛ baiyo bai* | You know everything |

For the first time in these prayers the word *thubu* ('worship') is mentioned. *Thubu* denotes prostrating and expressing a longing for God. In desperation, the worshipper has come to seek and implore God to send his angels as support during this time of anguish. In dedication of his/her entire being (both the physical and spiritual), the worshipper expresses inability to bear his/her burden and goes on to name it. With confidence that sacrifice and prayer will solve the problem, a plea is made to God to eradicate the trouble at home. After making his/her request known, the worshipper leaves everything in the care of God who is all-knowing.

## Conclusion

The Limba, like many Africans, believe in God, who is the highest being in the supernatural hierarchy. He is properly called *Kanu Masala*, but is more frequently called by the shorter form *Kanu*. *Kanu* exists and lives above. He is Almighty and Omnipotent, the Creator and Sustainer of all things, who is therefore all-knowing. He is the Chief that rules from above, their Teacher and Father. The names or epithets, and attributes of *Kanu* portray his character, abilities, qualities and peculiarities.

Some traditionalists juxtapose their belief in *Kanu Masala* ('God Almighty') with a belief in *Kanu Wopothi* ('god below'). The latter is considered less powerful and is seen as being mischievous. This is not a personal being, but a descriptive category applied to any evil or mischievous spirit. Unlike *Kanu Masala*, *Kanu Wopothi* is not generally understood to be an object of worship.

*Kanu Masala*, who alone occupies the top position in the supernatural hierarchy, is worshipped through sacrifices, offerings, prayers and libations. The Limba approach him through the ancestors, and with the aid of angels (*Malekɛŋ*), which are the subject of Chapter 5.

# 5

# Angels

## Introduction

Angels (*malekɛŋ*) are spirits who act as direct agents of God's will, and share an intimate relationship with God. Very few African societies speak directly about angels. However, most Africans speak about 'gods', 'spirits', 'divinities', or 'deities' with characteristics similar to those of the angels found in Judeo-Christianity. The Limba, however, do not have words or synonyms for 'gods', 'deities', or 'divinities'. They talk more about angels in terms that are similar to Judeo-Christianity and Islam.

The Yoruba speak of *orisa* ('divinities', 'deities' or 'gods') who are believed to be ministers of *Olodumare* ('God') with responsibilities similar to those of angels.[1] The African gods, deities or divinities are believed to be created by God and are subordinate to him. These spiritual entities 'intimate but subordinate relationship with God is conceptualised in terms of Father/Son, Chief/messenger or lord/servant relationships'.[2] Their status is not very different from the Christian idea of angels. In Nuer Religion the 'little gods' are the *malaika* ('angels') from the Arabic word *Mal'ak*.[3]

Herbert Lockyer, a British missionary to Kenya, recounts a story of angelic encounter told to him by a native Mau-Mau who converted to Christianity:

> One dark night the men of the Mau-Mau tribe were climbing the hill up to the school to capture and kill the missionary children, and fulfil one of their vows by eating a white man's brain. Suddenly men in white robes appeared all around the school, with flaming swords, and the natives ran back down the hill. Then the new Christian asked, 'Who were these men; were they angels?' A missionary replied, 'We do not have enough men on the staff to surround the school, and we have no flaming swords,' with wide eyes the native shouted, 'They were angels!'[4]

This story suggests that, although the belief in angels appears to be less prominent in African religion, some ethnic groups, like the Mau-Mau people, hold some belief in angels. The Mau-Mau man's question and the missionary's response suggest that the Mau-Mau man's knowledge about angels may have predated his conversion to Christianity. A solid effort by scholars to examine Africa angelology might reveal even more groups with such a belief. Although African belief in angels clearly predates the modern arrival of Christianity, however, it is uncertain to what degree it predates the early interaction with Islam or how much of the concept may be adapted from Islamic beliefs.

Although Limba traditionalists talk about Angels in terms that are similar to Christianity, the church does not consider this to be a point of commonality. Rather, it has dismissed the traditionalist's belief in angels, and based on Ezekiel 28; 2 Peter 2:4; Judges 6, believes that the angels known to traditionalists are actually fallen angels, more commonly referred to as 'demons' (Matt. 4:24; 7:22; Mark 1:32, 34; Luke 4:41).

I will proceed to discuss two main issues on the subject of angels in LIR — the nature and the role of angels.

## The nature of angels

The Limba believe that angels are spirits with wings (*bapey*), who are also capable of assuming human likeness. They can rightly be described as hylomorphic because they have both a spiritual and a physical nature. They are spirits because they dwell with God, they have wings because they fly (*akain*), and they assume human form because this is how they appear to people, whether physically, or in dreams. They appear to people in physical human form as 'strangers' who help them in times of great need.[5] An example of one such encounter is the following account by a Limba interviewee:

> I remember before the war when I was home, it was the time when my youngest daughter was to be initiated into the *Bondo* society. That year, the farming season was bad. My crops did not do well and a portion of them were eaten by animals. I had no money for the ceremony to take place. Three weeks before the scheduled date as I was walking home from my farm and entering my village, I came across a man I have never met in my life. He was wearing white and carrying a bag. We exchanged greetings, and he asked me for directions to *Makɛrɛ* village, two villages from ours, which I gave. But before he left he asked me if I could offer him a cup of water to drink. I took him to my place and gave him some water, he drank and thanked me. I then accompanied him out of the village to ensure that he took the right road. In appreciation of my hospitality, he opened his bag and gave me a substantial amount of money, more than what I needed for my daughter's initiation ceremony. I could not believe what was happening to me. One thing that was puzzling about this man was that his face was very difficult to look at and he could not give me his name or address. There is no doubt in my mind that he was an angel sent by *Kanu Masala* to help me.

This story shows that angels protect people, have the ability to communicate, and have human needs such as thirst.

The Limba also believe that angels possess moral attributes. Angels as *Patibeŋ Kanu* ('Children of God') are endowed with love (*matimo*), and they are kind and good (*hayʃhʃ*). Even the angel of death (*maleka wo bilɛ hutuka*) is considered good because he fulfils God's mission. There are male and female angels. Irrespective of their closeness with God, angels are the only kind of supernatural being that does not require worship or veneration. Like humans, they are under God's instruction and were not created for worship or veneration.

## The role of angels

Angels have several roles to play. Their primary role is that of a messenger/servant (*batʃntiwʃ*). The Limba believe that as messengers/servants of God, angels are the carriers of God's message, and the fulfillers of God's plan. Angels relay God's messages mostly in dreams. As messengers/servants, angels are mediators between God and humankind which puts them in special relationship with God, of whom they are agents, and with humans who, in most cases, are the object of their service.

It is on account of this mediatory role that the angels and the ancestors are sometimes confused. In much of ATR, 'a similar role seems to be given the ancestors, whose continued existence in a metaphysical state takes them "nearer to God" and allows them to help their descendants'.[6]

God also assigns angels to look after particular individuals. This duty entails caring for (*atima*), protecting (*apaŋ*), guiding (*adinki*), guarding (*akinkinti*), and helping (*masite*) the person. Although God does not delegate the duty of seeking the interests of people to the ancestors, as he does to the angels, the roles of angels and the ancestors as mediators, and caretakers of humankind, overlap. Unlike the ancestors, the role of angels as caretakers and protectors goes beyond death. An angel's final job is to take the deceased to *katilɛ* ('the home of dead'), after which the angel returns to God to give a report of his/her duties.

Until recently, the positions of angels and ancestors within the supernatural hierarchy were a matter of debate among the Limba. Although there are still a few who continue to debate this, at present, the majority of traditionalists believe that angels, because of their nature and relationship with God, are higher spiritual beings than the ancestors who are human spirits and have attained their spiritual status by human design.

# Conclusion

Angels[7] occupy the second place after the Supreme Being in the supernatural hierarchy of LIR. Unlike most other Africans, the Limba do not teach about or believe in 'gods', 'divinities', or 'deities'.

Angels are hylomorphic, that is, they are nature spirits with wings, but are also capable of assuming human form. They are believed to be spirits because they are with God, but may also assume human likeness because that is how they appear to people, whether in dreams or in person. They communicate and have human needs. There are male and female angels. As children of God, they possess the moral attributes of love, kindness, and goodness to people.

Angels are God's messengers and servants. In that regard, they carry God's messages and fulfil his plans. In their capacity as messengers and servants, angels play the role of mediators between God and humankind; they care for, protect, guide, guard and help people. When an angel completes his/her service to the individual assigned to him/her he/she takes his/her charge to the place of the dead (if the deceased is qualified to go there). Chapter 6 addresses those individuals who reach this place of the dead.

# 6

## Ancestral spirits/ancestors

### Introduction

The word which the Limba most frequently use for the ancestors is the plural *Fureni be/Hureni* (lit., 'old people'). It has been suggested, that, *fureni be* is a lengthened form of the word *furu/huru* ('breeze/wind/spirit'). The word *furu* is from the root *fu* ('to sleep, to spend the night'). Synonyms for *Fureni be* include *bila, biya beb]r] be* and *betiyɛ be* all of which mean old people. An alternate word for *Fureni be/hureni* is *nbembɛŋ* ('Forefathers, Great grandfathers').[1]

As in most African cultures, the ancestors are of central importance in the lives of Limba traditionalists. Their presence 'is felt all through Africa in spite of Christianity and western sophistication'.[2] Africans are still attached to their ancestors. Therefore, to take the ancestors away from them is to 'destroy their roots in the past, their culture, their dignity and their understanding of *communion sanctorum*'.[3] It is not surprising, then, that this is the point at which Christianity has encountered the stiffest resistance in Africa.[4]

Christian Limba leaders, like their AOG forebears, have unanimously condemned ancestor veneration as a heathen and superstitious practice. As such, the church attempts to completely avoid the use of the word 'ancestor' because in Limba vocabulary the word *fureni* ('ancestor') and its synonyms are only used in reference to the venerated dead. Therefore the church feels strongly that the use of the word in the church's vocabulary would create a great misunderstanding. The designation 'hero of faith' is instead used when dealing with any biblical passage that uses the word 'ancestor' or 'ancestors'.

This chapter will first discuss which of the three terms 'the dead', 'ancestral spirits' or 'ancestors' best suits the Limba context. It will then discuss the requirements for and process of becoming an ancestor, the role of the ancestors, the question of whether the reverence afforded ancestors properly constitutes worship or veneration, and the rituals involving the ancestors.

### The dead, ancestral spirits or ancestors?

Scholars are divided as to which designation appropriately represents the status of the venerated dead. Although Finnegan[5] uses the term 'ancestors', in a few instances when discussing the spirits of dead relatives of the Limba, she prefers the general term 'the dead'. She states that when an adult who is not a witch dies, a ceremony is performed on the third day during which, the deceased goes to be with the other dead in an unknown place called *katile*. She goes on to say that the burial rites of a known witch[6] are, 'correspondingly, somewhat different'. Finnegan's statements infer that children and witches do not attain ancestorship, thus it stands to reason that the Limba do distinguish between their dead as to who qualifies to attain ancestorship. Two years later, writing about the ancestors she states:

> They cannot be represented as a separate category of beings with special supernatural characteristics of their own juxtaposed to humans, for in Limba eyes the dead are merely human beings who were once alive and now are dead and buried, basically resembling their children who are now on earth ... Possessing essentially human qualities as they do, there is no point in introducing the dead into the stories as a special category. For in spite of the important part played in Limba life by prayers and sacrifices to the dead, they are at root not special separate beings at all, but the human beings of the old days – 'they are us'.[7]

This statement sharply contradicts the contemporary Limba view that tends to separate the ancestors from the general body of the dead and humankind.[8] A majority of the Limba I made contact with during my fieldwork represented the ancestors as a separate category with special supernatural characteristics of their own juxtaposed to humans. They are closer to God than humans and therefore possess a supernatural entity. 'They are understood to have maintained their human qualities, yet they are thought to be much more *spirit* ...'[9] Therefore, the term 'the dead' is a misnomer. In a wider perspective, Mbiti has argued that:

> 'Ancestral spirits' or 'ancestors' are misleading terms since they imply only those spirits who were once the ancestors of the living. This is limiting the concept unnecessarily, since there are spirits and living-dead of children, brothers, sisters and barren wives, and other members of the family who were in no way the 'ancestors'. One would strongly advocate the abolition of the two terms ... and replace them with 'spirits' or 'the living-dead' whichever is applicable.[10]

No matter how brilliant and useful the terms 'spirits' and 'the living-dead' could be to designate the ancestors; from the worldview of the Limba (as well as most other Africans), they are not adequate replacements for the terms 'ancestral spirits' or 'ancestors'. Death itself does not qualify a person for ancestorship. In Limba view, not every person that dies necessarily becomes an ancestor. As will be discussed later, certain conditions should have been met while the deceased was alive and a ceremony of inclusion into the rank of ancestors must follow the death of such an individual.

For the Limba, the terms 'ancestral spirits' or 'ancestors' are appropriate to differentiate 'the ancestors' from the ordinary dead and the spirits of ghosts and witches all of which are categorised as 'human spirits', because they were once human.[11] The general category of non-ancestral spirits also includes nature spirits and non-ancestral human spirits.

The ancestors in Limba view are the spirits of those individuals (both male and female)[12] who have successfully gone through the stages of life to attain prominence and who, after death, have been included in the community of the venerated dead.[13] The visibility of the graves (*thaloma thaŋ*), the movement of the ancestors *furu* ('breeze') which they do not see, but feel, and the appearance of the ancestors in dreams are the reasons they believe that the ancestors are in their midst and are accessible.[14] Their proximity does not constitute a threat in any way.

In view of the aforementioned, I join the likes of Geoffrey Parrinder, W. T. Harris, Harry Sawyerr, Edward Fashole-Luke and Anthony J. Gittins,[15] to name a few, in recommending the use of the terms 'ancestral spirits'/'ancestors' interchangeably in reference to the venerated dead. It is now pertinent to discuss the Limba view of who is qualified to be an ancestor.

## How does one become an ancestor?

The qualifications for becoming an ancestor and the methods of installation as an ancestor vary slightly among the Limba. As in many African societies, death itself does not make the individual a Limba ancestor. Usually, a potential ancestor is recognised as such before death because of his/her achievements, status, moral standards and positive contributions to society. It is on the basis of these qualifications that the living decide who becomes an ancestor. For the Limba, the following requirements are taken into consideration. The deceased must:

- Have attained old age,[16] hence the term *fureni be* and its synonyms, *bila, biya beboro be* and *betiyo be* ('old people'). Being an adult does not by itself qualify a person to become an ancestor. Technically, a person is considered an adult after initiation, but in reality this is not true until the age of forty.[17] The Limba believe that death at a ripe old age is a natural death and is God's death. This idea parallels the current Limba view, 'to say that death is through 'Kanu' would therefore be rather like our speaking of a 'natural' death – Kanu kills old people, for one expects them to die'.[18]

- Have been a married adult and had at least one child.[19] Marriage in Limba view conveys higher economic and social status. A child is important so that the name of the deceased will be remembered in prayer and offering and not be lost. The rationale is that a person cannot be an ancestor to the ethnic group unless that person is an ancestor to a member of the group. At the household level of ancestral veneration the oldest son or a surviving brother calls to the deceased.

- Have been a member of a recognised secret society: the *Gbangban* for men, the *Bondo* for women.[20] By becoming a member of a secret society, an individual joins the ranks of the forebears, from 'whose life-blood the existence of the community was derived and on which it continues to be sustained with the aid of the contemporary leaders'.[21]

- Have performed a heroic task during his/her lifetime. Heroism constitutes professional expertise and outstanding ability or prowess. The ancestor of an ethnic group may include a master hunter, a master witch catcher, a master healer and many others.

- Not have been a witch. Witches are considered to be destroyers of personal and communal harmony. They kill and destroy by spiritual means. The Limba are afraid of witchcraft, which makes life more stressful to cope with because the power of witches transcends distance and no one knows when he/she will become a victim of witchcraft.[22] Because of 'their evil ways' witches cannot live with God. They do not have a place in God's presence as good spirits do, and will not be permitted to enter *Katilɛ* to join the other dead.

- Have died from natural causes, and not unnatural causes such as an accident or suicide. Deaths from diseases considered to be unclean (small pox, leprosy, epilepsy, tuberculosis, etc.) are also considered unnatural deaths and are indications of God's punishment of the wicked and sinful.

The first four requirements indicate that a person's achievements and/or status in life determine his/her future in the spirit-world. The last two requirements prohibit 'bad deaths'. When a person who has met all of these requirements dies a 'good death', the final step is the performance of the necessary funeral rite for the attainment of ancestorship. This rite is the process by which deceased persons are installed as ancestors, and once the proper rites are performed, the deceased takes his/her place among the ancestors.[23]

In most Limba societies, this inclusion occurs three days after the person's death. Upon death,[24] and before his/her burial, the prospective ancestor is considered *kubeli* 'a corpse' (as in the case of all Limba dead). After burial in *huloma ha* ('the grave'), the dead person becomes *hure* ('a ghost'). At the ceremony on the third day (*kudigbiŋ*), it is believed that the deceased joins the other dead at an undisclosed place of the dead called *Katilɛ/Katiyɛ*. The deceased is then considered *fure wo* ('an ancestor'). In the hinterland, arrangements are made for burial to take place within a day. The prospective ancestor is buried by his or her respective secret society amidst great wailing and singing. After the burial, a hen is killed over the grave. On the third day those who were unable to attend the burial itself, find time to attend this important funeral rite of passage.

At household, compound, village or chiefdom level, it is very important that the oldest available person leads this particular ceremony because he/she is considered to be the closest to the ancestors.[25]

At all levels, the ceremony of induction may follow this order: the leader begins by saying: 'Excuse us, let it be so' (three times). It is customary to approach the supernatural with these words in order to show deference, and for fear that God or the ancestors might be disturbed by the worshippers.[26] The names of current ancestors are called; usually the walk of life of the candidate determines which particular ancestors are to be called upon. For example, if the deceased was a chief, a hunter, a diviner or priest, his/her ancestral predecessors will be called upon by name. This is followed by a general reference to *Kanu* and to the rest of the ancestral spirits that were not named, 'All of you/to you[27] all as you go around: You old people'.[28] This statement identifies the focus of the veneration as God and the ancestors who are believed to be 'moving around' as spirits. Although God and the ancestors are known to reside in the sky and the place of the dead respectively, as spirits they are capable of roving around. This is one of the many times that God and the ancestors are jointly referenced in Limba worship. In most cases, God is addressed, in prayer, through the ancestors. This action buttresses Finnegan's findings that *Kanu* is worshipped in prayers and sacrifices through the ancestors, and at times concurrently.[29]

The leader proceeds to determine the willingness or readiness of the ancestors to listen to, and accept, the veneration that is about to be offered by the throwing of kola nuts. If the result is positive, the leader can proceed with the rest of the ceremony. The first stage is concluded by expressing thanks to both *Kanu* ('God') and the ancestors for their willingness to listen to what they are about to say.

Next, the death is officially reported. Although it is believed that the ancestors are aware of what goes on, they still need to be informed officially by invocation and prayer of important occurrences in the community. The ancestors are then invoked to accept the deceased into their ranks. The achievements and qualifications of the deceased are mentioned and the same kola nuts are again thrown to ascertain the mind of the ancestors. If this indicates that the ancestors accept the inclusion of the deceased, the items for the sacrifice are offered.

First, water is poured as libation with the words: 'Here is water – it is not tears'. Which are repeated three times as the libation is being poured. The reason for the libation and for the clarification that 'it is not tears' is the same as that discussed earlier in 'Worshipping *Kanu*'.

At household level, if the family can afford it, a hen is killed and cooked. If not, red and white kola nuts and rice-flour will suffice. Usually at compound, village or chiefdom level, a sheep or cow is killed and the meat is shared. The number of animals slaughtered depends on the size of the crowd. When the ceremony is concluded, musicians and dancers take over to entertain mourners and guests. This may go on until the early hours of the following day.

Some people have a shrine in their homes where stones representing the family/clan's ancestors are kept.[30] After the death of a would-be ancestor, a stone representing him/her is added to the receptacle or the place in the house where the other stones are kept. This system enables the family/compound to keep records of the number of their ancestors. This system makes provision for honouring a deceased family member who although he/she did not meet the community's requirements for becoming an ancestor, was not a witch and did not die from 'unnatural' causes.

The time, energy and resources invested in these ceremonies, and the continued trust and belief that Africans place in the ancestors demonstrate the essence of ancestral spirits in traditional spirituality. What part do the ancestors really play in the lives of believers? Let me proceed and consider their role in Limba view.

## The role of ancestors

The ancestors are very closely involved in all of Limba life. They manifest an interest in the welfare of the communities to which they belonged, and still belong.[31] They do not only belong to the village, but also order the lives that are led there. Even though spatially they are primarily associated with their graves, because of their spiritual nature, they are capable of following their children wherever they go. This makes it possible to call on them anywhere, even from the far reaches of the world. Not only are they ever-present, they are also conversant with everything that goes on in the community. The traditionalists' relationship with the ancestors is not one of paranoia, but of intimacy and deference as is evident in their relationship with their living elder kin. The ancestors are around for the good of the people, not to afflict them. They are in a better world, in God's realm because they are good spirits.[32]

The ancestors inherited certain things from God and these they bequeath to the community, namely: farming methods, hunting skills, skills of interpreting weather conditions and the seasons of the year, story-telling, the rules of their secret societies, songs and dances. They continue to uphold all of the social institutions, techniques, values and ideals of Limba life. Like good parents, the ancestors reprimand the living when they are aggrieved or neglected and the living do nothing to make amends.[33] Suffering or punishment from the ancestors is for the welfare of the victim. As a parent punishes a child for his/her welfare, the ancestors consider their living relatives as their children and do their best to help them. They are the closer link between the people and God.[34] The ancestors plead with God to help the living, to give them things such as children, wealth or food. In this context the ancestors are seen as earthly parents who plead with the chief to help their children. They communicate directly with God, and for their children's sake, intercede with God who is in control of everything. The ancestors cooperate with *Kanu* and represent the social ties within the community. In Limba view, as in that of most African peoples, ancestors are good spirits who continue to interact and seek the welfare of their people in several ways. Mbiti aptly describes the role of the ancestors in some African communities as follows:

> They return to their human families from time to time and share meals with them, however, symbolically. They know and have interest in what is going on in their family ... They are guardians of family affairs, traditions, ethics and activities.[35]

Gabriel Setiloane expresses it this way:

> Ah ... yes ...! It is true.
>
> They are very present with us ...
>
> The dead are not dead; they are ever near us;
>
> Approving and disapproving all our actions,
>
> They chide us when we go wrong,
>
> Bless us and sustain us for good deeds done,
>
> For kindness shown, and strength made to feel at home.
>
> They increase our store, and punish our pride.[36]

It can rightly be said that the Limba and other African peoples have a high regard for their ancestors. This leads to the question: 'Do the Limba worship or venerate their ancestors'? This issue will now be discussed.

## Ancestor worship or ancestor veneration?

Finnegan states:

> The exact relations between Kanu and the dead are not clearly defined. In a sacrifice Kanu is often called on as well as the dead, and some Limba, when the question is raised, tentatively suggest that perhaps the dead convey the requests of the living to Kanu in somewhat the same way as a father intercedes for his children with a dominant chief.[37]

Today, the Limba more clearly define the relationship between *Kanu* and the dead. No one debates the fact that *Kanu* is higher than the ancestors and that he is in control. Although the Limba offer the same sacrifices and prayers to the ancestors as they do to *Kanu*, although most often they are offered concurrently,[38] although in these acts of sacrifice and prayer they express their submission and dependence on both *Kanu* and the ancestors, and although this would seem to constitute worship, most Limba will argue that they are venerating the ancestors and not worshipping them. An interviewee clarified it in these words: 'I wish to make it clear that we do not worship the ancestors as we do in the case of God, we merely venerate them as our dead relatives who brought prosperity to our communities and who continue to care for us'.

The question of whether Africans worship or venerate their ancestors has been a matter of interest for several decades. Fashole-Luke[39] poses the question: 'Do Africans worship their dead ancestors or do they venerate them'? To him the question is not just academic because it involves, 'the problem of whether African ancestral cults are merely idolatrous practices', and 'the problem of whether the rituals and practices offered to the ancestors constitute true worship'. He challenges the reader to assess 'whether the quality of the so-called worship offered to the ancestors is of the same nature as that offered to the Supreme Being'. His considerations are vital in attempting to explore an adequate answer to the question.

After a close look at ancestral rites, practices, and prayers, Sawyerr[40] argues that ancestral cults constitute true worship. Much later in another published work,[41] after discussing his views and the views of several other scholars on the appropriateness of the term 'ancestor worship' he concludes that, 'Africans do worship their ancestors as they do their divinities', and this worship, he continues, 'consists of prayers, sacrifices, and divination on communal occasions or prayers and divinations on private occasions'.[42] In Sawyerr's understanding, the rituals and practices offered to the ancestors both in public and in private constitute legitimate worship and are of the same nature as those offered to God.

Parrinder, after considering the various scholarly debates on the issue, suggests: 'Perhaps the African attitude to the different classes of spiritual beings might be expressed approximately in terms used in Roman Catholic liturgy … It might be helpful to speak of Latria for the Supreme Being alone in Africa, with *Hyperdulia* for the gods and *Dulia* for the ancestors'.[43] *Latria*, *Dulia* and *Hyperdulia* are terms that were developed to differentiate between different types of honour in order to make more clear which is due to God and which is not. *Latria* is used to designate the honour that is due God alone, *Dulia* is used in reference to the honour that is due humankind especially those who lived and died in God's friendship (i.e., the saints). *Hyperdulia* is a combination of the words hyper and dulia meaning 'beyond dulia'. This is reserved for the honour given to the Virgin Mary, who is worthy of honour higher than the *dulia* given to other saints.

On the basis of these distinctions Catholics have sometimes said: 'We adore God but we honour his saints'. Fashole-Luke in a similar view states:

> The basic axiom of the Christian faith is that worship should be offered to God alone; but throughout the history of the church there have been rituals and prayers offered to saints which sometimes come very close to worship. Critics of the cult of saints and martyrs have often described these rituals as 'Saint Worship', but their practitioners have replied that it is neither Christian worship in a debased form, nor does it contradict the basic Christian premise that God alone is worshipful. This reply is grounded on the distinction between various qualities or levels of worship, so that a Christian can honestly say that he worships only the true and living God and venerates the saints. This does not mean that veneration of the saints is not genuine; it is merely an acknowledgement that it is at a lower level than worship of God. We suggest, therefore, that this distinction is equally valid in African religious beliefs and practices concerning the ancestors and provides us with an adequate paradigm for understanding these rituals and practices: worship of the Supreme Being, veneration of the ancestors.[44]

Fashole-Luke further argues that, 'the phrase "ancestor worship" is emotionally charged, conjuring up primitive and heathen ideas of idolatry', while in contrast, 'the phrase "ancestor veneration" is neutral', and does not present the negative images provoked by the former phrase. He strongly recommends scholars discard the phrase 'ancestor worship' and adopt the phrase 'ancestor veneration' in discussions pertaining to African ancestral cults.

Having considered the arguments of Parrinder and Fashole-Luke, 'ancestor veneration' seems a more appropriate term for the African regard shown to ancestral spirits than does 'ancestor worship'. The Limba venerate their ancestors on account of the mediatory role that they play between God and the living, and the service they render as elders of their families. The ancestors deserve veneration for what they are and do for their people. Here follow some rites of ancestor veneration.

## Ancestral rites

Like God, the ancestors are reached primarily through sacrifices and offerings, which are made for various purposes and at different levels.[45] Ancestral sacrifices may be offered in response to the advice of a sacred specialist whose advice was sought out for the appropriate response to some present or imminent misfortune. They are also offered for regular and recurring purposes including, the accession of a new chief, the dedication of a new house and at important points in the rice farming cycle. Smiths, hunters, diviners or the owners of swear make their own special sacrifices to dead predecessors.

At chiefdom and village/town levels, a sacred specialist or occasionally, the oldest person present, leads the ceremony. At compound level, the oldest person in the clan conducts the ceremony. At household level, the oldest son, or the brother of the deceased, leads the ceremony, which may be held at either the house or the graveside. It is common to find a small shrine in a home where food is occasionally placed for an ancestor. On a personal level, a competent individual who knows the procedures and formalities may offer sacrifice to an ancestor or ancestors. However, most people prefer to engage the services of a sacred specialist to perform the ceremony on their behalf because of his/her religious status.

At all levels, the ceremony follows a similar order starting with an invocation, followed by a libation, a prayer, the offering of gifts and a concluding prayer. At chiefdom and village/town levels, music and dancing precede and follow the ceremony. In most cases, kola nut (*huthugeŋ*) and rice flour (*hudɛgɛ*) are used to contact the ancestors. Because the ancestral rites are nearly identical at all levels, and are very similar to those offered to God, I will avoid eminent repetitions by considering only the unique household and personal graveside (*kahuloma/kaboŋa*) ceremonies.

## Household ceremonies

The Limba, like other ethnic groups in Sierra Leone, go to the cemetery to speak to an ancestor or ancestors.[46] In the hinterland people go to the cemetery as often as they want. In Freetown, most people go to perform ceremonies at the cemetery only on New Year's Day. In general, Limba traditionalists believe, that it is more respectful and effective to go to the graveside when time permits in order to speak to the deceased than to attempt to do so from home. The family will take along red kola nuts, rice-flour, fruit and water for the ceremony.

A family may go to the graveside to offer sacrifice for help in resolving family disputes or for straightening out a recalcitrant family member who is causing trouble for him/herself and for the family or community. In these situations the family consults an ancestor who was capable of resolving family dissensions amicably or whose advice the troubled family member was known to heed.

The oldest son or the brother of the deceased or the oldest family member present will lead the ceremony. The kola nuts will first be opened and, as they are being rolled on the deceased's grave, the leader may say the following words:[47]

| | |
|---|---|
| *Pa Sori, yu fambul dɔn kam fɔ si yu* | Pa Sori, your family has come to see you |
| *Wi want fɔ tuk to yu* | We want to talk to you |
| *Mak wi si yu mind thru dɛn* | Let us see your mind through these |
| *kola ya so* | kola nuts |

As usual, the ancestor is named. In this case he is called Pa Sori.[48] As expected; his family came to speak with him because they needed help. The ancestor's compliance is sought using kola nuts. From the contents of the prayer that follows, it may be concluded that Pa Sori gave the visitors the go-ahead to continue their ceremony. This favourable response is followed by the pouring of a libation, after which, the reason for the veneration is made known:

| | |
|---|---|
| *Pa Sori*, wi n] kam f] dist]b yu pis | Pa Sori, we have not come to disturb your peace |
| *Wi gɛt prʔblɛm we yu no bot* | We have a problem that you know about |
| *Yu na bin di pʔsin we bin de hɛp wi* | You were the person helping us |
| *Di trʔbul we you lɛf na di hos* | The trouble that you left in the home |
| *de go ]n* | still goes on |
| *As no yu bin abul f] mek pis* | As you were the peacemaker, |
| *we done cam to yu* | we have come to you |
| *Yu de naw na di tru w]l hɛp wi* | You are now in the true world |
| *]si G]d de* | where God is |

In Limba spirituality, the good dead are always presumed to be in peace. Therefore, the visitors make it clear that they have not come to disturb the peace of the deceased. They came with an old problem that the deceased already knew of, and which he had tried to help resolve while he was alive. Now that he is in the true and better world where earthly occurrences are no longer hidden from him,[49] the family believes they can count on him for help even more than before because he is in a better place and has the resources to help resolve the problem. After making their purpose known, they make a request:

| | |
|---|---|
| *Mek G]d gi yu the pawa f] hɛp wi* | May God give you the power to help us |
| *dis tɛm* | this time |
| *Hɛp wi sɛtul dis prʔblɛm* | Help us settle this problem |
| *N] tay ya pan wi* | Do not be weary with us |
| *Hɛp the fambul f] ti nap tranga* | Help the family to stand strong |
| *Luk wetin wi bring f] yu* | Look what we brought for you |
| *Mek G]d hɛp wi ]l. Emen.* | May God help us all. Amen. |

The first line shows that the venerators attribute power to God and not to the ancestor. If the matter is going to be settled once and for all, it is God who will give the deceased the power to fix it. Pleas are made for patience, because the venerators are concerned that they might have already wearied the deceased with their problem and for help to enable the family to stand strong in times of challenge and struggle. The sacrifice is then offered and the ceremony is concluded with a request for God's help for both the venerators and the ancestor.

## Private ceremonies

When a deceased relative appears in a dream[50] and complains about being mistreated, the person who has offended the deceased goes to the grave to make amends. He may take along a sacred specialist with the usual kola nut and rice-flour. If the individual decides to go alone, he/she may start by saying:

| | |
|---|---|
| *Mi papa/mama a dɔn kam fɔ tuk to yu* | My father/mother I have come to talk to you |
| *ɛn sɛtul di prɔblɛm we a dɔn kawz* | And settle the problem that I have caused |
| *A tek Gɔd naym beg yu* | I take the name of God to beg you |
| *fɔ padin mi fɔ di bad a dɔn du* | to forgive me for the bad I did to you |
| *Na Gɔd in naym a beg fɔ padin* | In God's name I am begging for forgiveness |
| *Mi na mɔtal man a de mek mistek padin mi* | I am human I make mistakes forgive me |

The opening statement shows that the individual has come to talk to either a parent or an older deceased person.[51] The deceased was offended through either neglect or some other unacceptable behaviour by the venerator. The phrase 'I take the name of God to beg you',[52] is a tool to encourage a positive response where this may be difficult to obtain. Among the Limba as well as among the other ethnic groups of Sierra Leone, no one expects to be turned down when asking for forgiveness or making another request in the name of God. This is thought to ensure a positive outcome.

The worshipper proceeds to acknowledge his/her failures and throws the sides of the spilt kola nut on the ground to determine the result. When a positive result has been obtained, the ceremony is concluded with an expression of thanks, and as in the concluding phrase of the previous ceremony's prayer, God is asked to help both the worshipper and the ancestor:

| | |
|---|---|
| *Tɛnki, tɛnki, a gladi fɔ padin mi* | Thanks, thanks, for forgiving me |
| *Mek dadi Gɔd mek we fɔ wi ɔl* | May God make a way for us all. |

## Conclusion

The ancestors continue to play a vital role in the Limba worldview. These are the ancestral spirits of adult dead relatives who during their lives had attained physical and/or moral prominence, and have made positive contributions to their communities, and on the basis of these qualifications, they have been included in the community of the venerated dead. They are believed to be very active in the affairs of the living as mediators between God and the living, as guardians of the culture, institutions and values of the ethnic group. In that respect, the Limba like most African traditionalists venerate their ancestors.

The rituals used to venerate Limba ancestors are very much the same as those used to venerate God. However, a close look at the prayers offered during ancestral veneration makes it clear that the ancestors are regarded as subordinates to God.[53] For example, the last lines of the closing prayers of the household and private graveside ceremonies: 'May God help us all' and 'May God make a way for us all' show that the venerators pray for God's help and God's way for themselves and for the ancestors as well.[54] Having dealt with the ancestors, it is now appropriate to move to a study of non-ancestral spirits in Chapter 7.

# 7

## Non-ancestral spirits

### Introduction

The Limba, like most African peoples, believe that their spiritual world is full of a myriad of spirits.[1] 'We have hundreds of spirits roving around us', the traditionalist would say. These non-ancestral spirits are believed to be quite different from ancestral spirits.[2]

Finnegan states that non-ancestral spirits 'are not and never have been human'.[3] According to Limba pneumatology, this is not true of all non-ancestral spirits. Ghosts, who are considered non-ancestral spirits, like the ancestors, were once human and fall under the category of 'human spirits'. These 'human spirits' live outside the social order of the village, unlike the ancestors (who are in the village and fall within the social order). For this reason, unlike the ancestors, the 'human spirits' are considered to have more in common with animals than with humans and they relate only to individuals who have 'double sight' *thaya thale* (lit. two eyes or four eyes in English, two in front, two in back of the head) to see and communicate with them. Non-ancestral spirits fall into the category of *Kanu Wopothi*.

The church, which regards all such spirits as 'evil' and/or 'demonic' holds the traditionalists responsible for encouraging evil spirits by having personal and collective relationships with them and for venerating them because of their powers.

This chapter will examine the various categories of non-ancestral spirits, their characteristics, and how they are venerated.

## Categories and characteristics of spirits

### Nature spirits

Non-ancestral spirits are classified as either 'nature spirits' or 'human spirits'.[4] 'Nature spirits'[5] are believed to be either celestial[6] or terrestrial[7] beings.[8] They were created as they are and are either associated with natural features, or rove disassociated.[9] Because of the 'mysterious, fearsome and somatic nature'[10] of *thabekede* ('mountain/hill top'), *thasili* ('lake'), *gb]nk]ni* ('forest'), *ŋagb]r]* ('cave') and *kutɛnɛ/ŋatɛnɛ* ('cotton tree'), spirits are commonly believed to inhabit them.[11]

Nature spirits are varyingly considered good, bad, or ambivalent in their operations.[12] The good spirits are called *kukahi/mabakaŋ*, and the bad ones are called *waali/mbaaliŋ/mbaayiŋ*. In general, nature spirits are characterised by an unpredictable ambivalence and must therefore be treated cautiously.

The acquisition of special skills and good fortune is often attributed to good spirits. It is believed that *bathaya* (a person gifted with a 'spiritual eye'), will take 'a good spirit' to become wealthy, or renowned or to attain certain skills. It is a common notion that people with outstanding abilities or talents in the community have 'taken a spirit'. For example, sacred specialists, people with unsurpassed skills in athletics, hunting, music, craftsmanship, or education, as well as the leaders of secret societies, are all believed to have obtained their outstanding abilities from spirits.[13] What is generally said to have happened is that, a double-sighted person wandering in the bush meets a spirit that says it is willing to help him or her get whatever he/she wishes. When an agreement is reached between the two parties, the person returns home carrying a smooth stone representing the spirit he/she has taken.

Although people may be aware of the causes of a particular misfortune, cases of suffering, accidental or inexplicable deaths, as well as the deaths of young people, are usually considered to be the acts of evil spirits. Natural disasters, such as floods and the consequent destruction are attributed to the anger of nature spirits.[14] Destruction caused by thunder and lightning, wind and rain, is similarly thought to be the work of spirits.[15]

The following are the most commonly consulted spirits in Limba pneumatology:

- *Ninkinanka*[16] is the spirit consulted by chiefs for power and influence. To gain skill and prominence in his chieftaincy, a chief has to be in constant touch with the supernatural. Apart from this understanding, traditionalists believe that the chief, as a powerful figure, derives his power from a greater power that makes ruling possible. This power may be the Supreme Being, the ancestors or the spirits.

- *Yaar]* is the spirit that possesses other prominent men in the community. Prominence is difficult to attain exclusively through human power or influence. Traditionalists believe that rich or famous people have taken the spirit *Yaar]* to make them what they are, and to maintain their status.

- *Kolidonso* is the spirit for hunting. Good and excellent hunting skills are attributed to the patronage of the spirit *Kolidonso*.

- *Sokoro*[17] is a dwarf spirit that is also contacted for hunting purposes. As the counterpart of *Kolidonso*, *Sokoro* is believed to be equally powerful, but much shorter in stature which makes him very swift to find game.

Clan and personal spirits also fall under the category of nature spirits. Some spirits are thought to stand in a special relationship with certain clans for example; *Kumba* is connected with households in Bumban and Bafodea, and the spirit *KJyande* is identified with the Biriwa chiefdom.[18]

The most popular and revered of all nature spirits is *Gbaŋgba*. It is the spirit of the male secret society and also the main spirit of the ethnic group. Although it is not known how, the females have, along with the males, come to accept *Gbaŋgba* as the main spirit of the Limba. As the main spirit of the Limba, it is not surprising that *Gbaŋgba* is feared by a majority of the people, and also why the *Gbaŋgba* secret society is found only in the Limba homeland. There are also several other kinds of spirits, which are referred to as *Thumbu, Sumuyenke, Kondeyo, Hukoko,* and by several other names.

## Human spirits

The next category of non-ancestral spirits is 'human spirits' (*kuyimay*). These are the dead who have not been integrated into the ancestor cult. These include witches, wicked dead relatives and ghosts. Such individuals are believed to become malevolent spirits[19] roving around in the night or day to bewitch or injure the innocent, especially their enemies or infants.

### Witchcraft

Witchcraft (*thawɛthɛ/huwɛthɛ/huwɛthi*)[20] is practised by a man or woman called *bawɛthi wo/ bayaku wo* ('a witch')[21] who may potentially afflict people by mystical means through the power and encouragement of evil spirits[22] usually at night guarding against discovery. It is said that a witch leaves the body spiritually when 'asleep and goes out to attack another person, infant or adult' while their victim is also asleep.[23] Parrinder[24] has strongly dismissed such a belief as a delusion adding that: 'People do not leave their bodies or destroy the souls of others. So in fact there are no witches, though many people believe in them'. Parrinder, however, failed to give any evidence in support of his argument.

To most Africans witchcraft 'is the greatest wrong or destruction on earth'.[25] In the Limba worldview as in many African belief systems; suffering, sickness and death usually 'have their origin in witchcraft'.[26] Witchcraft is considered the 'reverse of normal values and behaviour' of the community.[27] For these reasons practitioners of witchcraft are always be considered evil and anti-social.

In Limba society, as in many African societies, the belief in witchcraft is very strong. Finnegan reported that, most Limba traditionalists, if asked why they believe in witchcraft would 'often reply by saying that after all the witches confess'[28] and 'no one could confess to anything so terrible if they were not guilty',[29] even today; this is still the most common explanation of this belief. Although witch-hunting is rare in Limba societies, there have been cases where accused witches have been made to confess under physical and psychological duress. However, because of modernisation, although a confession is seen as 'an indication of witchcraft practices', it does not on its own establish culpability for a crime.[30] Legally, Limba authorities are required to 'look very carefully at the circumstances of the confession and at corroborating evidence'[31] before taking any action.

The Limba believe that they are surrounded by witches acting invisibly. Witches are believed to acquire their power through their 'double eyes' which make them capable of seeing beyond the physical and ordinary. However, not all people with double eyes practice witchcraft. As mentioned earlier, many people with exceptional abilities are believed to have 'double sight'. This includes sorcerers and traditional healers.[32] It is also believed that twins and triplets posses 'double sight'. These individuals 'may possess the same powers as witches, but they are not necessarily malevolent'.[33] Most of them are good people who use their abilities to expose witches and those trying to harm others through mystical means. Some use their double vision to secure wealth and fame through the spirits. The Limba consider double-sightedness a gift from God. However, like many of God's gifts, while most people use it for good, some people misuse and abuse it.

Witches sometimes take on different forms to commit their mischievous acts. They, like other spirits, are capable of taking on forms of animals, reptiles and birds,[34] therefore some spirits are associated with animals[35] like leopards, elephants, lions, snakes,[36] owls[37] and vampire bats.[38] Most ethnic groups in Sierra Leone believe that even the bravest and strongest beasts are normally afraid of humans. Because of this belief, if the Limba hear of a wild animal attacking a person; it is thought that, the animal or reptile is not ordinary, and a witch must have entered it. A witch who takes an animal or reptile form is called 'baɲahi wo/bakahe wo'. Witches also deprive people through spiritual means by stealing their crops, plaguing and killing their cattle, causing harm and destruction to anyone who is seen as a threat to them politically or socially. Wicked like-minded people may procure the services of witches to eradicate a political opponent or a rival in love affairs.

## (a)    Process of witchcraft

When a witch is full of envy, malice or bitterness, at night, he/she assumes a spiritual form and leaves his/her physical body lying in bed while he/she goes and eats the internal parts of his/her victim by spiritual and mystical means. At times, a witch may use a gun[39] called 'kufaŋki' to kill a victim. If he/she is successful, the victim becomes a walking corpse and eventually dies. Sometimes, a witch's plan may backfire if another double-sighted person catches him/her in the act and decides to stop or destroy him/her. If he/she decides to stop the witch, the good 'double sight' individual follows the witch and blocks him from entering the house of the proposed victim. If this happens the witch should count him- or herself lucky. Alternately, if the 'double-sighted' person chooses to destroy the witch, he/she prevents the witch from entering his/her own house after a destructive trip. If he/she does not enter the house and take on his/her mortal body by daybreak, he/she will die. It is believed that witches even fly great distances to find their victims, the power of flight being achieved through the use of groundnut/peanut shells.[40]

### (b)    Eradication and prevention of witchcraft

The Limba, like most Africans,[41] seek to eradicate witchcraft because of the destructive results. This is usually done by having the witch named and caught after which the act of witchcraft is then reversed by a sacred specialist. There are several ways this may be accomplished. If the death of a person or an animal, or the destruction of something is declared to be the work of a witch, a diviner called, *basakapu* (a person who exposes witchcraft through a spirit in a box) is summoned to name the culprit. Depending on the community, if the accused denies the charge, a series of tests may be conducted to declare the truth, or a 'swear'[42] may be invoked to pursue the miscreant. If the offender is caught using a 'swear', he/she must undergo an elaborate and expensive ceremony to remove the eminent curse of the 'swear'. In most cases a person found guilty of witchcraft is required to make a public confession, and it is up to the village to either forgive or banish him/her.

The Limba are taught from childhood to protect themselves and their interests from witchcraft and evil spirits by procuring protective charms. Although a witch is considered to be powerful and is feared by most people, it is also believed that in the natural human existence he/she 'is vulnerable to certain charms and spells and could be repelled by them'.[43] Most Sierra Leoneans 'view the Limba as more involved in 'medicine' and the supernatural than any ethnic group in the country'.[44]

In general these charms are called *taliŋ beŋ* ('medicines'). There are several categories of *Taliŋ beŋ*. *Sɛbɛ* are objects used for protection of one's home or person. They may be worn as amulets or pendants or may be hung over the doors of houses in leather bags that have had tiny chunks of kola nut spat on them. *Kulʼŋki ko* are objects commonly buried on farms. *Ɗakurɛ*, and *kumanki/kuwanki* are objects visibly hung around farms to protect them against thieves. *Kulaba* is a combination of white, red and black pieces of cloth sewn together to be hung outside a house and to be fashioned into under vests and slips worn to protect people from bodily and spiritual harm.[45] People also wash and rub their bodies[46] with potions known as *Manɛsi*. Charms may also be sticks, stones, pieces of traditional cloth, or almost anything a person thinks is powerful.[47]

*Taliŋ be* are used to secure a feeling of safety, protection and assurance. A person's use of religious charms reflects invisible values and beliefs. These charms serve as 'visual aids'[48] that give confidence and security to the user.

The spirit of a powerful person is believed to live on after his/her death with the same passions as he/she had when alive. For this reason, people make sure that when a convicted witch dies, steps are taken to prevent him/her from surviving death to return and cause more mischief.[49] To this end, a sacred specialist (*basakapu*) is usually summoned and an offering is made to the ancestors to deactivate the power of witchcraft possessed by the deceased.[50]

## Ghosts

A ghost (*hure*) is 'an apparition or spectre of a dead person'.[51] Like many Africans, Limba traditionalists believe that a spirit becomes a ghost[52] when a person has not received proper burial and is resultantly 'wandering about between this world and the next'.[53] While ghosts in other traditions plague people 'and bring sickness to children',[54] ghosts in Limba tradition are harmless, but are notorious for stalking and harassing their targets until something is done to appease them. Usually, this is accomplished by performing a second burial rite.[55] Because of their habit of harassing the living, ghosts are considered to be evil spirits. Stories of ghosts haunting homes, offices and people are still common among most peoples in Sierra Leone. Finnegan concludes that in Limba perspective:

> Spirits of every kind share the same characteristics – that of being away from the village, potentially dangerous though often giving their favourites great riches, associated rather with individuals than a village or lineage as a whole; they are unlike both the dead who belong to all, and *Kanu* who is over everything.[56]

# Offering to nature spirits

An offering (*kudamaŋ*) is made periodically or as required to appease the spirits or as thanksgiving for a fortune received from the spirits. *Kudamaŋ* is offered to benevolent or malevolent spirits by the chiefdom/village/town, compound, household, or individual in caves (*ŋagbɔrɔ*),[57] or forests (*gbɔnkɔni*), near lakes (*husili/thasili*), or springs (*katha sosi*), under huge/cotton trees (*kutɛnɛ/ŋatɛnɛ*),[58] on mountains,[59] at shrines[60] (*thagbɔm/ŋathɔkɔ*) which have full-time priests, society bushes, and blacksmith's houses. *Kudamaŋ* is usually made in the perceived 'home' of the spirit to which it is made, it is seldom made at the family/clan shrine where the clan spirit (*nthɔngbakile*) dwells. Items offered to these spirits are much the same as those used for sacrifices offered to *Kanu* and to the ancestors. Let us consider some of these ceremonies.

## Forest spirits

Offerings to the spirits of the forests are made by those who have taken a spirit to become outstanding hunters or by those who believe that contacting the hunting spirits before a hunting expedition (*hudonso*) will ensure its success. A hunter (*badonso*) who has one of the hunting spirits (*kolidonso* or *sokoro*) may decide to give thanks to the spirit or may make an offering for forgiveness if the spirit has been neglected or offended. Either kind of offering may be either a blood offering or a bloodless offering, depending on the advice received from a sacred specialist, or on the wishes of the hunter.

During the ceremony, the spirit's name is called and the hunter, or the sacred specialist on behalf of the hunter, expresses his thanks for all the good the spirit has been doing for him. This is followed by the offering of gifts. If the purpose is to ask for forgiveness from the spirit, the hunter does that in the usual way someone might ask for forgiveness. The hunter determines whether he has been forgiven by the spirit or not through the use of kola nut in the same way as in the worship of God and the veneration of the ancestors. Another way in which the spirit may communicate is through the appearance and action of vultures. If vultures appear at a particular time and start eating the meat offered it indicates that forgiveness is in place. If they do not appear at the appropriate time, it may indicate the contrary.

## Water spirits

The spirit which controls rivers, lakes and streams is called *Mami Wata* ('Mother of Water').[61] Flooding that is not caused by rain is attributed to the work of the water spirit. Because *Mami Wata* is considered to be an agent of the 'god below', some people do not bother to appease her but take their concerns directly to God or to the ancestors. Others go to the stream, river or lake from which the problem emanated to make an offering and to offer prayers to appease *Mami Wata*. Also, if a river has dried up on account of a drought, the community may choose to pray to God and the ancestors or to go to the river banks and present an offering. Such an offering, like most others, can be either a blood or bloodless sacrifice.

The worshippers begin by informing the spirit of their presence, and the nature of their problem. Because it is generally presumed that disaster strikes when the spirits have been displeased or offended, the worshipers, often ask the spirit for forgiveness even though they are not sure of the wrong they have done.

The spirit is then asked to accept the offering and forgive the people of their wrong. The confession and offering is intended to put an end to further calamity. The ceremony is then concluded as the throat of the sheep is slit and the blood is drained and sprinkled on the river. The meat is left on the banks for vultures to eat.

# Conclusion

The Limba believe in a myriad of non-ancestral spirits which are classified as either nature spirits or human spirits. Nature spirits were created as they are, and are believed to be associated with natural objects like mountains, waters, forests, huge trees and caves, and with natural phenomena like thunder and lightning, storms and rain. Nature spirits are either benevolent or malevolent. Good spirits are said to be helpful to individuals and communities and must be honoured for their patronage and be appeased when offended. When offended or neglected, malevolent spirits become malignant to individuals and/ or communities, causing misfortune, suffering, death, and destruction. The Limba have personal and communal spirits that seek the welfare and interests of the individual and community. Offerings to return thanks and appreciation to benevolent spirits are sometimes made in any of the places mentioned above. Offerings are also sometimes made to drive away malevolent spirits.

Non-ancestral human spirits include the spirits of witches, wicked dead relatives and ghosts. The Limba believe in, and fear witchcraft. Witches are believed to possess animals, reptiles, and nocturnal birds to perpetuate mischief. So the Limba traditionalists do their best to protect themselves against the power of witches, and if possible, they try hard to eradicate witchcraft and its practitioners. To protect themselves from the power of witches, the traditionalists seek help through sacred specialists who prescribe the use of religious charms and objects. The Limba are renowned in Sierra Leone for their expertise in and obsession with traditional charms and objects. Ghosts are the spirits of the dead who did not receive proper burial rites. Although they are considered harmless, their habit of taunting the living has caused them to be classified as evil spirits. Offerings are not made to non-ancestral human spirits.

African pneumatology is anthropocentric and the spirits are defined morally by their relationship to man, whether they bring harm or good and almost any spirit may move from one classification to another based on their actions.[62] The chief harm inflicted by spirits is physical. God often appears to be silent in Limba pneumatology.

# 8

## Humankind

### Introduction

The Limba believe that there is a purpose for human existence; every individual has a role to play in the universe. In that regard, humankind (*wɔmɛti*) 'is at the very centre of existence', and the Limba 'see everything else in its relation' to humankind's central position.[1] Humans in the journey of life must deal with the supernatural, animate beings, and inanimate objects. This puts them in a position where they must strive to maintain a balance between personal identity as unique individuals on the one hand, and communal identity on the other.[2] This advocates 'the integrative notion of "person" as a being-in-plenitude who can assert his/her being only in concert with other beings'.[3] The Limba traditional worldview as it relates to humankind may be considered from the viewpoint of humanity's origin, and purpose in life.

The church does not seem to be overly concerned with the traditionalists' understanding of humankind as it has neither taken specific issue with, nor spoken out against, any of the following elements which will be discussed in this chapter, namely: the origin and nature of humankind, and humankind's relationship with God, animate beings, and inanimate objects.

### Origin and nature of humankind

Earlier, under the topic '*Kanu* the Creator' (see 4.4.1), the Limba belief that *Kanu* created humankind was discussed. This belief is so strong and prevalent in their worldview that there is hardly a Limba who thinks otherwise. The Limba believe that *Kanu* created them out of the earth,[4] thus they are products of the earth hence the word *wɔmɛti* (humankind) which literally means 'one created from the earth' or 'one of a town or village'. In general, humankind is believed to have originated from God, and is superior to and more intelligible than any of God's other creatures.[5]

According to Limba worldview, a person consists of a body (*kɔrɔ*) and breath (*siba*).[6] The body contains the breath, which comes from God and makes humankind a living being.[7] *Siba* gives life to the body and without its presence the body is lifeless. In addition to the body and spirit, humankind is endowed with a spiritual nature that enables him/her to relate with the supernatural.

## Relationship with God

The relationship between God and humankind in Limba view is based on the belief that humans are God's creation and that God provides and continues to provide for human existence.[8] Although objective proof is understandably lacking, the Limba claim to be autochthones created from the earth in their present homeland,[9] unlike all other Sierra Leonean ethnic groups who they believed were created somewhere else and later immigrated to their present place. This, the Limba claim provides them with a special relationship with God. Further, the Limba claim a special relationship with God because their ancestors told them that God himself came down and formed all their social and religious institutions, and showed them the skills necessary for living.[10] They also claim to have inherited their moral and religious ethics from God. Because of this special status and relationship with God, the Limba believe that they are obliged to sustain a harmonious relationship with God; therefore, all individuals are encouraged to strive to be at peace with God and others.[11] From the moment a person wakes in the morning, to the time they go to bed in the evening, everything must be done according to God's wishes.

## Relationship with other creatures

Humankind as a creature of the earth is part of the natural order. Humans share the universe with animate beings and inanimate objects which are all part of God's creation. Since humans are a part of nature, they are 'expected to cooperate with it'.[12] It is 'the need to remain in harmony with nature'[13] that has caused Africans to incorporate the environment and its inhabitants into their 'religious perception of the universe'.[14] For Africans, 'sacredness extends to their environment and all the means of sustaining life, that is, the sacredness of all creation'.[15] To be in harmony with nature is 'to be on good terms with one's entire social and spiritual world'.[16] Therefore, in Limba view, humans, as the highest and most intelligent creatures, have a responsibility to take care of God's universe and all that is in it. Every individual must be a caretaker of God's creation; humans must take care of the earth and God's entire creation because the animals do not have the ability to do so.

Limba people are both spiritually and physically connected to the earth. It is the place where their ancestors are buried, and it is the source of their livelihood. It is from this perspective that the Limba speak out and take a tough stance on ecological[17] issues. One interviewee made her frustration known this way:

> There are two things that are paining me about the way we treat the earth and what God has given to us. People are going from bush to bush cutting down trees for firewood to cook food. If you go now to some villages in my chiefdom, they look like deserts. The trees which are protecting these villages and giving them other benefits have been cut down. We know that wood is vital to cook our

food; I believe that there are other available means of providing fire for cooking. The other problem is with the pollution of some rivers and streams. Just take a walk along the shores of the stream around us. Without a doubt you will see trash and at least one dead domestic animal floating on it. There are a few more things that happen in rivers and streams that I cannot say here. If we are saying the earth is God's and He has delegated the upkeep of it to us, then let us do it the right way

From these words, it is clear that some Limba are 'treating nature as a mere object of exploitation for the satisfaction of human needs'.[18] As a whole, the Limba strive to maintain a physical and spiritual balance with nature. The goal is to live with sacred awareness and an ethic of eco-sustainability. However, for economic reasons and because of negligence and apathy, some are not putting into practice the teachings and beliefs they have inherited. The frustration expressed above is primarily about two issues which call into the question Limba stewardship of God's earth:

- The indiscriminate cutting down of trees for firewood has led to forest depletion and has left some villages looking like deserts. They have been stripped of their trees making these communities vulnerable to even the mildest storm that blows. Wood is the most common fuel used for cooking by people without electricity or kerosene stoves.

- The improper disposal of garbage and other waste has led to the pollution of many rivers and streams. Most people think that because rivers and streams empty into the ocean, anything dumped into them will be carried there and eventually rot away.

Some traditionalists believe that the careless handling of nature by humankind causes the prevalence of diseases like cholera and tuberculosis in Sierra Leone. Although most of the published series on ecology[19] have not addressed ATR and ecology, the contribution of ATR to the 'ongoing world-wide concern with environment cannot be overemphasised'.[20]

Limba traditionalists believe that God created the animals, which are a very important part of nature, and should be treated with respect. Every Limba clan, like those of many African societies,[21] has a taboo (*thana/kasi*), which forbids clan members from eating particular animals or birds. The infraction of a taboo is an offence called *kadɔkʃ]/kakʃ]*. In general the intentional destruction of any animal, reptile, or bird is considered a sinful act known as *kamalʃ]*.

However, in spite of these and other restrictions that are intended by the Limba to prevent the abuse of animals, and to foster harmonious relationships between humans and animals, the actual maltreatment of both domestic and wild animals is prevalent in Limba societies. This is because, as noted earlier in this chapter, the Limba believe that humankind is superior to animals and far more intelligent than them.

## Conclusion

*Kanu* created *WJmɛti* ('humankind') out of the earth, hence the word *wJmɛti* which literally means 'product from the earth'. In Limba view, humankind is the highest created being of *Kanu*. A person consists of a body, and breath, which gives life to that body and makes humankind a living being.

As God's creations, humans are endowed with a spiritual nature that seeks to be in constant harmony with the Creator and creation. Animate beings and inanimate objects are part of the sequence of creation. Therefore there should be harmony between humankind and the rest of the universe.

Humans are expected to cooperate and live in harmony with the rest of creation including animate beings and inanimate objects. The Limba believe that human beings are superior to and more intelligent than the rest of creation and should therefore take care of God's other creatures. The Limba are connected to the earth spiritually and physically because they were created from it and because their ancestors are buried in it. This requires the Limba to have an ecological conscience. The meaning and purpose of life is a mystery that is only deciphered and fulfilled by the presence of God.

# 9

## Lifecycle

### Introduction

In Limba culture, religion pervades every aspect of life from conception to the afterlife.[1] For the Limba, life is a 'holistic' journey, which begins and ends with God who is consulted every step of the way. Awareness of the divine presence and intervention in their daily lives is reflected in the rites of passage which mark important stages and events in the life of the Limba.[2] The religious tenets of the Limba, like those of most Africans, have formed the matrix of every aspect of Limba life. Mbiti rightly observes:

> Wherever the African is, there is his religion: he carries it to the fields where he is sowing seeds or harvesting a new crop; he takes it with him to the beer party or to attend a funeral ceremony; and if he is educated, he takes religion with him to the examination room at school or in the university; if he is a politician he takes it to the house of parliament.[3]

In ATR, 'all acts from birth to death and thereafter bind the person as a communal being to everyone around themselves, especially those who have passed on to the metaphysical world and those still to be born'.[4]

Most Limba traditionalists believe that God not only created them, he also instituted their culture and showed them how to fend for themselves. God gave them the skills of growing rice, tapping palm wine, offering sacrifice, and preparing food. In this regard, 'there is no sharp dividing line between sacred and secular such as is usually assumed in the West. Material and spiritual are intertwined, the former as a vehicle of the latter'.[5] In LIR as in other African religions, 'there is no formal distinction between the sacred and the secular, between the religious and non-religious, and between the spiritual and the material areas of life'.[6] The inseparability of the sacred and the secular in ATR is another factor that ensures that the longevity of ATR will match that of the culture. In every part of African society religion plays a vital part, and each 'society is maintained by its religious outlook'.[7] The pervasive nature of religion makes it an inevitable component of everyday life. For the Limba, life is religion and religion is life. Life cannot be divorced from 'Religion' and 'Religion' likewise cannot be divorced from life. This worldview was clearly echoed by Magesa when he said that African religion is 'quite literally life and life is religion'.[8] Religion permeates the whole life of Africans – 'their personal, family, and socio-political life'.[9] It is a living organism, so to speak, that regularly operates in the life of the society. Because religion is the life-blood of the society, the Limba believe that life must be lived holistically'. Although religion gives them spiritual and physical strength during times of distress, hardship and disappointment, which without a doubt, helps them to understand the reality of life and provides significance to the mystery of life, these are not the factors that compel them to stay connected to the supernatural. In other words, religion is not practiced only in times of need, or so that they can deal with life's troubling and challenging experiences. *Kanu* is served not merely for what he can do, but for who he is.[10] LIR is an ongoing process in times of joy as well as in times of sadness.[11]

Although the church officially condemns traditional rites of passage as devilish and misleading because they are not centred on Christ and the teachings of the church, it seems, if only subconsciously, to recognise their importance to the psycho-social development of the Limba. For this reason, the Church has replaced many of these traditional rites with new rites celebrating the same stages of development, but with a distinct Christian flavour and focus. The one exception to this practice is the secret societies, which the Church views as unredeemable and therefore condemns outright.

## Pregnancy and childbirth

For the Limba the religious journey starts at conception.[12] As soon as a woman knows that she has conceived,[13] religious observances begin. These observances are necessary for two reasons. The first is that the conception and eventual birth of a child is understood to be 'not merely a result of man and woman coming together in the act of sexual intercourse', but 'as the result of a blessing from God and the ancestors'.[14] In that regard, the sayings: *Kanu wɔnte dɛ na bilɛ sɛmbɛ ba duŋgu si* ('God alone has the power to give life'), and *Kubri iŋ sɛmbɛ sa duŋgu si* ('Money/wealth and power cannot give life') are common among the Limba. At conception, thanks are given to God who has granted the couple/family the greatest gift in the world that neither money nor human efforts can procure. Usually thanksgiving for a pregnancy is made through prayers only, but sometimes a sacrifice[15] of rice-flour, kola nuts and water is made at home. Wedding prayers in the hinterland and in the Western Area include a special prayer for the gift of a child for the newlyweds. After a year of marriage, if the woman has not conceived, the couple/family usually attributes it either to sterility or to the work of witchcraft. In either case, a sacred specialist is invited to call upon God, the ancestors and patron spirits on behalf of the couple/family to bless the womb of the woman. A ritual consisting of exorcism and cleansing is done.

The second reason that religious observances are required at conception is to thwart the clandestine activities of evil spirits. The news of a woman's pregnancy is not received with ultimate joy until the child is born.[16] In other words, the pregnant woman, her husband and the families on both sides are apprehensive until the child is born.[17] During this period of uncertainty, prayers and small-scale sacrifices are made to God – the One responsible for all pregnancies and births, and 'to ensure normal gestation and delivery'.[18] Further, for her protection and that of the baby, the pregnant woman must adhere to certain taboos:[19]

- She must hang lime fruit on a string around her neck for protection against evil forces.

- She must not go out for a walk at night because it is believed that evil sprits are more active during the night and through witchcraft might enter the womb to destroy the foetus.

When a child is born at home, the mother should make sure that fishing net is placed on the door where the child is, within a day after the birth. This is intended to catch malevolent spirits that may attempt to enter the child's room to harm it.

Because life is from God, the foetus has the right to life from the moment conception takes place.[20] A majority of Limba traditionalists are strongly opposed to abortion. An interviewee has this to say:

> Abortion has no place in our tradition. We can never destroy God-given life … Anyone who destroys God's creation that way is doomed for a life full of trouble and misery. In fact, that person is no different than a witch who goes out to eat a child in its mother's womb. To us there is zero tolerance when it comes to abortion.

However, a westernised and educated interviewee views things somewhat differently:

> Abortion I believe should only be accepted on medical grounds. If the mother is getting problem with the conception and if it is not aborted will result in tragedy, I recommend that abortion is the best way to go. I believe like other traditionalists that life is from *Kanu* and we do not have any right to destroy it. But there are circumstances at times that call for that action. For instance, coming back to the war we were just discussing. Traditionalists took people's lives through supernatural means because it was necessary to do so – because our lives at that time were at risk, something drastic had to be done to save ourselves. This situation is not different from the mother whose life is at risk to abort a pregnancy that threatens her life. Our people I know will never see my logic. In fact they will call me *poto* 'White man' because of my ideas. I only do not justify getting rid of a pregnancy that was a result of rape. Also, it is wrong when girls who go for abortion because our custom teaches that it is wrong to have a baby out of marriage. They know that it is wrong to have a child if you are single, then they should abstain from sex. Equally, abortion for the sake of poverty makes no

sense to me. We all know that in our culture you have to take care of your child until he/she gets married. Then you should be financially prepared to take full care when it comes.

## Naming ceremony

The child is usually named by the father who informs the ancestors and presents the child to God – because the child belongs, not only to the family, but more importantly to God and to the ancestors.

The naming of the child is followed by a thanksgiving sacrifice[21] consisting of kola nuts and rice-flour mixed with sugar and salt, presented to God through the ancestors. An older person then takes the child outside the house to be shown to the world. After all the rituals, family and friends share a meal of rice and soup, palm wine and/or other drinks provided by the father. Some families after this naming and 'out-dooring' ceremony will go a step further and take the baby to a sacred specialist to seek additional protection. The specialist will provide different kinds of phylacteries to be worn by the baby, and potions to rub on the baby's body for protection against evil forces. The parents, especially the mother, will continue to visit the sacred specialist occasionally to keep him informed of the child's progress until the child is weaned and a sacrifice is offered.

The ceremonies that 'accompany pregnancy, birth and childhood' signify 'that another religious being has been born into a profoundly religious community and religious world'.[22] In Limba culture, as in many African cultures, much goes on in the child's life between birth and puberty: 'Many rites are performed and many prayers are said to enhance' the child's vital powers. The child also 'learns the traditions and patterns of the life of the family, the village and the clan, through pure curiosity . . . but also through various forms of instruction from parents, the neighbours, the grandparents, and peers'.[23]

## Secret societies

The next important phase of a child's life journey is his/her initiation into a secret society (*Kahu*). This initiation plays a crucial role in his/her road to adulthood.[24] Limba people claim that the major secret societies of *Gbangban* (*Poro*),[25] *nabo* and *Kofo* (*Darri*) for men, *Bondo*[26] and *Humɛndaŋ* for women[27] have no human origin. They simply say that 'We met it',[28] the Limba therefore believe that secret societies were established by God and are maintained by him.[29] In that respect, some educated Limba are strongly convinced that these institutions should be rightly called 'Secret Sacred Societies'. These societies are 'secret' in the sense that no member of the opposite sex, or a child who has not yet been initiated, may know about the rituals or take part in the dances. They are not 'secret societies' in the sense of having a concealed or limited membership, but this does not mean that all persons of an appropriate age and gender are included in the society's rituals.

Initiation into these societies is meant to equip an individual for adult life;[30] through learning certain medicinal, magical and technical skills patterned by these societies; and to honour the initiates. The men's societies are not operated in Freetown, where only the women's *Bondo* society is seen.

Because secret societies are considered sacred, the process of initiation is preceded by certain religious activities. The bush is cleansed from evil forces and consecrated to prevent unwelcome spiritual forces from entering it and causing havoc.[31] As God is the only one who has control over the powers of evil in the bush, He must be contacted for help. A sacrifice is then offered to God through the ancestors for the well-being of the participants, both the officials and the initiates. Having the necessary religious ceremonies done before the candidates are initiated, is an attempt to present the officials, the candidates and the bush to God's care and control. The 'idea of rebirth is characteristic of many of these initiation rites'.[32] In general, after the emergence from the bush, initiates are considered to be adults.

## Gbangban society

Among the three major men's secret societies, namely *Gbangban, Nabo* and *Kofo, Gbangban* is the most widespread and is found in all regions in the hinterland. It has different categories. Most members belong to the lower categories: *Huyɛnki, Hukoko* and *Kondeyo*. A few members belong to the higher and more complex categories: *Sindama, Ɖaraŋara* and *Nabamba*. Members are typically initiated around puberty. Initiation into a secret society is an important part of the passage from childhood to adulthood. Once initiated, the member is expected to act as a responsible adult; however, he remains in the care and under the control of his parents until he marries.

In the *Gbangban* society, there are two divisions in the bush (*hɛli*). *Thɛŋkidɛŋ* serves as an open court and a partially holy place. *Tharumba* is the most sacred or holiest place. The candidates are taken without previous notice to *thɛŋkidɛŋ*. They remain there for the entire initiation period which lasts three to six months. While in the bush, the prospective candidate is called *Gbaku* ('chief') and is given the treatment due any tribal chief or authority. The initiation programme is intended to equip the initiates to face the realities of life. During this period, the initiates undergo intense grooming and nurturing as well as difficult ordeals which are meant to prepare them to face life's hardships. It is during this time that many cultural and religious teachings are passed down to the initiates.

The final rite is called *kuŋ]ti-kamandi* (lit., 'to be plunged into or immersed in water'). This is a cleansing or purifying ceremony to make the newly initiated candidates clean and fit to once again associate with other members of the general community. *Kuŋ]ti-kamandi* is said to be so dreadful that no one ever desires to go through it a second time.

The night before graduation, the initiates together with their families/patrons spend time in *Tharumba* (the most sacred part of the bush). At graduation, the graduates wear a traditional gown known as *huroŋko*, with a traditional cap (*Kuhaka*).[33] The cap signifies that the initiates take full responsibility to comport themselves as people who have entered the secret society. If a person commits a crime in the community (especially in Freetown where not every male is expected to have entered a secret society), the first question that is asked is, *E wunde tut]k]y?/ E wo tut]k]y kuhaka?* ('Has he worn a cap?'). If the answer is 'yes' the offender faces a more severe punishment, but if the response is 'no', the offender is considered, and disciplined as a child, regardless of his age or position within the community. Graduates are respected and are expected to contribute to society in a meaningful way.

Titles are used for all those who play a part in the ceremony. At graduation time, the outgoing initiates are referred to as *Badiŋitɔk]y]* ('freshman'). Later when all is over, they will be known as *Bathɛkɛlɛ* ('an undergraduate').[34] The parents/guardians are known as *Boyhiki*. There are usually sponsors or benefactors who are known as *Basemeŋ*. The person that relates with the public and community on behalf of the society is called *Basampɛrɛ*. Last but not least, the elders, teachers and councillors are known as *Bethanthɛ*.

## Bondo society

*Bondo* is the most common secret society for women and is found throughout the country wherever the Limba have an organised settlement. This situation has allowed for some flexibility with rules in urban areas like Freetown.

Unlike in the men's societies in most communities, the date of the initiation is not usually kept secret from the candidates because it is considered a joyful occasion. The night before the ceremony, there is a big celebration with music and dancing in the village. The older women play their drums and sing until daybreak when the candidates are taken to the bush. In the Western Area, the celebration usually takes place in the bush to avoid disturbing the peace.

The main event of the initiation is the act of 'cutting'. Society elders called *barigha/sowei*, 'circumcise' the girls by removing the clitoral hood, and at times, part of or the entire clitoris itself.[35] For several days after the initiation, until they are healed the girls are tended to by the older women called *siŋkabondo*. Later, they are taught morality, religious songs, dancing and cooking.

Because initiation into the *Bondo* society traditionally marks the passage from childhood into womanhood, in the hinterland, most girls are initiated between the ages of 13 and 16 and are thereafter considered eligible to marry. In the Western Area, many girls are initiated much earlier according to the wishes of their parents. In many cases girls in Freetown are initiated at eight years of age and some are initiated even younger. The rationale behind this practice is that the initiation process discourages premarital sexual activity. Thus, the goal is to initiate the girl before she has the opportunity to lose her virginity.

After about a week the girls are brought back to the village with their bodies smeared with white clay. They are now referred to as *babɔŋkani beŋ* ('new initiates'). The *babɔŋkani beŋ* dance in the village/town as they are watched by their families, future spouses and friends, who give them gifts and money. After the occasion, the Bondo officials take them back to the bush for further instruction and training. The time spent in the bush varies from community to community. In the hinterland, it may last as long as two months, but in the city, or where the girls attend school, it is typically much shorter lasting between one and two weeks.

Three days before the final ceremony, the girls are secluded in a hut or house close to the village/town where they sing and dance about all they have been taught. When the days of seclusion are over, they become full members of the society and are known as *semaiŋ*. The day that they leave seclusion and re-enter the community, they are dressed in fine clothes and jewellery according to the financial means of their family or sponsor. In Freetown, most of the girls' families get their friends and acquaintances to buy and wear *ashoby* (the same colour dress) as a way of celebrating with them. The crowd dances and sings popular songs accompanied by drums. The initiates and Bondo officials are given gifts by the girls' families or sponsors.

In the hinterland, after the ceremony, the girls are eligible to be given in marriage because most often they are initiated at an accepted age for traditional marriage. In the Western Area, where the girls are often initiated at a very young age, and the legal age for consensual marriage for both men and women is eighteen, marriage is not considered after coming out of the *Bondo* society. African secret societies are an 'important cultural bastion'.[36]

# Engagement and marriage

After the formal procedures of engagement (*kuliathi/kudethi*) have been followed (see Chapter 1), water is poured as a libation to the ancestors in order to ensure their approval.[37] The visitors then present the bride price (*nahulu*),[38] followed by prayers and the serving of food.[39] The bride price 'is the seal on the transfer of rights and obligation from the bride's father/guardian; it is the transfer that marks a legal marriage from other forms which, although they may be equally permanent, were not as acceptable traditionally to the kin concerned'.[40] Traditionalists in Freetown still follow the above marriage (*hudɔŋ/kuyɛntande*) procedures.

In most African cultures, marriages are believed to come from God.[41] In the Limba traditionalist worldview, it is 'believed to be God's responsibility' to make marriages, whether prearranged or otherwise happen.[42] A good husband or a good wife is believed to be a gift from God, and this is the reason the Limba continue to depend on God for his guidance in choosing the right partner. It is believed that only the help of God enables a family or a suitor to find a perfect match. The Limba often say, 'It is God who finds the right spouse for you'. Beauty, good looks and charm are not enough, only God is able to determine the right life-partner for a person.

Occasionally, if a man has run out of patience, and can no longer wait for God to provide him with a suitable partner, he may take another spiritual route to find her. In such an instance, the impatient man solicits the help of a sacred specialist to win the heart of the one he loves. The man pays a sum of money to the priest or diviner who makes powerful charms for him to steal the heart of the lady in question. The client is given lotions and objects to wear, which, it is believed, will not only attract the desired woman, but also capture her heart from the moment she sniffs their scent.[43] The diviner may also make a mixture of herbs for the client to secretly place in the food of the person he wants to win over.

Conventionally, it is the man who approaches a woman and expresses his interest in her, not the other way around. However, if a woman comes to a man and expresses her interest in him, the traditionalist believes that this is a sign that the woman has been sent by God. Under normal circumstances, a Limba woman would never tell a man that she has an interest in him, but if, God has engineered the plan, she will not find it difficult to approach a man.

Because God created marriage, and directs people to their rightful partners, it is believed that he is also the one who sustains marriages. For this reason, at all Limba weddings God is asked for his blessing, and for the creation of a peaceful and stable home.

## Farming

Like many Africans, the Limba take their religion to the fields when they are 'sowing seeds or harvesting a new crop'.[44] The land and the techniques for farming have been inherited from God, therefore, the Limba believe that in spite of human efforts, *mɛnɛ Kanu tha mɛn* ('if God does not agree')[45] there will not be a good harvest. Various ceremonies are performed yearly during the rice-farming season at strategic places on the farm.

Before work on the land begins, a sacred specialist may be called to inspect it. If it is found that evil spirits are living on the land or in the area, *Kudamaŋ*, (an offering of rice-flour, egg, kola nut, white cloth or at times chicken) is made to inform the spirits of the family's intention to farm on the said land, and to ask the spirits for peace and prosperity as they work.

If *Kudamaŋ* is necessary, it must be offered on the day work on the farm is scheduled to begin. This is because the bush (*hu-kariya/heli/feli*) should not be left unattended after the event in case, evil spirits would otherwise return to repossess the land.

If a piece of land or bush proposed for farming is declared free from evil spirits, at the time of brushing and clearing of the bush, the head of the family offers a sacrifice for the welfare of the farm and its workers, and for protection against witchcraft or evil spirits at a ceremony called *Kul]ŋki*. An object called a *Kul]ŋki ko* is buried in the centre of the farm for protection. The supernatural power of the *Kul]ŋki ko* watches over the farm protecting it from any form of evil or destruction. A banana tree is usually planted to mark the spot where the *Kul]ŋki ko* is buried.

Before hoeing/ploughing starts, a sacrifice of kola nuts, cooked rice and rice-flour is offered to the *Kul]ŋki ko*, to indicate a readiness to start hoeing/ploughing the farm. This is done because the *Kul]ŋki ko* is literally seen as God taking care of the farm. On the day of the sacrifice, as usual, food is cooked for everyone to eat. No one leaves the farm until the end of the day's activities. No food is allowed to be taken home or to the village, it should all be consumed on the farm. After the ceremony, if heavy winds start blowing without rain, it is considered a good sign signifying that the *Kul]ŋki ko* is happy and that the year will be a prosperous one for farming and harvest.

In some other Limba communities, before the farming season begins, the choice and location of the bush is made known to the ancestors through a sacrifice of kola nuts and rice-flour with prayers. A small portion of the bush is cleared and a farming 'curse' to scare away thieves in the form of an object known as *ŋakurɛ* is placed on top of a tripod until harvest. As the Limba are afraid of the power of any form of 'curse' no one comes close to a farm where the *ŋakurɛ* is hung.

When the harvest has been brought in, each family or person will give thanks to God and to the ancestors for the harvest. The first batch of harvested rice should not be eaten, but should be cooked and offered to God through the ancestors as a thanksgiving sacrifice in gratitude for a good harvest and for God's protection throughout the concluded farming season. After this ceremony of thanksgiving, the family can harvest for themselves and their helpers.

Other villages, for their end of harvest religious ceremony, take their prepared meal early in the morning to a designated cave to offer thanksgiving to the ancestors. Usually an elderly person leads the ceremony. Although the religious ceremonies vary from community to community, religion plays a vital role on the Limba farm from the start of the season to its end.[46]

## Employment

Those Limba who are not farmers, as well as those who live in the cities, try to find employment in the private or government sectors. Because there is a high level of bureaucracy and political interference in these sectors, Limba applicants who lack political backing, often resort to traditional religious methods to secure a job.[47] The applicant approaches the sacred specialist with the belief that only God can make the impossible possible.[48] This belief gives the applicant the faith that God is greater than the officials handling the application, and has the power to touch their hearts to employ him/her.

For some applicants, visits to the sacred specialist do not end once they have been employed. In a job culture where employers/supervisors may sack employees at will, employees are in a constant struggle to ensure that they keep their jobs. With the guidance and help of a sacred specialist, prayers and sacrifices for job security are offered to God through the ancestors, and the employee is given either a religious object or a potion to mystically make those in authority like him/her. It is wrongly believed that almost anyone who rises rapidly to a high-ranking position is either dealing with a spirit or being helped by a sacred specialist.

## Ethnic politics

Although voters know clearly the qualifications for a chief, and the reasons why a particular candidate is elected, or 'why they themselves support one rather than another, it is commonly said that it is not the people who choose the chief but "it is God" (*Kanu na*)'.[49] For this reason, sacrifices are offered for the chief on his installation, and when he dies.

The process of a chief's installation varies from region to region. One thing that is common in all regions is that the coronation of a Paramount Chief in a chiefdom or a Limba tribal head in Freetown, is that the occasion requires a major sacrifice.

The chief officially assumes office when he is presented with the staff of authority by the government, but the Limba do not consider his office effective until he returns from a period of seclusion known as *Kantha*.[50]

At the end of *Kantha*, the chief is accompanied around the town in a procession showing him to his subjects as they sing, dance and cheer for him. The climax of this function is the sacrifice in the evening or following day. This sacrifice is meant to:

1. Formally present the new chief to God through the ancestors.

2. Return thanks to God for choosing the new chief.

3. Pray for long life and protection for the chief.

4. Pray for peace and stability in the land.

When a Limba chief is being installed[51] in any area of Sierra Leone, the following prayer may be said:

| | |
|---|---|
| *Masala, nbɛnbɛŋ beŋ…* | God almighty, our ancestors (the ancestors are then named). |
| *Hɛ/fɛ miŋ se iŋ mal]holima* | Today we have come with joy/happiness |
| *Yi na dunku mina gbaku wo* | You gave us our chief |
| *Miŋ sa ŋi bayo bali miŋ kiŋ* | we cannot do anything without |
| *ba sa tepe bena ba gbaku wo* | first telling you about the chief |
| *Sarakaŋ baŋ hɛ/fɛ na ba* | Our sacrifice today is to |
| *bena kalani* | thank you |
| *Iŋ ba dethia mal]holima* | And to find favour |
| *ba gbaku wo iŋ kubɔriko* | for our chief and our community |

God and the ancestors are both mentioned in this opening prayer because it is God, through the voters who chose the chief, and the ancestors who will keep the chief safe and prosperous. The worshippers are in a pleasant mood because they have a new chief. Nothing will be done without first bringing the chief to God and the ancestors for dedication. Although God and the ancestors are aware of human happenings, they are required to be officially informed of important occurrences. The worshippers have come to thank God and the ancestors and to seek their favour for the chief and for the community.

The following words may be said in intercession:

| | |
|---|---|
| *Wali, Wali, Wali,* | Thanks, Thanks, Thanks |
| *Masala kiŋ ba miŋ* | The Almighty is for us |
| *Masala miŋ thiyina mamo* | Almighty we give thanks |
| *Yina Kanu wothimo mina* | You are the God who loves us |
| *Miŋ kute hɛɛra ba yina* | We have seen peace because you have |
| *dunkuŋ mina gbaku* | given us a chief |
| *Yi sɛtiki gbaku mayoŋ* | You took our previous chief |

| | |
|---|---|
| *Fɛ/hɛ yi dunkuŋ mina gbaku* | Today you have given us a new chief |
| *Wali yoo, Wali yoo, Wali yoo* | Thanks! Thanks! Thanks! |
| *Thiya gbaku thaduba* | Put blessing on the chief |
| *Dunkuna ni f]s] iŋ sɛmbɛ* | Give him strength and power |
| *Dunkuna ni* | Give him wisdom |
| *Dunkuna mina f]ma mal]holima* | Give us all happiness |
| *Yina dunkunɛ mina gbaku* | You gave us a chief |
| *Miŋ sise ni fɛ kɛnda* | We have brought him to you today |
| *Wali, wali, wali* | Thanks, thanks, thanks |
| *L]ntha, l]tha, l]ntha* | Let it be so, (three times) |

God is thanked[52] because he is a God of love who has brought peace to the people by giving them a chief to replace[53] the (deceased) one he has taken. This is followed by intercessory prayers for God's blessing on the new chief, for strength and power to rule well, for wisdom[54] to rule wisely and decisively, and finally, for happiness for the chief and his subjects. The chief is once again acknowledged as a gift from God and is presented to God, for blessing as he starts his job. This is followed by repeated thanks, and the prayers are concluded with the usual words.

The chief as God's choice is considered to be his human representative. He is always prayed for[55] and is believed to be under the protection and guidance of the ancestors. At his death, elaborate funeral and religious ceremonies are held. The following prayer is usually said at the funeral:

| | |
|---|---|
| *Miŋ se iŋ nkinikiniŋ ba mandiŋ* | We have come with great sorrow |
| *Pati be kɛnda se iŋ huberina* | Your children have come with cry |
| *Yina lehinɛ mina* | You created us |
| *Miŋ k]tɛ kafaido mɛti tɛ* | We know that this world is not home |
| *Hutuka wo ka gbaku sise* | The death of the chief has brought |
| *huberina mandiŋ* | a great cry |

| | |
|---|---|
| *Dunkuna mina thɛbinalima* | Give us peace of mind |
| *Miŋ sa kɔtho te mal]k]maŋ huŋande* | We do not know when the time will come |
| *Katha ni ka katilɛ* | Take him to the place of the dead |
| *Haali furenibe sɛkiti ni* | Let the ancestors accept him |
| *Dunkuna ni hemuwe* | Give him rest |
| *Mase hub]riko* | Help the family/community |
| *Dunkuna mina yoo thɛbinalima!* | Give us peace of mind! |
| *Miŋ ka yiŋ sɛmbɛ baŋ pindi tuka* | We don't have power to prevent death |
| *Mase mina ba sɛkiti tuka* | Help us to accept death |
| *N]ŋ gbaku wo dethia* | May the chief find |
| *maloholima iŋ yi* | peace with you |

The death of a chief brings great sorrow. The effect of his death reaches far and beyond his chiefdom's jurisdiction. As God's children, they have come with their cry, and with the understanding they are strangers in this world. At this time of great loss, they need peace of mind. No one can tell for sure when death will come. The people then intercede on behalf of their chief asking that he might be taken to the place where the ancestors live, that the ancestors will accept the chief, and that he will be given rest.[56] They also intercede for the chief's immediate family and for the community asking that they will be able to cope with such enormous loss, and be given peace of mind.[57] As the people do not have the power to prevent death God's help is required to accept death as an ultimate reality, and finally if the chief did find peace with God during his life time, the people ask that he will find it now.[58]

## National politics

Any study of LIR in politics would be incomplete without a discussion of its contribution to Sierra Leone national politics[59] especially from 1968–1992. In national politics, Limba politicians take their religion 'to the house of parliament'.[60] Sierra Leoneans have generally attributed the incorporation and promotion of ATR practices into national politics to two Limba heads of state: Dr Siaka P. Stevens and Major General Joseph S. Momoh. These two men who were both leaders of the All Peoples' Congress (APC) party[61] encouraged the idea of traditional religiosity as a way to achieve and maintain power. They made some government and political organisations see 'in traditional religion a potential source of reinforcement and legitimation for their activities'.[62] The supernatural became a very important element in politics, which encouraged many members of parliament to ally themselves with diviners or soothsayers.

Throughout APC rule, both high-ranking politicians and those of lesser influence sought out the help of diviners and fortune-tellers to win and keep their seats, or to gain the favour of those in higher authority when seeking more lucrative political positions.[63] The belief that it was not possible to attain political prominence without the help of these sacred specialists brought a great deal of deception into politics with sometimes disastrous results.[64] Political predators busied themselves trying to hunt down their supposed enemies/victims. It is believed that some politicians engaged the services of sacred specialists to kill their opponents through spiritual means. Sacred specialists took advantage of the situation to make themselves rich by sending messages of concern to politicians advising them of the traditional steps to take. These messages often warn politicians about their enemies who were trying to get rid of them; they predicted coups and assassination attempts.[65]

The pouring of libation was reintroduced at public and state functions during the APC regime.[66] At these functions, libation was poured to seek God's guidance, blessing and protection.

## The role of Limba indigenous religion in Sierra Leone's civil war

Sierra Leone's ten-year civil war (1991–2001), commonly referred to as the 'rebel war', attracted great international attention. Its suggested causes, cultural, political, and sociological dynamics and impacts are well documented.[67] In that regard, I will only discuss the role played by LIR on the battle field.

Sierra Leone's army had participated in the two World Wars under the umbrella of the British, and had sent platoons on UN and regional military and peacekeeping missions, but the army had been considered primarily 'ceremonial' and had never before fought a large scale war on a home front. Several months after the 1991 outbreak of civil war, it became evident that the army was ill-equipped and largely unprepared for combat. At the time the war broke out there were approximately 3 000 soldiers and although that number was subsequently increased to 16 000, there was still no strong military or police presence in the hinterland, and the people there were left vulnerable to the sporadic attacks by the Revolutionary United Front (RUF) guerrilla fighters. On account of the lack of logistics and an unprepared army, the APC government came to believe that their only hope for victory was some form of supernatural intervention.[68] This led the government to make a public announcement on national radio encouraging all citizens, especially those in the hinterland, to use whatever traditional means or power they had to combat the rebels.

This call by the government gave birth to several ethnic defence groups in the hinterland. The *Tamab]r]* group was formed by the Kuranko and Yalunka people in the north. This group was later joined by some Limba people who were said to have been recruited from Warawara Bafodea Limba Chiefdom, a place which is particularly noted for its attachment to traditional beliefs in Sierra Leone.[69] The *Gbeti* and *Kapra* groups were formed by the Temne in the north. The *Kamajoi* was formed by the Mende people in the south and the east, and the *Donsa* was formed by the Kono in the east. Members of these groups were mostly hunters who belonged to secret societies and were believed to be experts in traditional spirituality and medicine. On the battle field, they used not only conventional arms and 'witch guns' but, through spirituals means used killer bees to attack and destabilise the rebels. It is believed that some rebels even died from the painful stings of the bees. The supernatural ability to turn daylight into darkness was another effective method used by these fighters to prevent the rebels from seeing where they were going. The traditional fighters could see the rebels but the rebels were unable to see the approaching traditional militia. It is also believed that many rebels were killed through these means. Although each ethnic defence group employed its own strategies, one thing that was common among all of them was the use of a protective traditional outfit called *huronko/ronko* – a fearsome traditional brown or red gown with black vertical stripes, prepared by sacred specialists, and drenched in herbal medicines believed to make the user invincible.

The traditional militias were not the only ones to use African traditional means to fight. The rebels also made use of their own traditional religious powers to frustrate the efforts of the ethnic defence groups.

The involvement of these traditional militia groups on the side of the government and the nation, did not sit well with many evangelical Christians. It was the opinion of the evangelicals that Christian prayers should never be mixed with devilish traditional spirituality. In fact, nation wide, there is an ongoing debate on the part traditional spirituality played in bringing an end to the civil war. In some people's view, the reason why the traditional militias were not able to bring an end to the war was that the rebels themselves resorted to traditional spirituality to fight back – making it difficult for the former to win.

Although Sierra Leoneans are divided as to whether traditional spirituality, Christian or Muslim prayers brought the war to an end, one belief commonly held by all the faith groups is that the war was brought to an end through God's intervention.

## Judiciary process

Before the advent of the British in Sierra Leone, chiefs judged all cases in the Limba homeland. Although many of the more serious cases are now removed to the courts, it is still believed that *Kanu* also gives wisdom and courage to the court president or chairman to judge well. In many court sittings, prayers are said before the commencement of proceedings. Before the pronouncement of the verdict on high profile or complicated chiefdom cases, such as land disputes, rebellions, or malicious destruction of property, God is consulted for his guidance and wisdom through a sacred specialist.[70]

In some instances when a verdict is hard to reach, and it is the opinion of the majority that the accused might have committed the crime, but there is no tangible proof to link him/her to it, if the accused continues to stress his/her innocence, the court may recommend the invocation of a 'swear' (*kud]ri/kuth]nk]ni/duku*)[71] as a kind of self-operating justice. Because most Limba are afraid of the power of a 'swear', the accused will quickly confess if guilty. A 'swear' is considered an effective means of preventing or punishing the most profoundly anti-social of crimes, therefore, its use is not only limited to the courts. Out of the court system 'swears' are used for various reasons to obtain justice, for example a victim of theft, a man who suspects his wife of being unfaithful, and to pursue witches. The source of the supernatural power of the 'swear' is still a matter of debate among the Limba. Some argue that because of the inhumane actions of the 'swear', its power comes neither from *Kanu wobekede/kathinthin* ('God above') nor from the ancestors, but comes instead from *Kanu wopothi* ('god below') evil and malevolent spirits.

Some Sierra Leoneans do not trust the national judiciary system because the judges or jurors and/or sentencing outcomes are often influenced by politics. This is especially likely with high profile matters like treason, homicide or the misappropriation and embezzlement of public funds. For this reason, the family and friends of the accused desperately search for renowned sacred specialists to offer sacrifice in order that their loved ones might receive justice and be acquitted.[72] Similarly, people who feel that their needs will not be met by the justice system, or that they will not receive a fair trial, because of prejudice and injustice in high places, turn to God for help and deliverance with the belief that God is the only one who can prevail over any human institution or power.

## Health

It is by God's grace that people stay well or healthy,[73] therefore when the traditionalist is asked, *Nama/mɛ k]t] koŋ?* ('How is your body?'), the usual response is either, *yan ndo pet]y sɛmbɛ ba Kanu* ('I am well by God's power'), or simply, *kalaŋ Kanu* ('thank God').[74] In most African societies, 'the manifestations of good, such as health . . . are attributed to God'.[75] Although in Sierra Leone it is generally assumed that wealthy people live longer than poor people because they can afford to pay for expensive medications and the best available medical attention, the

Limba believe that 'money cannot give you health, only God can'. Even when people are cured by western medicine because they can afford the expensive medical treatments, the Limba still believe that it is God who made the healing possible. Both western and traditional healing systems are believed to be under God's control because it is through divine intervention that both the medical staff at the hospital and the traditional healer are able to heal their patients.[76] Some traditional healers claim that, 'their knowledge of medicines derives from God'.[77]

For the traditionalist, sickness is a religious matter and not just a physical or mental condition. When sickness occurs, it shows 'that there is an imbalance between the metaphysical and the human world as the flow of numinous power/life force has been disturbed',[78] and it is for this reason that Africans take a holistic approach toward sickness.

In the hinterland when a traditionalist is seriously ill, he/she usually calls the herbalist/medicine man or woman,[79] who is believed to possess supernatural powers and to depend on God for guidance to find the right herbs.[80] The traditionalists believe that although traditional healers do not always diagnose what is wrong with the patient, the healers' faith in God and his/her reliance on God for direction in finding the herbs to cure the victim, is what gives the patient and his/her family hope and satisfaction.[81] It is believed that it is God who chooses the medicine through the healer, so it does not matter whether or not the patient or the healer actually knows the cause of ailment.

African healing is believed to be directed by God's providence, and anytime someone is cured it reminds the African of God's presence within the community. However, there have been many cases where traditional and spiritual healing did not work at all.

## Death and burial

At death (hut]ka)[82] the breath/life (siba) leaves the body, which is buried, decays and stays in the grave. For the Limba, as for most African peoples, death at an old age is seen as God's death[83] and 'a dignified event'.[84] In that regard, although everyone feels the pain of parting, there is a general satisfaction and appreciation to God for the gift of a long life.

On the other hand, the Limba attribute the deaths of young people, and untimely or unnatural deaths, to witchcraft, the effects of swearing, or the work of evil spirits. Currently, there are two existing views about the cause of such deaths. Some believe that although God himself does not take the person's life, he is responsible for the occurrence of such a death because he is the only one who has the power to prevent or allow it. Others believe that a loving God would neither take such life nor be responsible for the premature death of an infant or a young person.

The Limba have several stories about the origin of death in the world.[85] A common story is that of *The Toad and the Snake*:

> Kanu did not want the Limba and all animals to die, so he made two medicines – one for the Limba people and another for the animals. Kanu decided to give the snake the medicine to take to the Limba. The toad got up and objected to that decision on the ground that the swiftness of the snake would cause the medicine to spill. The snake countered by saying he would not spill it and his swiftness would get the medicine to the Limba people in a timely fashion. In spite of his good argument, the toad did not allow the snake to carry the medicine. The toad took the medicine for the Limba when he jumped; it fell off of his head and spilled. He then took the empty bowl to Kanu to be replenished. Kanu said, 'I will not be able to get more now, I told you not to take it, you disobeyed, you went and just spilt it – I will not be able to get more now.' Death came to the Limba because of the toad who spilled the medicine. The snakes do not die naturally because their medicine was not spilled. If snakes are not killed, when they get old they bathe in the medicine which was carried to them from Kanu.[86]

In this story, death comes because an unnamed medicine from God did not reach the Limba as a result of the unreasonable judgement of the toad. That is why the shorter version of this story is entitled *The Toad Did Not Love Us*.[87]

Usually when a person dies, the Limba, like most Africans, spend a great deal of time, energy and resources to ensure a proper funeral[88] for the departed so that the spirit of the departed 'may be contented in the world beyond and will not return as a dissatisfied ghost to plague his family'.[89]

In most African societies, 'the phenomena of death and burial (*amanki*) rites usually bring people of diverse beliefs together since people come from various walks of life irrespective of their religious leanings as sympathisers, mourners, friends, and relations'.[90] In the Limba homeland and in the Western Area, a wake normally takes place the night before the funeral and burial and goes on to until about 2:00 a.m. At all Limba wakes, mourners and sympathisers are well fed.

All Limba traditionalists believe that, it is God who is responsible for the safe passage of the deceased to the abode of the dead (*katilɛ/katiyɛ*). In that respect, when death occurs, sacrifices are offered to *Kanu* through the ancestors on the third (*kudigbiŋ*), seventh (*nhureŋ*) and fortieth (*huboka*) days after death.[91] Because God was called when the deceased entered the world, he must also be called when that life ends. These ceremonies are observed as a way to relate with the supernatural on behalf the deceased. Along with the sacrifices that are involved in these ceremonies, wailing and prayers of petition for comfort, peace, and protection for the living, and for a cordial reception of the deceased by the ancestors at *katilɛ* are also made.[92]

## Widowhood rites

The Limba practise widowhood rites as part of a period of mourning also called *huboka* ('cry'). In the hinterland where, as already noted, burial usually takes place on the same day the death occured, three days after the death of her husband, the widow is taken to a stream/river to be cleansed and released in a ceremony called, *afuŋa kugbarido/ba pɛŋi kuggarido* ('to be released from evil'). In the Western Area, where burial is not as urgent, the ceremony can take place a little later, preferably on the seventh day after the husband's death. This ceremony is believed to release the deceased husband and the surviving wife from each other, 'otherwise the living will remain miserable in their frustrated devotion, and the departed soul will be unhappy'.[93] It is a time of closure.

At the end of the ceremony, the widow changes her dress and puts on either a black or grey coloured dress for the next phase of the *huboka* which ends on the fortieth day after her husband's death. She again changes her dress to another colour which she will wear until the anniversary of the funeral which brings ends her mourning period called *athɛti boka* ('breaking the crying/mourning'). During this year long time of mourning, the widow is expected to sleep on the floor in the living room and out of the bedroom she once shared with her departed husband. She is also expected not to have any sexual encounter or remarry. For as long as the prescribed time of mourning is not completed and until she has performed the required rites, the widow continues to be the 'property of the spirit of her deceased husband with full marital rights'.[94] Any man who has sexual intercourse with a widow during this period will be cursed because it is believed that the deceased husband's soul will not rest until the widow has completed her mourning rites. Only then is she free to remarry.[95]

In some Limba dialects, like the Warawara Limba people, the widow is free to start courting another man after the cleansing and releasing ceremony but is not permitted to marry until after the fortieth day of her husband's death. Although she may see another man, she is expected to abstain sexually until then.

## The next world

When speaking about the hereafter, Limba traditionalists commonly use the phrase 'the next world'. Unlike many other African societies, the Limba do not speak about reincarnation.[96] The Limba are extremely vague about the issue of the next world. It appears Limba traditionalists have no knowledge about the final destination of the soul/breath (*siba*). In fact, like most

Africans,[97] Limba religiosity only makes provision for life beyond the grave if the deceased is accepted as an ancestor. As stated earlier, at death, the spirit leaves the body, and the buried body decays in the grave. For the Limba, as well as for other Africans, the grave appears to be 'the seal of everything, even if a person survives and continues to exist in the next world'.[98]

## Conclusion

Limba traditionalists do not distinguish between the secular and the sacred, rather they embrace all of life, integrating both, and seeking to find harmony or balance between them. In other words, existence for the traditionalist is 'religious participation and the world is a religious phenomenon...'[99]

The Limba dependence on God is evident throughout the entire lifecycle. Because God is the only source of life, this dependence begins on the child's behalf, even before conception. On account of God being the ultimate Sustainer of life, a person's descendants or surviving relatives perpetuate this dependence even after death. Religion deals with both private life and community life. It cannot be confined at home and the Limba take it with them wherever they go. Religion controls and harmonises both society and the individual. It provides spontaneous answers to the numerous challenges of humankind's daily life.

God is the provider of everything that is necessary for life. It is God who gives knowledge and the skills necessary to attain success in agriculture, career, politics, and sports. God provides wisdom in making life's decisions and guides people to their marriage partners. Through this same wisdom, God guides rulers and courts to make just laws and verdicts. In any of these areas, if a person is experiencing difficulty, God's favour may be entreated through religious ritual. Training in such religious ritual is one of the functions of the secret societies, which, it is believed, were instituted by God to preserve Limba culture and religion and to provide training in moral and social ethics. Throughout all of life's endeavours the Limba must depend on God for sustenance and well-being. At death the breath leaves the body, which is buried and decays in the grave. The Limba are vague about the final destination or end of the breath.

# 10

## Sin and salvation

### Introduction

The Limba community, like any African community, is governed by rules most of which were established by the ancestors or the elders of the community for the guidance of its social and religious life. From an African ethical standpoint, violation of any of these rules constitutes sin (hakε) or wrongdoing,[1] and sin consequently 'creates disharmony and brings about the disintegration of the society'.[2] Sin injures the African 'philosophical principle of: I am because we are, and since we are, therefore I am'.[3] In view of that, sin is regarded as an agent destructive to spiritual, personal and social harmony. It is therefore condemned. However, as African societies are *sensu communis*, provisions are made by which an offender may be made whole and restored to the community.[4]

The church supports the traditional Limba view that sin is destructive and has severe consequences, but it sees the solutions proposed by ATR as inadequate and condemns LIR as a sinful and hopeless endeavour that leads its practitioners to eternal damnation.

This chapter will examine the Limba concept of sin, its categories and consequences, as well as the remedy to sin, and the Limba concept of salvation.

### Sin and its categories

In Limba worldview, hakε ('sin/offence') is any wrongful act or behaviour directed against the supernatural, an individual, or the community. This may include acts against living or non-living entities. This is in line with Mbiti's observation: 'It seems that sin in African religion refers almost exclusively to the area of relations between human beings, with spiritual realities and with nature'.[5]

In Limba cosmology, no one is born with hakε. Children are always regarded as innocent, and are referred to as 'angels' because of their sinless nature. As the child grows, he/she becomes maladjusted as a result of bad influences.[6] At an early age the child is taught which acts, behaviours, and words are considered wrong or unacceptable. When the child does wrong, he/she is reprimanded and/or punished. In Limba society it is not until a child is initiated, or becomes a teenager that he/she is considered capable of committing 'sin'.

Although deliberate sin almost always emanates from evil or wicked thoughts, for the Limba as for most Africans, sin 'has to do with real life situations' and is not considered from an 'abstract metaphysical' viewpoint.[7] Therefore, evil thoughts or motives are not considered sin until they are expressed in words or actions.

Although technically any wrongdoing may be referred to as '*hakɛ*' the Limba use different terms to refer to certain categories of sin:[8]

- Sins against God or the ancestors are called *hakɛ*. Because God created all that is and intends his creation to live in harmony and respect, any intentional act against any part of God's creation is considered a sin directly against God.[9]

- Sins against other humans are called *hakɛ* or *yulubu*.

- Sins against nature, the spirits or the secret societies are known as *adʃkʃ*.

- The infraction of taboos or clan norms is called *kadʃkʃ/kakɛ*.

- The intentional destruction of animals, reptiles or birds is referred to as *kamalʃ*.

- Intentional crimes of other natures are known as *aspi bali/athaki bali*.

- An accidental/unintentional wrong action of any nature is *anʃti kasi*.

- Sexual sin in general is classified as *nkedaŋ*. Particular sexual sins like adultery and fornication are known as *hubaliŋina/abalaŋaŋ*.[10] Marrying or having sex with a close relative is known as *kuthʃmbʃ* ('incest'). Rape is called *keŋdaŋ*.

## The consequences of and remedies for sins

On a personal level, sin destroys the good reputation of a person. It makes him/her a bad person and an outlaw of the community. As sin is a socio-religious concept, the offender is considered spiritually and socially unfit and he/she is 'avoided by the rest of the community'.[11] Sin not only affects the offender, it also affects his/her community,[12] and most adversely his/her family or clan.[13] It is believed that certain sinful actions result in curses that, if not remedied will pass on from one generation to another. The belief that the sins of a parent will follow the child and children yet unborn is strong in Limba traditional worldview. It is for these reasons that the Limba seriously frown upon sin, and every effort is made to teach about its consequences[14] and to prevent its occurrence.

In order for harmony to be restored, the offender must make provision for forgiveness or atonement and achieve peace with God/the supernatural, the community, and the self.[15] This is accomplished 'either through personal or communal rituals of cleansing',[16] or through the offering of sacrifice (depending on the nature of the crime). These acts and rituals are the 'natural means of restoring the vitality' of the individual and the community.[17]

In most Limba communities, when a sin/offence/crime is committed, the first step to restoration is a confession (*huthembɔkɔ*) of the act. In the Limba worldview, confession shows humility and honesty. It expresses an open feeling of grief and shame. This expression of feelings is called *ath]ŋ kulahu* ('eating shame').

If a Limba traditionalist is the victim of an offence that requires a confession, and the offender refuses to confess, the traditionalist most often will say, *yan pɛy ka Kanu ba k]s]ŋ] wo thiya woŋ* ('I leave my case with God who is the righteous judge').[18] Confession is followed by an acceptance (*yɛrikɔy bath]nk]y*) of responsibility for the crime committed (whether intentional or unintentional), a genuine repentance, a request for forgiveness (*mapɛniyɔ*), and a willingness to undergo the appropriate ritual, or to offer the prescribed sacrifice for atonement.

The process by which an offender's sin against God and the ancestors is expiated and forgiven has been discussed previously (see 4.6 'Worshipping *Kanu*' and 6.5 'Ancestor veneration').

Sins committed against a parent, or against an older member of society carry a curse (*danka*) if they are not dealt with through the normal means of confession and restitution. When confession and apologies have been made, the victim of the crime lays his/her right hand on the offender's head or back, and publicly acknowledges the apology. Because water is considered as a symbol of purification, the offended person then sips a mouthful of water and sprays it on the offender's head. If the victim is the offender's parent, custom dictates that the child must give a piece of cloth to his/her parent 'to cover the parent's embarrassment'.

When a sin is committed against a person other than a parent, the elders are called upon to mediate. If it is a serious offence like adultery, trespassing, the intentional killing of someone's livestock or the use of abusive and profane language against someone, the offender is required to bring a customary gift to present to the victim as a sign of respect and humility. The elders present will ask the offender to either lie prostrate on the floor or kneel in front of the victim and confess the sin committed and ask for forgiveness. The offender stays in a prostrate or kneeling position until the victim touches his/her head and says 'I have forgiven you, get up and have a seat'. The victim then calls for water and drinks some of it as an indication that his/her bad feelings have been 'cooled down'. Or he/she can spit out some of the water indicating that his/her bad feelings have been 'washed out'. The climax of the process is a handshake and an embrace or the sharing of a kola nut. All rituals of forgiveness are concluded with a warm handshake and an embrace. When someone deliberately destroys an animal; or a bird, he/she is required to make a sacrifice in a ceremony called *kuloy ko ka kamalɔ* (cleansing from an animal sin).

The victim of a 'swear' must undergo either *adɛkɛŋ kubul]* ('partial cleansing') or *kuloy/kugbilisi/ kuloki/kusasi mandi* ('full cleansing'). Either ceremony can be performed by a specialist known as a *batheki/baduku, bad]ri/bath]nk]ni* ('a diviner'). If a community or family is experiencing the effects of a curse, the diviner first identifies the source of the curse, and when the culprit is found, performs an elaborate cleansing ceremony called *Masiyaŋ* ('to throw water') to put an end to the contagion.

Sins against nature, spirits, or secret societies, and sexual sins of any kind are ritually absolved likewise by a full cleansing ceremony *Kugbilisi/Kuloy*. Sacrifices are also offered to the supernatural for the forgiveness of certain sins and offences.

As a result of these rituals and sacrifices, 'the offender is re-accepted, reconciled, brought close to the party and to the wider community'.[19] In the African *sensus communis*, the socio-religious well-being of the individual affects the well-being of the community. In other words, 'the well-being of the community as such is a reflection of the morality of the individuals who constitute it'.[20] It is this state of personal and communal well-being that from the Limba point of view constitutes salvation.[21]

## Salvation

Salvation (*Kuyaŋkaŋ*) is freedom from wrong doing, deliverance from evil forces, and a state of well-being with oneself, the supernatural, and the community. It is a 'state of being at peace with the spirit world by living one's life in line with the traditional decorum'.[22] It is also a deliverance from the 'physical and immediate dangers that threaten individual or community survival, good health and general prosperity or safety'.[23] As noted earlier, for the Limba, 'good health and general prosperity' are blessings from God, and that is understood as *Kuyaŋkaŋ*. Dr Siaka Stevens, the first Limba head of state, and the most corrupt politician in the history of Sierra Leone once said: 'God has blessed me with children, grandchildren, power, wealth, good health and long life. This is what I call true blessing'.[24] For Dr Stevens, 'salvation meant wealth, health, and prosperity with no reference to moral scruples'.[25]

The African concept of salvation is highly based on 'contemporary realities'.[26] Salvation is not something to be experienced at 'the end of time'.[27] There is 'no anticipation of a final day when the present cosmic order will be "judged, or dissolved" and replaced by "a new heaven and a new earth"', and 'there is no clear hope of a hereafter free from suffering'.[28] Rather, salvation 'has been experienced in the past, and it is being experienced in the present'.[29] In a nutshell, salvation is conceived 'in terms of concern for the ills and successes of community life'.[30] To be saved is to be 'delivered from sin into fullness of life', and be 'empowered to live a community-centred life'.[31]

## Conclusion

Limba communities are governed by rules which guide the socio-religious life of the community. Any breach of these rules is considered an act of wrongdoing or sin. The

Limba despise sin because it destroys the spiritual and social well-being of the offender, the community, and in some cases the offender's family. Sin separates the offender from the supernatural, and from his/her fellow human beings. The Limba see sin of whatever nature as an offence against God and the ancestors. For these reasons, sin is frowned upon and is not treated lightly. For an offender to be restored, he/she has first to confess and accept the crime, and must be willing to go through a ritual or offer a sacrifice in order to be cleansed. Only then can the offender be forgiven, and restored.

The offender's reconciliation with the victim, and with the supernatural, and his/her restoration to the community is regarded as salvation. It is a state of harmony within the self, the supernatural, and the community. Salvation is not only redemption from present ills; it is also a continued experience of well-being and peace, both internal and external, for the individuals and the community as a whole.

# 11

# Sacred specialists

## Introduction

Sacred specialists[1] play an important role in LIR. In most cases, sacred specialists play a part in the traditionalist's life from conception to death. They are very important in the religious life of the community. They are helpers and guides to the people for the maintenance of the sacred values of the society. Sacred specialists are found in almost every Limba community. They are held in high esteem because of their relationship with the supernatural and for the mediatory role they play between the people and the supernatural. Sacred specialists are believed to have received their special ability either from *Kanu* or from spirits, as the case may be.

The church condemns sacred specialists as evil personages and workers of iniquity. They are considered to be the devil incarnate because they work under the influence of Satan to promote deception and false religion. This chapter will study the various kinds of Limba sacred specialists, and their specific duties.

## Priests

The Limba consider their priests (*Banabeŋ*)[2] to be called apart for the purpose of relating with the supernatural on behalf of the people.[3] Their primary duty is to offer sacrifice. Limba priests may be either male or female;[4] both priests and priestesses are allowed to marry.[5]

Priests may be either lay priests or professional priests. Lay priests may be the head of a household and officiate at domestic or family ancestral shrines where they lead in the presentation of household offerings and prayers and the pouring of libations for important events.

Professional priests, on the other hand, are responsible for all community rituals and spiritual matters. They minister in community shrines and at public rituals.[6] There are two categories in the professional priesthood. The chief celebrant at grand funeral ceremonies (e.g., when a chief or one of the big men in the community passes away) is called *Bagbendek]l]*. He is regarded as the Chief Priest. His assistant is known as *Bagbayha*. Although the Limba say that the priesthood is open to both males and females it is rare for a female to become a Chief Priest. Professional priests can also perform a 'swearing' ceremony on behalf of someone. In the men's *Gbangban* society, it is the duty of the ceremonial priest to invoke the spirits. He is referred to as *Bakurɛ*.

Regardless of rank, the goal of all Limba priests is the same. They connect people to the supernatural through sacrifices, prayers, offerings and libations. Some candidates for the priesthood are required to undergo long and rigorous training[7] which is conducted by more experienced priests and elders. Others enter the priesthood without such rigour. Those who are proven to be called by divine means through the ancestors or spirits do not require the same training. Some are set apart from childhood.

# Diviners

Limba diviners (*bamandi, badetimandi*),[8] along with smiths, hunters, herbalists, twins and secret society officials, are gifted with *bathayɛŋ* ('double eyes or four eyes') that give them a supernatural vision of the worlds that are normally invisible to ordinary eyes, namely, the worlds of the spirits, of the dead, and of witches.[9] All people with double eyes are called *bekele*.[10] The majority of Limba diviners[11] are male, but there are a few female diviners.

A diviner is a 'specialist who seeks to diagnose disease, or discover the solution to problems, by means of inspiration or manipulation of objects through various techniques'.[12] He/she is the agent of 'unveiling mysteries of human life'.[13] The diviner 'stands at the crossroads between the spiritual and human worlds'.[14] In that regard, the diviner serves as 'the intercessor, mediator, and bridge of communication between the two worlds. As an agent with access to both the human and spiritual worlds, s/he explores and exploits the mystical world to normalize, ameliorate, restore, and reconcile estranged relationships for a harmonious and habitable universe'.[15] In general, Limba diviners, like diviners in most African traditions, play the roles of 'counsellors, judges, comforters, suppliers of assurance and confidence during people's crises, advisers, pastors and priests, seers, fortune-tellers and solvers of problems, and revealers of secrets like thefts, imminent danger or coming events'.[16]

Diviners are feared by witches and evil spirits because of their ability to expose them and their evil plots. In most Limba communities, when an unexplainable misfortune does occur, a diviner is called to ascertain the cause of the misfortune and to prescribe the necessary solution, or to expose the thief.[17] Limba diviners are vital in helping their clients to decipher various messages from the spiritual world that are intended for them, especially those from the dead.

The Limba have several kinds of diviners, each with their own special methods to manipulate and control 'the spirit world for the benefit of human and spiritual communities'.[18] Although each diviner has his/her own special divining method, all Limba diviners use objects as mediums to interpret their results.[19] The following are the most familiar kinds of Limba diviners and the methods of divination they use:

- *Bamandi* divine by the casting of stones in a process known as *nɛki mandi* ('looking water').[20] The belief behind this method is that, as water is clear, the truth will be revealed clearly. During this process of divination, water is put into a receptacle to signify that belief.

- *Babɛrɛ* are women sooth-sayers who also divine using stones.[21]

- *Basakapi/Bawuy]* divine and expose witchcraft through small receptacles believed to be inhabited by spirits.[22] They are renowned for handling complicated and difficult witchcraft matters and for cleansing[23] the defiled or the cursed.

- *Bad]ri/Bath]nk]ni* are those who own and use 'swears'.[24] The process of obtaining a 'swear' is lengthy and expensive because the smith, who makes and sells the 'swear', has spiritual powers, and will first have to prove that the customer possesses the power to operate a 'swear'. Several tests will be done to prove the customer's ability. If the tests are passed, the 'swear' is purchased at a high price.

## Herbalists

Limba herbalists (*Bapɔlo*, *Bataliŋ*) are men and women who cure the 'sick using medicines made from wild plants gathered in the bush'.[25] Herbalists, like diviners, are known as *Bekele* because they are believed to be born with supernatural vision to 'see the devils in the bush that are invisible to others, communicate with them, and learn the powers of wild plants'.[26] There is some overlap between the activities of herbalists and those of diviners, because both possess the gift of healing.[27] Herbalists are believed to have the 'widest knowledge of the curative properties of herbs, plants, bark and roots'.[28] Limba herbalists 'dispense protective and curative medicines'[29] and are capable of curing minor, life-threatening, mental, and witchcraft-related illnesses.[30] Herbalists continue to serve the needs of many with their ability to deal with 'unnatural' or 'spiritual illnesses' and through their ability to recognise the agency of witchcraft and the power of traditional symbols, they 'serve to perpetuate traditional beliefs and practices'.[31] Recently, an association of medical doctors and traditional healers was formed. This alliance between the two professions is a positive step in the right direction.

## Conclusion

Sacred specialists are people who are believed to have received spiritual abilities either from God or from the spirits. Because of their spiritual giftedness, sacred specialists play a vital role in the life of the individual and the community. They are human mediators between the supernatural and the people. In some cases they play a part in a person's life from conception to death. They also help and guide people to maintain personal and communal religious values.

Priests, diviners and herbalists are the three main categories of sacred specialists in LIR. In the priesthood, there are lay and professional priests. Lay priests are usually heads of families/compounds without community status for their priesthood. Professional priests have community status and are believed to receive their call either from God or from the spirits, or have received training from an experienced priest or elder. Both kinds of priests connect people to the supernatural through sacrifice, prayers, offerings and libations. The Limba have male and female priests.

Diviners are people with outstanding spiritual eyes that enable them to see and know what transpires in the worlds of the spirits, of the dead, and of witches. Because of this capability, witches fear diviners. Diviners discover the solution to problems through inspiration or the manipulation of objects using various techniques. In addition to their role as fortune-tellers and seers, they also counsel, comfort, and give assurance and confidence to people; they expose thieves, and interpret messages from the spirits and from the dead. Although the five different kinds of Limba diviners use objects as mediums to achieve their results, they use different methods of divination.

Herbalists, as the name implies, are sacred specialists who use herbs and wild plants from the bush to make medicines for protective and curative purposes. They are believed to have an outstanding knowledge of the curative properties of herbs, plants, bark and roots. They are gifted in curing minor, life-threatening, mental, and witchcraft-related illnesses.

# 12

## Concluding remarks

### Introduction

This book has attempted through a survey of published works, fieldwork, and the author's own experience as a Limba, to fill a gap in the extant literature about the ethno-religious landscape of Sierra Leone, by providing an introductory systematic study of the fundamental tenets of LIR. This chapter will recap the findings of chapters 1 through 11, and will conclude with a few recommendations for a positive dialogue and understanding among traditionalists, Limba Christians, and the church.

### Recapitulation

The book began with an attempt to gain an overall understanding of the 'socio-history' of the Limba people. Background information was provided on the origin, present homeland and outside settlements, language, political administrative structures, economy, and other socio-cultural characteristics of the Limba.

Chapter 2 examined the external and internal influences that have affected and continue to affect Limba culture and religion. Islam though an immigrant religion was able to present itself as an African religion by retaining many aspects of Sierra Leone traditional culture with an overlay of Muslim belief and practice. This peaceful co-existence between the Muslims and indigenes resulted in intermarriage, the formation of new clans, and a reciprocal adoption of cultures and practices. In contrast, Christianity was presented as imperialistic, insensitive, and exclusive – which has resulted in the destruction of pertinent Limba cultural traits, and an ongoing struggle between the church and African culture and religion. It was through the church that western education came. Traditionalists now blame that education for the post-modern ideologies expressed by the young and educated which challenge and condemn long held worldviews and elements of culture. Interaction with other ethnic groups, and the dialectical divisions of the Limba are internal factors that have also affected Limba culture and religion.

Chapter 3 presented a picture of the current state of the traditional Limba religious belief system and its components as it is currently affected by these internal and external factors. It was discovered that for the Limba traditionalists, religion is a way of life deeply rooted in their hearts and minds, and is expressed through their words, actions and symbols as a means of maintaining a cordial relationship with the supernatural, the community, and the self. It is on this basis that, in spite of the changes and challenges it continues to encounter, LIR still thrives. The mapping out of the components of LIR provided the perimeters in which the framework for the rest of this study was built.

Chapters 4 through 11 systematically explored the core of Limba traditional religiosity. Foremost in the Limba worldview is the belief in a Supreme Being known as *Kanu Masala* ('God Supreme'), who lives above in the sky. He is referred to by several other names and titles which express various aspects of his character, qualities of his nature, his abilities, his activities, and the nature of his relationships with the Limba. On account of *Kanu*'s values and in appreciation of his continued provision for his creatures, especially humankind; the Limba offer worship to him as a means to stay connected and to maintain a relationship with him.

Unlike most Africans, the Limba claim to have a clear teaching about Angels, the second highest spiritual influence in their supernatural hierarchy. Little is yet known about angelology in LIR which opens the opportunity for further studies in this area.

Just below the angels are the ancestors. These are the spirits of the venerated Dead who achieved their status through their outstanding contributions to the community, and who continue to seek the welfare of the living and are believed to be intermediaries between God and the living.

The question of whether or not the ancestors are worshipped was discussed. Sawyerr[1] is one the African theologians who strongly argues that ancestral veneration rites constitute worship. Contrary to this argument, some scholars interested in African religion have commented that although the veneration offered to ancestors may exhibit signs of worship, in the mind of the African traditionalists who carry out the practice, it is veneration. In that regard, 'worship' has been challenged as an inaccurate label to apply to ancestor veneration, because the 'Africans themselves know very well that they are not 'worshipping' the departed members of their family'.[2] Ancestors are not objects of worship; rather they are intermediaries, and considered 'a conveyor belt, a medium to reach an end, not the end itself'.[3] They are not venerated because they are dead; rather, the ancestors are venerated due to their proximity to God which gives them the ability to seek the interests of their families.

Last in the hierarchy of the supernatural are the non-ancestral spirits who are believed to be numerous and living in the world. These spirits been classified into two categories – nature spirits and human spirits. The former are believed to be created as such and may be ambivalent, and the latter are the spirits of dead humans including ghosts and witches, and are considered to be malignant.

Outside of the supernatural realm is humankind believed to have been created by *Kanu Masala* from the earth with a body and breath, which is the source of life for the body, and with a spiritual nature which gives him/her a yearning to be in constant harmony with God. Although humans are considered superior to and more intelligent than all of God's other creatures they are expected to embrace and live in harmony with the rest of creation: both animate beings and inanimate things. As creatures with a physical and spiritual connection to the earth, on account of their origin and the place where their ancestors were laid to rest; humans are expected to exhibit an ecological consciousness.

For the Limba, life is full of puzzles, none of which can be solved without the help of God. Therefore, their dependence on God as the ultimate source and Sustainer of everything is evident throughout the entire lifecycle – from conception to death, and, in some instances, even after death. Throughout all of life's stages, God is a focal point. He is the source of everything, and in all of life's challenges the Limba depend on him for sustenance and well-being.

As humankind tries to maintain a cordial relationship with the supernatural, other animate beings, and inanimate objects, there are rules for the guidance of the socio-religious life of the individual and of the community. The ancestors and the elders established these rules and any failure to follow them is considered an act of sin. In that respect, sin is discouraged, and measures are taken to deal with it for restoration and harmony through prescribed procedures that the offender must follow. He/she must first confess to the crime, and be prepared to undergo the prescribed rituals or offer the sacrifice required for forgiveness. When the offender is forgiven and reconciled with his/her victim, with the community, and with God, then he/she is considered to be saved.

Salvation in Limba theology is a state of being in harmony with the supernatural, the community, and the self. It is deliverance from the physical and contemporary dangers that militate against the individual or community existence, and it is a state of spiritual and physical prosperity. Salvation is primarily based on contemporary realities which are experienced in the here and now.

In Limba communities and settlements, three categories of sacred specialists – priests, diviners and herbalists – act as intermediaries between the supernatural and humankind. They are believed to be gifted with 'double vision' that gives them the ability to see and reveal things in the worlds of the spirits, the dead, and witches, which are concealed from ordinary human eyes. They are also gifted with the ability to prevent the evil activities of malevolent spirits and witches, to communicate with the dead, and to provide help for the physical, spiritual, and social well-being of people. Both lay and professional priests were identified as were five different kinds of diviners who use objects as mediums to achieve their results, each using his/her own methods of divination.

Herbalists are the traditional doctors of the community. They are gifted with the ability of knowing and providing protective and curative medicines from herbs and wild plants found in the bush. They cure a variety of illnesses ranging from minor to life-threatening ones, including mental and witchcraft related ailments.

This study has shown that, LIR, like any other living religion, is both sacred and functional. Any religion, whether organised or organic consists of a wide range of beliefs, practices, and behaviours. More importantly, although there are divergences among religious systems, each religion is based on faith and mystery, as each religious system contains beliefs and practices that deny human logic and understanding.

## Recommendations

On the basis of my field work and interaction with the Limba traditionalists, Limba Christians, and Christian Limbas, I will conclude this study with a few general recommendations. Although these recommendations may not be new in African theological circles,[4] in the context of the Limba situation, they may prove to be helpful guides to map out possible strategies for mutual understanding among the Limba groups being discussed:

- On the basis that people can only speak about what they know, the clergy and the elders of the Limba churches must find ways and means to educate themselves about traditional values, and the methods of relating the Bible to these values as this study has attempted to do.

- As the church is already aware of the concerns of Limba Christians, its leaders should now be willing to sit and reassess their approach to LIR and their treatment of Limba Christians.

- The church must be willing to establish a dialogue with Limba Christians. The Limba churches and traditionalists must be able to sit together and work out their differences. In order for this dialogue to be effective each side must be willing to listen to the other's ideas, and volunteer their own.[5]

# Notes

## Introduction

1    It has been this way for several decades now. See R. H. Finnegan, *Survey of the Limba People of Northern Sierra Leone* (London: Her Majesty Stationery Office, 1965), 10; C. M. Fyle, *The History of Sierra Leone: A Concise Introduction* (London: Evans, 1981), 3; J. A. D. Alie, *A New History of Sierra Leone* (London: Macmillan, 1990), 10.

2    J. O. Awolalu, 'The Encounter Between African Traditional Religion and Other Religions in Nigeria', in *African Traditional Religions in Contemporary Society*, ed. J. K. Olupona (St. Paul, Minn: Paragon House, 1991), 111.

3    Ibid.

4    J. K. Olupona, 'Introduction', in *African Traditional Religions in Contemporary Society*, ed. J. K. Olupona (St. Paul, Minn: Paragon House, 1991), 1.

5    J. Opala and F. Boillot, 'Leprosy Among the Limba: Illness and Healing in the Context of World View', *Social Science and Medicine* 42 no. 1 (1996), 5.

6    For example, W. T. Harris and H. Sawyerr, *The Springs of Mende Belief and Conduct* (Freetown: Sierra Leone University Press, 1968) and A. J. Gittins, *Mende Religion: Aspects of Belief and Thought in Sierra Leone* (Steyler Verlag – Wort Und Werk, Nettenal, 1987) wrote on the Mende. R. T. Parsons, *Religion in an African Society* (Leiden: E.J. Brill, 1964) wrote about the Kono. This work has also made use of several other articles on these ethnic groups written by these scholars.

7    Similarly, J. O. Lucas, *The Religion of the Yorubas* (Lagos: C.M.S. Bookshop, 1948) and J. O. Awolalu, *Yoruba Beliefs and Sacrificial Rites* (London: Longman, 1979) have written on the ethnic religion of the Yoruba. S. F. Nadel, *Nupe Religion* (London: Routledge & Kegan Paul Ltd., 1954) wrote about the Nupe people; E. E. Evans-Pritchard, *Nuer Religion* (Oxford: Clarendon Press, 1956) has written on the Nuer; R. M. Downes, *Tiv Religion* (Ibadan: Ibadan University Press, 1971) wrote about the Tiv people; and several other African ethnic groups are fully documented.

8    Documented information found in historical, anthropological and ethnological works regarding Limba religion is limited in both quantity and scope. In a general socio-economic study of the Limba, Finnegan, *Survey of the Limba*, 106–22, wrote a chapter on Limba religion in their historical homeland. Two years later, R. H. Finnegan, *Limba Stories and Story Telling* (Oxford: Clarendon, 1967), 19–24, published an abridged version of Limba religion. S. Ottenberg, 'Two New Religions, One Analytic Frame', *Cahiers d'Etudes Africaines* 24 no. 4 (1984), 437–54 analysed the similarities and differences between the impacts made by Islam and Christianity on the Warawara Limba people of Bafodea. In another work, S. Ottenberg,

'Religion and Ethnicity in the Arts of a Limba Chiefdom', *Africa* 58 no. 4 (1988a), 437–65 examines their major visual and performing arts and explores changes they have undergone over the past century as a result of external religious and ethnic forces. A common thread in the above publications is their focus on Limba religion as practised in the hinterland. Because of their own unique focuses, little or no attention is given to the large number of Limba living in metropolitan areas like Freetown the capital city of Sierra Leone, which has the largest settlement of Limba outside their historical homeland, and where all the various dialects of Limba are found.

# Chapter 1: Socio-history of the Limba

1    Sierra Leone's major ethnic groups are the Mende, Temne, Limba and Krio.

2    Finnegan, *Survey of the Limba*, 12.

3    Regarding Limba ethnopoliticization, J. D. Kandeh, 'Politicization of Ethnic Identities in Sierra Leone', *African Studies Review* 35 no. 1 (1992), 94, writes: 'Limbanization of political and bureaucratic appointments, the security forces and mobility opportunities in Sierra Leone, a practice that dates back to the Siaka Stevens era, has undoubtedly meant greater access to state offices and resources for Limba elites'.

4    R. H. Finnegan, 'Limba Religious Vocabulary', *Sierra Leone Language Review* no 2. (1963), 11–15; '"Swears" Among the Limba', *The Sierra Leone Bulletin of Religion* 6 no. 1 (1964), 8–26; 'How To Do Things With Words: Performative Utterances Among the Limba of Sierra Leone', *Man* 4 no. 4 (1969), 537–51, and 'Speech, Language and Non-literacy: The Limba of Sierra Leone', in *Literacy and Orality: Studies in the Technology of Communication* (Oxford: Blackwell, 1988).

5    S. Ottenberg, 'Artistic and Sex Roles in a Limba Chiefdom', in *Female and Male in West Africa*, ed. C. Oppong (London: George Allan, 1983), 76–90; 'The Bride Comes to the Groom: Ritual and Drama in Limba Wedding', *The Drama Review* 32 (1988b), 42–64; 'The Dancing Bride: Art and Indigenous Psychology in Limba Weddings', *Man* 24 (1989), 57–78; 'One Face of a Culture: Two Musical Ensembles in a Limba Chiefdom Sierra Leone', in *Carrefour de Cultures: Melanges Offerts a Jacqueline Leiner*, ed. R. Antoine (Tubingen: Gunter Narr Verlag, 1993), 57–75; 'Male & Female Secret Societies Among the Bafodea Limba of Northern Sierra Leone, in *Religion in Africa: Experience and Expressions*, ed. T. D. Blakeley, W. E. A. van Beek and Dennis Thomson (London: Heinemann,1994), 363–87; *Seeing With Music: The Lives of Three Blind African Musicians* (Seattle: University of Washington Press,1996); 'Stories and Storytelling: The Limba', in *African Folklore: An Encyclopaedia*, ed. P. M. Peek and K. Yankah (London: Routledge, 2004), 441–2.

6    R. Fanthorpe, 'Locating the Politics of a Sierra Leonean Chiefdom', *Africa* 68 no. 4 (1998a), 558–84 and 'Limba "Deep Rural" Strategies', *Journal of African History* 39 no. 1 (1998b), 15–38.

7    W. A. Hart, 'Woodcarving of the Limba of Sierra Leone', *African Arts* 23 (1989), 44–53.

8    C. M. Fyle, *Alimamy Suluku of Sierra Leone, c. 1820–1906: The Dynamics of Political Leadership in Pre-Colonial Sierra Leone* (London: Evans, 1979); Fyle, *The History of Sierra Leone*.

9    Alie, *A New History*.

10    M. McCulloch, *Peoples of Sierra Leone* (London: I.A.I, 1950).

11    C. Fyfe, *A Short History of Sierra Leone* (London: Longman, 1979).

12    The other 16 are: Krio, Mende, Temne, Kono, Kuranko, Loko, Sherbro/Bullom, Kissi, Vai, Krim, Fula, Mandigo (or Mandika), Soso, Yalunka, Kru and Gola. Fyfe, *The History of Sierra Leone*, 3, excludes the Kru and puts the number at 16.

13    Alie, *A New History*, 1.

14    Ibid.

15    McCulloch, *Peoples of Sierra Leone*, 51; Finnegan, *Survey of the Limba*, 14; *Limba Stories*, 3; Fyle, *Alimamy Suluku*, 3; Alie, *A New History*, 10.

16    In tracing the history and traditions of the origins of the ethnic groups in Sierra Leone, the Limba was the only group among the four major groups whose origin, McCulloch, *Peoples of Sierra Leone*, 51; Finnegan, *Survey of the Limba*, 14; Alie, *A New History*, 9, could not trace. According to Alie, *A New History*, 9; Fyle, *The History of Sierra Leone*, 15, 49; cf. McCulloch, Peoples of Sierra Leone, 7; S. J. Yambasu, *Dialectics of Evangelization: A Critical Examination of Methodist Evangelization of the Mende People in Sierra Leone* (Accra, Ghana: AOG Literature Centre, 2002), 46, the Mende presumably originated from the Liberian hinterland. In Alie, A New History, 9, cf. McCulloch, *Peoples of Sierra Leone*, 50–1, the Temne claim to have immigrated from Futa Jallon, which is present day Republic of Guinea into their present day Temne homeland. In Fyle, *The History of Sierra Leone*, 34–5, 71–4; A. Wyse, *The Krio of Sierra Leone: An Interpretive History* (London: C. Hurst & Co, 1989), 1–5, and Alie, *A New History*, 78, the Krio, descendants of freed slaves from England, Nova Scotia, Jamaica and West Africa arrived in Freetown between 1787 and 1863.

17    Finnegan, *Survey of the Limba*, 14.

18    Ibid.

19    Fyle, *The History of Sierra Leone*, 10.

20    Cf. Alie, *A New History*, 10.

21    The observation of M. P. Banton, *A West African City: A Study of Tribal Life in Freetown* (Oxford: Oxford University Press, 1957), 48, to some extent is still valid. It has been noted for a very long time that the Limba are one of the hinterland people who have the heaviest emigration rate both long term and seasonal. For economic and social reasons, migration has long been a feature of Limba social strategies.

22    Finnegan, *Survey of the Limba*, 11, lists three.

23    Cf. Finnegan, 'Speech', 46; *Survey of the Limba*, 10; Alie, *A New History*, 8.

24    Ibid.

25    Finnegan, *Survey of the Limba*, 10.

26    *Poyo* is a white foamy drink extracted from the trunk of the palm tree.

27    Finnegan, *Survey of the Limba*, 10; 'Speech', 46; National Curriculum Development Centre, *Source Book for Four Sierra Leonean Languages* (Freetown: Print Sundry and Stationers, 1993), 82.

28    D. Westermann, *The Languages of West Africa*. (London: Oxford Press, 1952), 13; Finnegan, *Survey of the Limba*, 10; F. W. H. Migeod, *The Languages of West Africa* (London: Gregg International, 1971), 33; Fyle, *History of Sierra Leone*, 5; Fanthorpe, 'Limba "Deep Rural" Strategies', 18.

29    For example, *hulimba*, is an abstract noun that can refer to the Limba language, the Limba ethnic group as a whole, or a Limba person, singular (Finnegan, 'Speech', 46; cf. NCDC, *Source Book*, 69). *Malimba* is an adjective which means 'in the manner of the Limba', NCDC, *Source Book*, 71 or 'the Limba way'. For example, when a Limba wants something to be done culturally, he/she would say *Miŋ niyaŋ malimba maŋ* ('let us do it the Limba way').

30    NCDC, *Source Book*, 83. Properly, there are 12 dialects: Biriwa, Gbonkobo, Kalanthuba, Kamuke, Kelen, Safuroko, Sela, Sonkon, Thamiso, Thonko, Warawara Bafodia, and Warawara Yagala. However, the five regional dialects were identifiable as early as the mid-nineteenth century and have been generally accepted ever since (Alie, *A New History*, 10).

31    NCDC, *Source Book*, 83; Fyle, *The History of Sierra Leone*, 52. Most individuals who speak one dialect are also able to understand and communicate with individuals who speak another dialect. Overall, the similarities outweigh the differences. For a brief history of the development of the Limba language, sound system, word contraction, grammatical structure, type of sentences, tenses, language mechanisms and orthography, see NCDC, *Source Book*, 61–82.

32    Several earlier works, Finnegan, *Survey of the Limba*, 11; Opala and Boillot, 'Leprosy Among the Limba', 8, and Ottenberg, 'Religion and Ethnicity', 437, enumerate only seven chiefdoms, however, the current statistics provided by the Ministry of Local Government and Community Development (MLGCD) name 11.

33    Fanthorpe, 'Locating the Politics', 558–9. On the issue of political control by European Powers, Lamin Sanneh, *Piety & Power: Muslim and Christians in West Africa*. (Maryknoll, NY: Orbis Books, 1996), 86, has this to say: 'The existing state boundaries of Africa, for example, were created by Western colonial powers and inherited by the independent governments. These boundaries still provide the context of sate jurisdiction in modern Africa. Through the artificial colonial creation of tribes as an amalgamation of ethnic groups and nations as the fusion of tribes, states were established as the vehicle by which Africans could enter the twentieth century'.

34    Divisions that existed can be described as a dialect cluster with fuzzy edges. This was due to the movement of peoples, inter-cultural intermarriage, trade, warfare, and other social factors. The British were very conscious of ethnic differences in Britain (e.g., English, Scottish, Welsh, Irish and India) and applied much of the same model of governance in Africa. They also had the idea that the mixing of the 'races' as they called them in early days, was in general undesirable and might lead to conflict and disorder. For this reason, they sometimes tried to set up separate areas for each ethnic group in the cities, although this was often unsuccessful.

35    The Chiefdom Council system within this plan was originally patterned after the Nigerian model (Alie, *A New History*, 152; Fyle, *The History of Sierra Leone*, 114, 116–7).

36    Finnegan, *Survey of the Limba*, 43, 47–8.

37    Cf. Fanthorpe, 'Locating the Politics', 563.

38    Finnegan, *Survey of the Limba*, 43; Fyle, *History of Sierra Leone*, 117–8; Alie, *A New History*, 156–7.

39    As all chiefs are called *Gbaku*, a term which should be only used when referring to the Paramount Chief, many Limba now use the term *Bathanpi* ('one with the staff' or 'staff carrier') to distinguish the Paramount Chief from the junior Chiefs. According to the MLGCD, chiefdom rulers and officials are considered 'natural rulers'. Paramount chiefs and other ethnic rulers in Limba land are designated 'natural rulers' because the land they rule is their natural home. By divine providence, these leaders descended from the first families that inhabited the land. As the first families that God placed on the land, they are considered the owners and custodians of it. Therefore, it is customary to have the ruler come from one of those homes. Ethnic Limba rulers outside Limba land are usually designated 'natural rulers' because they do not fit the above profile.

40    Finnegan, *Survey of the Limba*, 23.

41    Ottenberg, 'Artistic and Sex Roles', 77.

42    Fyle, *The History of Sierra* Leone, 29.

43    Ottenberg, 'Artistic and Sex Roles', 77.

44    Alie, *A New History*, 213.

45    Capital offences such as murder, cannibalism and rebellion are beyond the jurisdiction of the tribal court and are transferred to the national government through the police. Divorce cases concerning marriages that were contracted in the church or mosque are also beyond the jurisdictional limits of the tribal courts, and are therefore referred to the national courts.

46    Fyle, *The History of Sierra* Leone, 119.

47    Finnegan, *Survey of the Limba*, 21.

48    Cf. ibid., 31–2.

49    Formerly, a witch was banished after three offences.

50    Cf. Fanthorpe, 'Locating the Politics', 563–5, Chiefdom Council structure of the Biriwa Limba.

51    Banton, *A West African City*, 14; Alie, *A New History*, 161.

52    Alie, *A New History*, 161.

53    Ibid.

54    Land disputes and major robbery cases are beyond the jurisdiction of a tribal court. In the Western Area, as in the chiefdoms, divorce cases concerning marriages that were contracted in the church or mosque are beyond the jurisdictional limits of the tribal courts, and are referred to the national courts.

55    *Alkali* is a Temne title from the Islamic word, *al quadi* meaning 'a judge' (Fyle, *The History of Sierra* Leone, 32).

56    Alie, *A New History*, 161.

57    NCDC, *Source Book*, 85.

58    Finnegan, *Survey of the Limba*, 10–1; 81–6; Opala and Boillot, 'Leprosy Among the Limba', 5.

59    Finnegan, *Limba Stories*, 8.

60    Fyfe, *Alimamy Suluku*, 4; Fyle, *The History of Sierra* Leone, 68.

61    A few start earlier in January and February.

62    Cf. Finnegan, *Limba Stories*, 8.

63    This custom is similar to that of the Mende people who have two major groups – the *kugbe* and the *bembe*, that provide assistance during the farming season. The *kugbe* is made up of both young men and women, and the *bembe* is a group of about a dozen or so young men (Alie, *A New History*, 22).

64    NCDC, *Source Book*, 89; Finnegan, *Survey of the Limba*, 123.

65    See Ottenberg, 'Religion and Ethnicity', 442–59, for visual and performing arts in Bafodea.

66    Cf. Hart, 'Woodcarving'.

67    C. G. Hargrave, *African Primitive Life: As I Saw It in Sierra Leone British West Africa* (Wilmington NC: Wilmington Printing Co., 1944), 88–96; Alie, *A New History*, 25–6.

68    Finnegan, *Survey of the Limba*, 26.

69    Cf. ibid., 56.

70    Alie, *A New History*, 20; cf. Finnegan, *Survey of the Limba*, 56.

71    Cf. Ottenberg, 'Artistic and Sex Roles', 78.

72    Finnegan, *Survey of the Limba*, 54.

73    Finnegan, *Survey of the Limba*, 52, stated that clans are strictly exogamous. This may have been the case for all clans at that time, as it is still true of the clans of the Warawara Limba (Ottenberg, 'The Bride Comes to the Groom', 43; 'The Dancing Bride', 59).

74    Such as the Conteh clan of the Biriwa to which I belong.

75    Fanthorpe, 'Limba "Deep Rural" Strategies', 29.

76    See E. G. Parrinder, *African Traditional Religion* (London: Sheldon, 1962), 92; J. Mbiti, *African Religions and Philosophy* (London: Heinemann, 1989a), 109. In the Bible, Jeremiah 20:15 suggests that the father was not present at birth.

77    For health reasons, the former practice of spitting kola nut into the child's mouth by the birth attendants (Finnegan, *Survey of the Limba*, 75), is longer in practice in most Limba communities.

78    Circumcision is practised in most parts of Africa (Parrinder, *African Traditional Religion*, 94).

79    In New Testament (NT) times, the child was named on the eighth day (Luke 1:59; 2:21).

80    The traditional Limba name for the ceremony is *agbɔrɔŋ* ('to shave'), because, on the day of the ceremony the head of the child is shaved before it is named and taken outside.

81    Cf. Parrinder, *African Traditional Religion*, 92; Mbiti, *African Religions*, 109–10. See Mbiti, *African Religions*, 110 for the symbolism of the placenta and umbilical cord.

82    This is true also in most African societies. See M. Cuthrell-Curry, 'African-derived Religion in the African American Community in the United States', in *African Spirituality: Forms, Meanings and Expressions*, ed. Jacob K. Olupona (New York, NY: Crossroad, 2000), 462. In the Old Testament (OT), the mother usually named the child (Gen. 29:31–30:24; 35:18; 1 Sam. 1:20), but the father sometimes did (Gen. 16:15; 17:19; Exod. 2:22).

83    For other African people see Parrinder, *African Traditional Religion*, 92–93; Mbiti, *African Religions*, 115; L. Magesa, *African Religion: The Moral Traditions of Abundant Life* (Maryknoll, NY: Orbis Books, 1997), 89–90.

84    Limbas are also fond of giving nickname(s) to people to portray someone's character, behaviour, special ability or favourite word. In this case the first name is followed by the nickname: *Sayo – Hughantama* (Sayo – the man of physical strength and might); *Sara – Bathagban* (Sara – the bookworm or the learned); *Hode – Gherema* (Hode – the guileful/duplicitous); *Yimba – Kupɛthɛ* (Yimba – the soft spoken); *Santigie Nyankuthɛgbɛ* (Santigie – be careful). Santigie Nyankuthɛgbɛ is a diviner/herbalist in Freetown who likes to tell his customers and acquaintances to 'be careful' with both the physical and spiritual worlds.

85    Magesa, *African Religion*, 90.

86    Christian Limbas adopted their naming and out-dooring ceremony from the traditionalists and modified it to portray Christian values. The ceremony is usually performed at the home of the child. It starts with a familiar hymn/song, followed by an opening prayer, the reading of scripture and a short exhortation based on the reading. The father of the child is asked to give the name of the child which should have already been written on a sheet of paper that is passed to the pastor who reads out the name. The child is then taken outside the house.

87    Finnegan, *Survey of the Limba*, 75, reports that the normal period for breast-feeding a baby is three years. While this was once the case, a majority of babies are now weaned by eighteen months. In Africa the period varies considerably (Parrinder, *African Traditional Religion*, 92; Cuthrell-Curry, 'African-derived Religion', 462).

88    This is a common practice in Africa where girls are 'betrothed since childhood', Parrinder, *African Traditional Religion*, 97; see also Parsons, *Religion*, 8.

89    Cf. Mbiti, *African Religions*, 132.

90    Cf. Finnegan, *Survey of the Limba*, 62–3.

91    In Africa, see Parrinder, *African Traditional Religion*, 97.

92    The practice of marrying several wives is common in Africa, see Mbiti *African Religions*, 138; V. R. Dorjahn, 'Changes in Temnes Polygamy', *Ethnology* 27 (1988), 367; and Magesa *African Religion*, 136–9. The patriarchs in the Bible practised polygamy (Gen. 4:19; 29:15–30; 2 Sam. 3:2–5), and sometimes had concubines as well (Gen. 16:1–2; 22:20–4; 2 Sam. 5:13).

93    For a discussion on the positive and negative aspects of polygamy see Mbiti, *African Religions*, 139–40.

94    In Africa leviratic union is common (Mbiti, *African Religions*, 140). However, it is not a proper 'marriage' in the African point of view because it is a temporary adjustment 'to fulfil an obligation to a deceased brother', Magesa, *African Religion*, 140. In the case of the Limba this is true because the surviving brother is not required to pay a bridal price nor go through the marriage procedures and rites to get the his brother's widow. In the Bible, if the husband died without a son, a leviratic law specified in Deuteronomy 25:5–10, required the brother of the deceased to marry the widow (P. J. Achtemeier, *Harper-Collins Bible Dictionary* [New York, NY: HarperCollins, 1996], 656); R. De Vaux, *Ancient Israel: Its Life and Institution* [Grand Rapids, MI: Eerdsman, 1997], 37–8; J. I. Packer, M. C. Tenney, and W. White, Jr., eds, *The Bible Almanac* [Nashville: Thomas Nelson, 1980], 435).

95    The Bible permitted divorce with certain exceptions. OT law only permitted the husband to initiate a divorce (Deut. 24:1–4), but in the NT, provision was also made for a woman to divorce her husband (Mark 10:12; 1 Cor. 7:13).

96    The causes of divorce among the Temne [V. R. Dorjahn, 'The Marital Game, Divorce and Divorce Frequency Among the Temne of Sierra Leone', *Anthropological Quarterly* 63 no. 4 (1990), 172–4], are quite similar to that of the Limba's. See Mbiti, *African Religions*, 141–2, for a discussion on some of the causes of divorce in Africa.

97    Alie, *A New History*, 23; Fyle, *The History of Sierra Leone*, 64.

98    Cf. Alie, *A New History*, 23.

99    Ottenberg, 'The Dancing Bride', 57–78; 'The Bride Comes', 42–64; 'Religion and Ethnicity', 437–65, portray the importance of Limba music in weddings, secret societies and other social activities.

100   See Finnegan, *Survey of the Limba*, 79–80; *Limba Stories*, 25–8 for a detailed understanding of some of these cultural traits.

101   Finnegan, *Limba Stories*, 25.

102   It is very rare for a man to cry in public. Men are very hesitant to openly express their emotions. When a man does show his sorrow, he does it quietly

103   In Western Area only the older women still sit on the floor. The younger women prefer to sit on chairs or benches.

# Chapter 2: Influences on Limba culture and Limba indigenous religion

1    In Limba the word *Dina* and its synonyms – *Namu, MabJrJ*, means both 'religion' and 'culture'. As such, it is hard to draw a dividing line between the sacred and the secular.

2    Alie, *A New History*, 31–46. See NCDC, *Source Book*, 205–6, for a discussion on the impact of foreign influence on the traditional life of the Temne people of Sierra Leone. Parsons, *Religion*, 226–40, addresses the effects of external influences on Kono Religion. For other African

people, see discussions on the impact of external influences on Tiv (Downes, *Tiv Religion*, 1–2) and Yoruba (Awolalu, *Yoruba Beliefs*, 183–96) religions.

3    Although there are Limba religio-cultural elements and values which find parallels in the Bible and which have been adopted by Limba Church, the church has maintained a hostile attitude toward traditional Limba practices. In sermons, teachings, discussions and songs, the Christian Limbas continue to dismiss Limba traditional practices as heathenism. See Ottenberg, 'Two New Religions', 437–54; 'Religion and Ethnicity', 437–65, for the external religious impact on the Warawara Limba. Magesa, *African Religion*, 4–14, discusses negative Christian attitudes toward African Religion and the latter's continuity irrespective of degradation. For a comparison of African cultural elements and values between ATR and Christianity, see J. S. Mbiti, 'Christianity and African Culture', *Journal of Theology for Southern Africa* 1 (1977); *Bible and Theology in African Christianity* (Nairobi: Oxford University Press, 1986); 'God, Sin, and Salvation in African Religion', *Journal of Interdenominational Theological Centre* 16 no. 1 (1989b).

4    Mbiti, *African Religions*, 211; see also page 222 for a detailed discussion on the causes and effects of modernisation on African religions.

5    J. S. Mbiti, *Concepts of God in Africa* (London: SPCK, 1970), xiv.

6    Awolalu, *Yoruba Beliefs*, 183–96.

7    G. Olson, *Church Growth in Sierra Leone* (Grand Rapids, Mich: W. B. Eerdmans, 1969), 47.

8    Fyle, *The History of Sierra Leone*, 27; S. D. Alharazim, 'The Origin and Progress of Islam in Sierra Leone', *Sierra Leone Studies* no. 21 (1930), 14.

9    Alharazim, 'Origin and Progress of Islam', 14.

10   Ibid.

11   Fyle, *The History of Sierra Leone*, 28.

12   Ibid., 31; Alie, *A New History*, 43.

13   Fyle, *The History of Sierra Leone*, 33.

14   Olson, *Church Growth*, 48.

15   D. E. Skinner, 'Mande Settlement and the Development of Islamic Institutions in Sierra Leone', *The International Journal of African Historical Studies* 11 no. 1 (1978), 57–8.

16   Skinner, 'Islamic Institutions', 58.

17   H. Fisher, 'Ahmadiyya in Sierra Leone', *Sierra Leone Bulletin of Religion*, 2 no. 1 (1960).

18   Alie, *A New History*, 101–2; Olson, *Church Growth*, 201–3.

19   Olson, *Church Growth*, 67–212; E. G. Parrinder, *Africa's Three Religions* (London: Sheldon, 1969), 124–6; Fyle, *The History of Sierra Leone*, 19; Lamin Sanneh, *West African Christianity: The Religious Impact* (Maryknoll, NY: Orbis Books, 1983), 60–83; Alie, *A New History*, 101–10.

20   Alie, *A New History*, 109; Olson, *Church Growth*, 94; Yambasu, *Dialectics*, 34.

21    Alie, *A New History*, 109; E. A. Turay, 'Missionary Work and African Society: James Booth in Thonko Limba', *African Research Bulletin* 7 no. 2 (1977), 36.

22    Ibid.

23    Ibid.

24    Olson, *Church Growth*, 96.

25    Ibid., 177.

26    Ibid., 179.

27    Ibid.

28    Ibid.

29    Olson, *Church Growth*, 178; Finnegan, *Survey of the Limba*, 106.

30    Finnegan, *Survey of the Limba*, 106.

31    Alie, *A New History*, 110.

32    K. E. Eitel, 'Contextualization: Contrasting African Voices', *Criswell Theological Review* 2 no. 2 (1988), 323.

33    K. J. Conteh, *A Short History of the National Pentecostal Limba Church: 1948 – 2001* (Freetown: Nabstech, 2002), 9–10.

34    Olson, *Church Growth*, 191.

35    Ibid., 192.

36    J. V. Taylor, *The Primal Vision: Christian Presence amid African Religion* (London: SCM Press, 1963), 16.

37    J. B. Kailing 'A New Solution to the African Christian Problem', *Missiology: An International Review* 22 no. 4 (1994), 492.

38    E. W. Fashole-Luke, 'Introduction', in *Christianity in Independent Africa*, ed. E. W Fashole-Luke, R. Gray, A. Hastings and G. Tasie (London: Rex Collins, 1978), 357.

39    Ibid.

40    Sanneh, *West African Christianity*, 170.

41    R. I. J. Hackett, 'Revitalization in African Traditional Religion', in *African Traditional Religions in Contemporary Society*, ed. J. K. Olupona (St. Paul, Minn: Paragon House, 1991), 146.

42    R. J. Schreiter. *Constructing Local Theologies* (Maryknoll, NY: Orbis, Books, 1985), 144.

43    Ibid., 145

44    Parrinder, *African Traditional Religion*, 12.

45    Several decades ago Nadel, *Nupe Religion*, 1, pointed out a similar situation about the Nupe people whose religious beliefs and practices differ considerably from region to region: 'Nupe are internally divided in various ways – by ethnic descent, by tribal segmentation, partly

by political allegiance, by the cleavage between urban and peasant population, and by the barriers of social class'.

46    This is similar to the ideas presented by Cultural Anthropologists F. Plog and D. G. Bates, *Cultural Anthropology* (2nd ed. New York, NY: Alfred A. Knopf, 1980), 16: 'While the culture of any society is by definition shared by all members of that society, culture is also differentially shared within the subgroups of the society'.

47    Mbiti, *African Religions*, 3. When talking about what is unique or different about a particular ethnic group, the Limba commonly make the statement 'my people practice so and so …'.

48    Mbiti, *African Religions*, x.

49    K. A. Opoku, 'African Traditional Religion: An Enduring Heritage', in *Religious Plurality in Africa: Essays in Honour of John S. Mbiti*, ed. J. K. Olupona and S. S. Nyang (Berlin and New York: Mouton De Gruyter, 1993), 78.

50    Mbiti, *African Religions*, x.

51    Magesa, *African Religion*, 7.

# Chapter 3: Components of Limba indigenous religion

1    Similar concern has been earlier expressed by Downes, *Tiv Religion*, 1, when he wrote: 'As Western influence increases with education, changes in religious thinking are taking place and it is of some importance to put what little is known on record before the rapidly changing customs and habits of the people render their own recollections more hazy, and the task of filling the many inevitable gaps becomes less likely of even partially accurate achievement'.

2    Cf. Parsons, *Religion*, 173.

3    Parrinder, *African Traditional Religion*, 25, represented the relationship between spiritual powers by a triangular formula. At the apex is the Supreme God, on one side of the triangle is the ancestors, and on the other side of the triangle are the gods or nature God, and at the base is the earth where the dead are buried and where humankind lives and its intermediaries. B. E. Idowu, *African Traditional Religion: A Problem of Definition* (London: SCM Press, 1977), 139, states that the beliefs in God, in the divinities, in spirits, in ancestors and the practice of magic and medicine are the five components that make African Traditional Religion. In Mbiti's opinion, the beliefs in God, spirits and divinities are part of the elements of African Religious beliefs (*African Religions*, 7). According to Magesa, *African Religion*, 35–6, 'God, the ancestors, and the spirits are all powers or forces that impinge on human life in one way or another'.

4    Christianity is also composed of beliefs, practices and teachings.

5    Not unlike Limba traditionalists, Christians believe in and teach about four kinds of spirits: God (John 4:24), the ancestors/saints [in the New Testament Abraham (Matt 3.9; Acts 7:2); David (Matt 11:10; Acts 2:29) and Jacob (John 4:12)] as ancestors. The church especially the Roman Catholics venerates the saints, angels (Heb. 1:14) and non-ancestral spirits (Eph. 6:12). Christian belief in God and in the communion of saints is enshrined in the Apostles' and Nicene Creeds. There is also a common belief in spiritual leaders as God's agents. The

activities of the Apostles in the Book of Acts are testaments to this belief. A similar leadership is accorded to Judges, Prophets and Kings in the OT.

6    This formula is similar to most African worldviews where 'the spiritual powers are ranked in hierarchies and approached according to need' (Parrinder, *African Traditional Religion*, 26).

7    It is only the positions of angels and ancestors, which are disputed, and whichever a person considers second, the other is third.

8    Other Sierra Leonean groups, like the Mende, consider three strands in the concept of the supernatural: a belief in the Supreme or High God, veneration of the ancestors, and belief in nature divinities (Harris and Sawyerr, *Spring of Mende Beliefs*, 3; cf. Gittins, *Mende Religion*, 40–1). The Kono believe in a Supreme Being, followed by lesser gods, ancestral spirits and impersonal powers (Parsons, *Religion*, 9).

9    Sacred specialists also play a vital role among Sierra Leonean ethnic groups: Kono: Parsons, *Religion*, 69, 81; Mende: Harris and Sawyerr, *Spring of Mende Beliefs*, 54–87; Gittins, *Mende Religion*, 179–202; Temne: R. Shaw, 'Gender and the Structuring of Reality in Temne Divination: An Interactive Study', *Africa* 55 no. 3 (1985), 286–303; 'The Politician and the Diviner: Divination and the Consumption of Power in Sierra Leone', *Journal of Religion in Africa* 26 no. 1 (1996), 30–55); ATR: Parrinder, *African Traditional Religion*, 100–9; Mbiti, *African Religions*, 162–82.

10   Cf. Parsons, *Religion*, 68–78; Parrinder, *African Traditional Religion*, 79–100; Mbiti, *African Religions*, 58–71; Magesa, *African Religion*, 201–9.

11   Cf. Mbiti, *African Religions*, 199–219; Magesa, *African Religion*, 161–91.

12   Finnegan, *Limba Stories*, discusses stories about God and about ethical relationships with both animate and inanimate objects because all of creation comes from the same spiritual force.

13   C. Nyamiti, *African Traditional Religion and the Christian God* (Spearhead Eldoret, Kenya: Gaba Publications, n.d.), 11.

14   Finnegan's discovery that Limba religious 'beliefs are not contradicted' by the influences of Islam and Christianity is still valid, almost four decades later (*Limba Stories*, 19).

# Chapter 4: The Supreme Being

1    While working as a missionary in Africa, E. W. Smith was asked by E. Ludwig, 'How can the untutored African conceive God?' Ludwig was surprised when Smith responded that it was irrelevant to persuade 'Africans of the existence of God: they are sure of it –' In disbelief he asked, 'How can that be?' He went on to say, 'Deity is a philosophical concept which savages are incapable of framing,' (E. W. Smith, 'The Whole Subject in Perspective', in *African Ideas of God: A Symposium*, ed. E. W. Smith (London: Edinburgh House Press, 1966), 1. While it is likely that Ludwig's statements simply express a gross misunderstanding of the African nature, if they were ever applicable, it is clear that they are now outdated.

2    In the NT, the basic assumption of God's existence is shared by scripture (if not always by Christians). On the basis of Hebrews 11:6, M. J. Erickson, *Introducing Christian Doctrine* (Grand Rapids, MI: Baker Book, 1992), 82–3, states 'that scripture does not argue for his

existence. It simply affirms it or, more often, merely assumes it – Thus existence is considered a most basic aspect of his nature'.

3    Mbiti, *African Religions*, 29. In African traditional life, 'even to a child the Supreme Being needs no pointing out' says an Ashanti proverb [E. Ikenga-Metuh, *God and Man in African Religion* (London: Geoffrey Chapman, 1981), viii].

4    Ikenga-Metuh, *God and Man*, viii.

5    Christian theologians have tried to prove God's existence through the following arguments: *cosmological* – that because there is wisdom and order in the universe there is a first Cause who planned it; *teleological* – that because there are significant ends and not accidental conclusions there is a Master Designer; *rational* – that because the universe moves with reasonableness there is a Mind behind it; *moral* – that because man feels there are some things he 'ought' to do there is a law Giver who put that moral sense in us; *ontological* – that because the idea of God exists there must be something behind the idea; *human* – that because humankind seeks to strive upwards often with considerable sacrifice there is a God who is Lord of this history. Although these arguments do have a cumulative effect and may bolster the reasonableness of faith, no single argument is sufficient to prove God's existence.

6    H. Sawyerr, *God, Ancestor or Creator: Aspects of Traditional Beliefs in Ghana, Nigeria and Sierra Leone* (Harlow: Longmans, 1970), 8, states: 'God's existence is never questioned' by the African.

7    My attempts to question some of my interviewees about their belief in the existence of God were met with strong resentment. One of my interviewees remarked, 'If you do not believe that the sun exists then you are out of your mind. Worse than that, if you do not believe that God exist you are considered a '*kaf'ri*' (*Kaf'ri* is an Arabic word to denote an unbeliever or atheist).

8    Cf. Awolalu, *Yoruba Beliefs*, 3.

9    Cf. Sawyerr, *God, Ancestor or Creator*, x. The Limba Church does not dispute the fact that Limba traditionalists have a belief in a God: the church's contention is that the traditionalists do not serve the one true God. The God who has revealed himself as the eternally self-existent 'I AM', the Creator of heaven and earth and the Redeemer of mankind. He has further revealed himself as embodying the principles of relationship and association as Father, Son, and Holy Ghost (Deut. 6:4; Isa. 43:10–11; Matt. 28:19; Luke 3:22). In that regard, the Christians do not equate the traditional God with their own. However, although the vital Christian teaching of the Trinity is not part of Limba religious concept, the traditionalists, continue to argue that the God of the Christians is the same God they serve.

10    Ikenga-Metuh, *God and Man*, 19.

11    Smith, 'The Whole Subject', 4.

12    In Judeo-Christianity, as in Limba tradition, the meaning of a name is crucial (Packer *et al*, *The Bible Almanac*, 445–7; Erickson, *Introducing Christian Doctrine*, 83. In biblical times, names were significant because 'they revealed character and identity and signified existence' (Achtemeier, *HarperCollins Bible*, 736). Names indicated who people were, their conduct, and the way they lived their lives. Care and attention to significance were very important

in the choice of names [Erickson, *Introducing Christian Doctrine*, 83; C. Houtman, *Exodus* vol. 1., (Kampen: KOK Publishing House, 1993), 71]. For the Israelites, the revelation of God's name and its continued use were of great significance because it was the means by which God could be reached and known (Achtemeier, *HarperCollins Bible*, 736). Theophoric personal names are a valuable guide to qualities associated with God, and the personal names containing God's divine name *Yahweh* depict his nature, character, and peculiar qualities (Achtemeier, *HarperCollins Bible*, 734). The tradition and terminology of God's names in the NT was 'inherited from the OT and Judaism as mediated by the Septuagint (LXX)' (Achtemeier, *HarperCollins Bible*, 734). However, this inherited tradition was greatly modified both by the 'understanding of the teaching of Jesus' and by the 'understanding of the person of Jesus as the definitive expression of God' (Achtemeier, *HarperCollins Bible*, 734). The names and titles of Jesus, tell us about his character, peculiar qualities, rank and power. For example, the name 'Jesus' (Heb. 'Joshua') means 'Saviour'. 'Emmanuel' (Heb.) 'means, God is with us' (Matt. 1:23). The title 'the Christ' (Heb. 'Messiah') means the 'anointed'. Jesus was the long awaited Saviour and Deliverer. The 'Lord' means 'master'.

13    This perspective is shared by many African peoples (Ikenga-Metuh, *God and Man*, 19–21; Awolalu, *Yoruba Beliefs*, 10).

14    Finnegan, *Limba Stories*, 107; cf. Ottenberg, 'Religion and Ethnicity', 441.

15    Smith, 'The Whole Subject', 3, has cautioned that 'Etymological methods are not invariably helpful and indeed may lead astray'. As truthful as this statement may be, the etymological explanation is of theological importance to the Limba and throws light on some of the attributes of God.

16    Similarly, in the OT, God is likened to the sun: 'For the LORD God is a sun and shield' (Ps. 84:11).

17    Mbiti, *Concepts of God*, 4; *African religions*, 31.

18    Similarly, Parrinder, *African Traditional Religion*, 34, states: 'An apparent identification of God with the sun has been thought to exist among peoples in the northern parts of Ghana and Nigeria. However, although they use a word for the Supreme Being which means "the sun", they are not sun-worshippers'. The same can be said in many African cultures. Among some East and West African peoples, the sun 'is such a potent epresent-ation of God that' he is 'simply named after it or in reference to it' (Magesa, *African Religion*, 59).

19    God's indiscriminate character is also a vital Christian teaching, for he 'makes his sun rise on the evil and on the good' (Matt. 5:45).

20    The Nuba people of Sudan also refer to God as *Masala* – 'the great Mother'; see R. C. Stevenson, 'The Doctrine of God in the Nuba Mountains', in *African Ideas of God: a Symposium*, ed. E. W. Smith (London: Edinburgh House Press, 1966), 215; Mbiti, *Concepts of God*, 334.

21    The Kuranko are another ethnic of Sierra Leone. As the closest neighbours in their homeland, they are also one of the ethnic groups with which the Limba have intermingled.

22    The Islamic, Kuranko and Temne sources show how foreign influences have impacted Limba culture. The full Temne name for God is *Kuru Masaba* ('God Supreme'). Like the Limba, the Yoruba refer to God as *Olokun* 'Supreme' and the Akan also call him *Nyame* 'The Supreme,

Omnipotent Being' [G. M. Setiloane, African *Theology: An Introduction* (Cape Town and Johannesburg: Blackshaws Ltd), 1986, 49].

23    The Limba Church adopted the use of the name *Kanu Masala* for the Judeo-Christian God. A majority of 'Christian missionaries in their teachings and translations of scripture have adopted African names of God' (Smith, 'The Whole Subject', 34). Missionaries to the Katonda and Banganda peoples adopted the local names for God (Parrinder, *African Traditional Religion*, 35). They 'proclaimed the name of Jesus Christ. But they used the names of the God who was and is already known by African peoples...' [J. S. Mbiti, 'Encounter of Christian Faith and African Religion', *Christian Century* 97 no. 1 (1980), 818]. L. Sanneh, 'Resurgent Church in a Troubled Continent: Review Essay of Bengt Sundkler's *History of the Church in Africa*', *International Bulletin* 25 no. 3 (2001), 114, writes that 'the adoption by missionaries of African names for God was key to the effective transmission of the Gospel. It implied the abandonment of arguments of European ascendancy and, too, of the moral logic of permanent colonial and missionary tutelage'. In the LXX, the often used word *Theos* ('God') a translation of the Hebrew word *Elohim* ('God') was also used for the gods of other nations, 'just as it was the standard word for the gods of the Greeks and Romans of NT times' (Achtemeier, *Harper-Collins Bible*, 735).

24    In some African cultures the name for God is sometimes the same as the word for sky. For example the Temne God *Kuru Masaba* the prefix *kuru* means 'sky' (Sawyerr *God, Ancestor or Creator*, 4). The Mende God *Ngew]* is likely derived from the words *ngele w]l]ng]* 'the sky is great' (Sawyerr, *God, Ancestor or Creator*, 4) or *ngele* 'sky' *w]]* 'long ago' a combination that means 'In the sky, from long ago' (Harris and Sawyerr, *Springs of Mende Belief*, 6). See also Gittins, *Mende Religion*, 49. The Supreme Being among the Tiv people is *A]ndo* which is the name for the 'above and firmament' (Downes, *Tiv Religion*, 17). The Nupe refer to God as the *Etsu na da sama* ('The God who is in the sky'). In Nuer Religion, the Supreme Being *Kwoth* is the Spirit who lives in the sky (Evans-Pritchard, *Nuer Religion*, 5). In Yoruba, *Olorun* means 'Lord of the sky or of the heavens' (Lucas, *Religion of the Yorubas*, 35–6).

25    The 'withdrawal theory of God' is common among the Africans. Some ethnic groups in Sierra Leone, 'Ivory Coast, Ghana, Togo, Dahomey and Nigeria, at least, say that God was formerly so near to men that they grew over-familiar with him' (Parrinder, *Three Religions*, 31).

26    Finnegan, *Survey of the Limba*, 107.

27    Finnegan, *Limba Stories*, 231–33.

28    Sawyerr, *God, Ancestor or Creator*, 9. In Judeo-Christian theology the transcendence of God is displayed in the concept that God dwells in heaven (Erickson, *Introducing Christian Doctrine*, 27). *Shamayim* ('heaven(s)/sky'), *ouranos* ('heaven/sky') is the abode of God. Rehab talking about Israel's God says: 'The LORD your God is indeed God in heaven above' (Josh. 2:11). Moses encouraged Israel to acknowledge and take to heart that 'the LORD is God in heaven above' (Deut. 4:39). At Jesus' birth the angels praised God: 'Glory to God in the highest heaven' (Luke 2:14). When Jesus was baptised by John the Baptist, a voice came from heaven (Matt. 3:17; Mark 1:11). Jesus taught his disciples to pray 'Our Father in heaven' (Matt. 6:9). He spoke of 'your father who is in heaven' (Matt. 5:16, 45: 6:1; 7:11; 18:14).

29    Finnegan, *Survey of the Limba*, 107; cf. Mbiti, *Concepts of God*, 15.

30    In ATR, the transcendence of God is considered in several ways: In terms of Time, Space, Distance, and Outreach, worship and exaltation, God's limitlessness, human's understanding of God and God's supreme status in relation to other beings, divinities, objects, and human institutions (Mbiti, *Concepts of God*, 12–6). God's immanence is generally conceived of as God's involvement in the affairs of the African (Mbiti, *Concepts of God*, 16–8).

31    Mbiti, *Concepts of God*, 12.

32    Sawyerr, *God, Ancestor or Creator*, ix. Like the Limba, Christians balance their belief in God's transcendence with their belief in his immanence. Although the Judeo-Christian God lives in heaven he 'is not far from each of us' (Acts 17:27b).

33    The Bakuta people of the Congo speak of two Supreme Gods: *Nzambi* above and *Nzambi* below who are often regarded as twins and they act heroic roles in many stories (Parrinder, *Africa's Three Religions*, 43).

34    Finnegan, *Limba Stories*, 274–5; states: 'Limba do not generally speak of *Kanu below*, but occasionally this term is used (especially in Kamabai, I think) to cover all the spiritual agencies other than Kanu (above), i.e. spirits, the dead and, especially, witches. This terminology may possibly be an effect of mission teaching'. The statement that 'Limba do not generally speak of *Kanu below*, but occasionally' may be true in the 1960s and perhaps in the early 1970s. This is no longer the case in the past three decades. As a Limba growing up in Sierra Leone, I was familiar with the phrase *Kanu below* before even starting my secondary schooling. The concept played a vital role during my fieldwork as will be shown in the discussion of non-ancestral spirits.

35    In the Bible, God is acknowledged as being 'God in heaven above and on earth below' (Deut. 4:39; Josh. 2:11). This speaks not so much of a perceived residence, but of God's domain. God controls both 'heaven above' and the 'earth below' (Gen. 24:3; Luke 10:21; Isa. 66:1; Matt. 5:34–5 and Acts 7:49). While Christians do not acknowledge a 'God below' they do identify a personal force responsible for much of the evil in the world: Jesus referred to Satan as the 'prince and ruler of this world' (John 12:31, 14:30).

36    See Finnegan, *Limba Stories*, 235–38.

37    Ibid., 274–6.

38    Cf. Mbiti, *Concepts of God*, 332. However, Mbiti misspells the word as '*Masaranka*'. The correct spelling is '*Masaraka*'.

39    Similarly, because the Abaluyia people sacrifice to God, they refer to him as 'the One to whom sacred rites and sacrifices are made (or paid)' (Mbiti, *Concepts of God*, 179).

40    Gifts offered to *Kanu Wopothi* are referred to as *kudamaŋ* (offering). These are offered as an appeasement.

41    God is also presented in the Bible as a God of sacrifice who requires sacrifice as a form of worship (Exod. 20:24).

42    See Mbiti, *Concepts of God*, xiii; *African Religions*, 30–8.

43    Some scholars have discussed God's activity of Creation as an attribute (Awolalu, *Yoruba Beliefs*, 13–6; Ikenga-Metuh, *God and Man*, 33–4, 40).

44    The Akan and the Ashanti describe God as 'the Powerful One' (Mbiti, *Concepts of God*, 9); the Yoruba call God '*Alagbara gbogbo*' which means 'All-powerful' [E. G. Parrinder, 'Theistic Beliefs of the Yoruba and Ewe Peoples of West Africa', in *African Ideas of God: A Symposium*, ed. E. W. Smith (London: Edinburgh House Press, 1966), 228], and the *Ng∫mbe* elders say '*Anjombe*' is 'All-powerful' [J. Davidson, 'The Doctrine of God in the Life of the Ng∫mbe, Congo, in *African Ideas of God: A Symposium*, ed. E. W. Smith (London: Edinburgh House Press, 1966), 167].

45    In Yoruba *Olodumare* means 'the Almighty' (Mbiti, *Concepts of God*, 8).

46    Sawyerr, *God, Ancestor or Creator*, 5, says that the African God is 'a God of Power and is the ultimate source of all power'.

47    God's omnipotence is evident in the Bible. In Genesis 17:1, God is called *El-Shaddi* ('God Almighty'). His omnipotence is seen in human life and personality (cf. Jer. 1:5; Gal. 1:15), in his ability to overcome apparently insurmountable problems (cf. Jer. 32:15–7; Matt. 19:26) and in his control of the course of human history (Acts 17:26).

48    Another meaning for God's name *Nyame* in Akan is 'Determiner' (Setiloane, *African Theology*, 46).

49    It is also clear that Christians share a belief that humankind lives by God's grace. Grace is God's unmerited favour and we are what we are because of that favour. Paul says 'But by the grace of God I am what I am' and he attributes his success to 'the grace of God that is with' him (1 Cor. 15:10). This all-powerful God calls for humankind's total submission to his will. Even Jesus submitted to the will of God (Matt. 26:42; Mark 14:36 and Luke 22:42).

50    A similar ideology is found among the Yorubas: things that receive *Olodumare's* approval are easy to do and the things that do not receive *Olodumare's* sanction are difficult to do (Awolalu, *Yoruba Beliefs*, 14).

51    Cf. Magesa, *African Religion*, 41.

52    For many Africans, 'life, and the power that is life or existence, flows from God' (Magesa, *African Religion*, 47).

53    Finnegan, *Survey of the Limba*, 107.

54    He is like the Kono God, *Yataa*, 'the one whom you meet everywhere' (Parsons, Religion, 165). Similarly, in Judeo-Christianity God is not subject to the limitations of time and space and 'there is no place where he cannot be found' (Erickson, *Introducing Christian Doctrine*, 84). God declares, 'Do I not fill heaven and earth?' (Jer. 23:24). Christians also believe that God is especially present when they gather to worship him. Jesus said, 'For where two or three are gathered in my name, I am there among them' (Matt. 18:20) and later commissioned his disciples saying 'I am with you always, to the end of the age' (Matt. 28:20).

55    Other African peoples like the Akan refer to God as 'He who knows all' and the Bacongo say 'God knows all' (Mbiti, *Concepts of God*, 3). The omniscience of God is also central to Judeo-Christian theology. Humankind is 'completely transparent before God ... He sees and knows us totally' (Erickson, *Introducing Christian Doctrine*, 85). There is nothing which escapes God's knowledge. Human beings cannot hide himself from God (Ps. 139:7, 13; Jer.23:24) and even what may be hidden from humankind is laid bare before God (Heb 4:12–3).

56    Mbiti, *Concepts of God*, 3.

57    Parsons, *Religion*, 165.

58    Mbiti, *African Religions*, 31.

59    Harris and Sawyerr, *The Springs of Mende Belief*, 13.

60    In most African societies, 'creation is the most widely acknowledged work of God' (Mbiti, *African Religions*, 39).

61    Finnegan, *Survey of the Limba*, 107. In the Bible the creative work of God plays a prominent role (Erickson, *Introducing Christian Doctrine*, 121). In Genesis 1:1, 'God created the heavens and the earth'. Unlike the Limba belief, the biblical account of creation shows God creating *ex nihilo* ('creation out of nothing'). The concept of creation *ex nihilo* is also reported among several African groups (Mbiti, *African Religions*, 39–40).

62    In Africa, myths and accounts about the order of creation vary widely (Mbiti, *Concepts of God*, 48–52).

63    Similarly the Nupe refer to God as *Tsoci* ('The Owner of us') (Setiloane, *African Theology*, 49). The Tonga refer to God as, Syatwaakwe ('The Owner of his things') [C. R. HopGood, 'Concepts of God amongst the Tonga of Northern Rhodesia (Zambia)', in *African Ideas of God: A Symposium*, ed. E. W. Smith (London: Edinburgh House Press, 1966), 74]. Similarly, the Ngoni call God 'the Owner of all things' (Mbiti, *Concepts of God*, 72).

64    H. Sawyerr, *Creative Evangelism: Towards a New Christian Encounter with Africa* (London: Butterworth, 1968), 12.

65    For information on the governing work of God as chief/king and judge, see Mbiti, *Concepts of God*, 71–8.

66    The Mende refer to God as *Maha-Ngewɔ*, 'God the Chief' [W. T. Harris, 'The Idea of God among the Mende', in *African Ideas of God: a Symposium*, ed. E. W. Smith (London: Edinburgh House Press, 1966), 278]. The Nupe call him *Etsu*, 'chief (Sawyerr, *God, Ancestor or Creator*, 6). One of the titles the Ambo used for God is *Pamba*, 'chief [G. W. Dymond, 'The Idea of God in Ovamboland, South-West Africa', in *African Ideas of God: A Symposium*, ed. E. W. Smith (London: Edinburgh House Press, 1966), 141]. The role of *Kanu* as Chief and Judge is similar to that of the Judeo-Christian God. In the OT, God is the Everlasting King (Ps. 10:16) who rules over creation (Ps. 47:7). As ruler of the universe, God cares for people (Ps. 145) and for other creatures (Ps. 147). In the NT, Jesus is described with royal terminology (Rev. 2:5; 3:21; 4:14; 17:14; 19:15–6).

67    The Mende refer to the Supreme Being as *Maha-yilei*, 'The one Chief (Harris, 'God among the Mende', 278)

68    Another title for God in Mende is *Mahawa*, 'the Great Chief (Sawyerr, *God, Ancestor or Creator*, 5; Harris, 'God among the Mende', 278).

69    Finnegan, *Limba Stories*, 9.

70    See Finnegan, *Survey of the Limba*, 20–35, for details.

71    Finnegan, *Limba Stories*, 239.

72   Finnegan, *Limba Stories*, 23–9, 246–7, contain the stories of *Kanu* teaching and advising the Limba how to cultivate their culture.

73   Finnegan, *Survey of the Limba*, 108. Likewise the Tiv, the Kakwa and the Acholi consider God as the 'Teacher' who showed humankind how to cultivate food and all the essentials of life (Mbiti, *Concepts of God*, 74–5). In the Bible, God is a Teacher and Adviser (Ps. 25:4–5). God is the one who imparts knowledge (Ps. 94:10; Isa. 40:14c) good judgement (Ps. 119:66), and skills (Ps. 144:1b).

74   Finnegan, *Survey of the Limba*, 107.

75   In ATR, 'God is father in terms of his position as creator and provider' (Mbiti, *Concepts of God*, 92). See also (Mbiti, *African Religions*, 48–49). In the NT, 'father' is used in most cases to refer to God (Achtemeier, *HarperCollins Bible*, 333). 'This Christian practice probably derives from the intimate term for father that Jesus used to address God (Heb. and Aram. *abba*; Mark 14:36; cf. Rom. 8:15; Gal. 4:6)' (Achtemeier, *HarperCollins Bible*, 333). Jesus did not only refer to God as 'Father', but he also taught his followers that God was their father (Matt. 5:16, 45; 6:1; 7:11 and 18:14), and to address God as father (Matt. 6:9; Luke 11:2).

76   Cf. Mbiti, *Concepts of God*, 93--94, 212.

77   Cf. Finnegan, *Survey of the Limba*, 111.

78   Among the Mende and Krio of Sierra Leone, water cultivates harmony, and it cools andrefreshes [H. Sawyerr, *The Practice of Presence: Shorter Writings of Harry Sawyer*r (Grand Rapids, MI: Eerdmans, 1996), 49].

79   Sawyerr, *Practice of Presence*, 49.

80   In Freetown disasters of any kind are investigated by the central government. Usually, the government encourages people to pray for the situation according to their faith or beliefs.

81   The Kono and Temne of Sierra Leone also pray to God and the ancestors concurrently (Taylor, *The Primal Vision*, 69).

82   This is the case on all five levels of sacrifice.

# Chapter 5: Angels

1   E-D. Adelowo, 'A Comparative Study of Angelology in the Bible and the Qur'an and the Concepts of gods many and lords', *Africa Theological Journal* 11 no. 1 (1982), 161–6.

2   Ikenga-Metuh, *God and Man*, 81.

3   Nadel, *Nupe Religion*, 247.

4   Herbert Lockyer, *All the Angels in the Bible: A Complete Exploration of the Nature and Ministry of Angels* (Peabody, Mass: Hendrickson, 1995), ix.

5   An example is the story above about the Mau-Mau man.

6   F. J. King, 'Angels and Ancestors: A Basis for Christology', *Mission Studies* 11 no. 1 (1994), 10.

7    Angels in Limba Religion and Judeo-Christianity are not only similar in nature; they are also similar in the roles they play. In the Bible, angels are portrayed 'as messengers or servants of God who are of unquestionable integrity, good will and obedience to Him ...(Gen. 16:7-13; 21:17-20; 22:11-18; Judg. 6:11-23; 1 Sam. 29:9; 2 Sam. 14:17, 20); (Adelowo, 'A Comparative Study', 158; cf. Lockyer, *All the Angels*, 3). In both traditions, angels are spiritual creatures that are capable of assuming human likeness. In human form, angels appear in dreams and physically to people, and they possess moral attributes. In Limba tradition, angels may be either male or female, but do not seem to have proper names. In Judeo-Christianity on the other hand, angels have proper names, and only male angels are mentioned. Angels in both traditions are God's messengers or servants who carry out various functions as directed by God. They help and protect people; and serve as mediators, guides and guardians. The systems agree that angels are not to be worshipped.

# Chapter 6: Ancestral spirits/ancestors

1    This parallels the Mende, *kɛkɛni*, and *ndeblaa* our 'Forefathers' (Sawyerr, *Creative Evangelism*, 2, 16; Gittins, *Mende Religion*, 62–3). Later Sawyerr, *Practice of Presence*, 44–5, refers to *kɛkɛni* as 'the fathers' and *ndeblaa* as 'the forebears'. Like the Limba word *nbembɛŋ* ('Forefathers', 'Great grandfathers') which serves as a synonym for *Fureni bɛ/Hureni*, the Hebrew word *'av* ('Father') is also translated 'Ancestor' (Gen. 10:21), 'Forefather' (Gen. 15:15), and 'Grandfather' (Gen. 28:13). In the NT, the Greek word *pater* ('Father') is also translated 'Forefather' and 'Ancestor' (Mark 3:9; Luke 1:73, 16:24).

2    G. M. Setiloane, 'Traditional World-view of the Sotho-Tswana', in *Christianity in independent Africa*, ed. E. W. Fasholé-Luke, R. Gray, A. Hastings and G. Tasie (London: Rex Collins, 1978), 407.

3    W. J. Hollenweger, 'Foreword', in *Religious Plurality in Africa: Essays in Honour of John S. Mbiti*, ed. J. K. Olupona and S. S. Nyang (Berlin and New York: Mouton De Gruyter, 1993), x; Setiloane, 'Traditional World-view', 406.

4    E. W. Fasholé-Luke, 'Ancestor Veneration and the Communion of Saints', in *New Testament Christianity for Africa and the World: Essays in Honour of Harry Sawyerr*, ed. M. E. Glasswell and E. W. Fasholé-Luke (London: SPCK, 1974), 209.

5    Finnegan, *Survey of the Limba*, 109–13.

6    The burial rites of a witch are different in order to ensure his/her spirit does not return to continue malevolent practices.

7    Finnegan, *Limba Stories*, 21.

8    Some African ethnic groups also demarcate between the dead who are ancestors and those who are not. Gittins, *Mende Religion*, 60–1, differentiates between the ancestors and the dead in Mende belief. He uses three terms, *ndJubla*, *halabla* and *kambɛihubla*, which are certainly used to refer to the deceased. *NdJubla*, in particular he says applies simply to the 'dead and buried' and does not carry any implications about ancestorship. They are the people who had not had the *tenjamɛi*, performed. The word is strictly applied to the non-ancestral dead. Ikenga-Metuh, *God and Man*, 76, tells us that the Igbo of Nigeria call the dead who have attained ancestorship, *Ndichie,* and these they venerate as benevolent spirits.

The dead who do not meet the requirements for ancestorship are called, *Ogeli*. These are wandering, malevolent spirits, which are frequently exorcised. H. A. Junod, *The Life of a South African Tribe* (vol 2. London: Macmillan, 1927), 373–75, states that the Thonga people of South Africa, differentiate between the ancestors who receive veneration from the living, and ghosts whose existence is considered malevolent.

9    Sawyerr, *Practice and Presence*, 44. In Krio view, the ancestors 'live in the world of truth and do discern truth and are therefore no longer subject to the effects of deception' (Sawyerr, *Practice and Presence*, 44).

10    Mbiti, *African Religions*, 81–2.

11    Cf. Gittins, *Mende Religion*, 53.

12    It is this understanding that makes the gender biased term, *nbembɛŋ* ('Forefathers' 'Great grandfathers') less popular because 'there is no gender differentiation; both male and female could be ancestors' [O. U. Kalu, 'Ancestral Spirituality and Society in Africa', in *African Spirituality: Forms, Meanings, and Expressions*, ed. J. K. Olupona (New York, NY: Crossroad, 2000), 57].

13    Cf. Finnegan, *Limba Stories*, 20.

14    Cf. Finnegan, *Survey of the Limba*, 109.

15    Parrinder, *African Traditional Religion*, 57–66, Harris and Sawyerr, *Springs of Mende Belief*, 13–33; *Practice and Presence*, 43–55), Fashole-Luke, 'Ancestor Veneration', 209–21, and Gittins, *Mende Religion*, 53–61.

16    Cf. Yambasu, *Dialectics*, 65. See E. B. Idowu, *African Traditional Religion: A Definition* (London: SCM Press, 1973), 187; Kalu, 'Ancestral Spirituality', 57, for a summary of the general requirements for ancestorship in ATR.

17    Cf. Sunberg, *Conversion*, 3.

18    Finnegan, *Survey of the Limba*, 108.

19    Cf. Yambasu, *Dialectics*, 65.

20    The *Gbangban* corresponds to the men's *Poro* societies and the *Bondo* corresponds to the women's *Sande* or *Bundu* of the Mende [K. L. Little, 'The Role of the Secret Society in Cultural Specialisation', *American Anthropologist* 51 (1949); Sawyerr 1968, *Creative Evangelism*, 1; *Practice Presence*, 44] and Temne [Vernon R. Dorjahn, 'The Initiation and Training of Temne Poro Members', in *African Religious Groups and Beliefs*, ed. S. Ottenberg (Folklore Institute, 1982), 35–62]. As in these other Sierra Leonean ethnic groups, the Limba secret societies are the principle ethnic cults. These societies are the defenders of their culture and society.

21    Sawyerr, *Practice Presence*, 44.

22    See the discussion below on 'witchcraft' under 'non-ancestral spirits'.

23    Yambasu, *Dialectics*, 64.

24    See the discussion on Limba view on 'death' under 'Lifecycle'.

25    At the Krio funeral rite, *Awujoh*, 'an old female member, preferably the oldest, of the family is generally the first to invoke the spirits, presumably, because she has the longest and the farthest memory of the family line' (Sawyerr, *Practice Presence*, 45).

26    In this regard, as a sign of respect to the supernatural, a priest always knocks at the door of the shrine to alert the spirits before entering it.

27    This is similar to the Krio concluding phrase of invocation, ɔl dɔn wan wi (you all, all those).

28    Cf. Finnegan, *Survey of the Limba*, 110.

29    Ibid, 108–9.

30    This is similar to the Temne *Boro ma sar* ('shrine of stones') a boat-shaped receptacle to mark the memory of their dead heroes (Sawyerr, *God, Ancestor or Creator*, 6).

31    Cf. Parrinder, *African Traditional Religion*, 58; Gittins, *Mende Belief*, 53.

32    Cf. Yambasu, *Dialectics*, 64.

33    Cf. Mbiti, *African Religions*, 83.

34    Ibid., 82.

35    Ibid.

36    Setiloane, 'Traditional World-view', 407.

37    Finnegan, *Limba Stories*, 21.

38    This is evident in prayers like: 'Kanu Masala and you dead… may we have cool hearts … if anything remains for me to say, may you complete it for me you dead; may you complete it Kanu Masala' (Finnegan, *Survey of the Limba*, 110).

39    Fashole-Luke, 'Ancestor Veneration', 210…1.

40    H. Sawyerr, 'Ancestor Worship II: The Rationale', *The Sierra Leone Bulletin of Religion* 8 no. 2 (1966), 33–9.

41    Sawyerr, *Practice and Presence*, 43–55.

42    Ibid., 55.

43    Parrinder, *African Traditional Religion*, 65–6.

44    Fashole-Luke, 'Ancestor Veneration', 211–2.

45    There is archaeological evidence that shows that the ancient Israelites deposited food near the tombs of their venerated dead [R. De Vaux, *Ancient Israel: Its Life and Institution* (Grand Rapids, MI: Eerdsman, 1997), 61]. This custom still continues among many Christians in the world. In Sierra Leone, on 1 January of each year, many Christians take food and gifts to the graves of their departed relatives.

46    For example, the Mende (Harris and Sawyerr, *Springs of Mende Belief*, 20–2), the Krio (Wyse, *Krio*, 12), and the Kono (Parsons, *Religion*, 26).

47    The prayers in this section are in the Krio language because that was the language the interviewee decided to communicate in. The Krio language as stated earlier is the common parlance in Sierra Leone. All Sierra Leonean ethnic groups speak Krio as well as their own language.

48    The term *Pa* is a title of respect when addressing an older man or somebody in position of trust. Sierra Leoneans used to call the former military head of state Capt. Valentine Strasser (who was in his twenties) by that title because he was the head of state. Male teachers and pastors are frequently called by that title. The term is frequently used in reference to an older man.

49    Cf. Sawyerr, *Practice and Presence*, 45.

50    Cf. Harris and Sawyerr, *Springs of Mende Belief*, 20–2.

51    It is common to hear people addressing a non-parent as father/mother. This is also a sign of respect reserved for the elderly.

52    I was told that usually when the name of God is sincerely used to ask the ancestors for forgiveness, no kola nut or any other means is needed to know the mind of the dead because the deceased or ancestors will surely respond positively. However, most traditionalists feel that worship without kola nuts will be empty, so they are always used even when God's name is invoked to win the favour of the ancestor(s).

53    Though the ancestors are intermediaries between the living and God, and may have more power and knowledge than humankind, 'they do not grow spiritually towards or like God' (Mbiti, *African Religions*, 160).

54    The Mende conclude their ancestral prayers with *ŋgew] jahun* (by the will of God), and the Krio *bai God pauer* ('by the power of God'). Like the Limba, 'this suggests that the ancestors are thought of as capable of fulfilling the requests expressed in the petitions, but also somewhat dependent, in the ultimate analysis, on the sovereign Will of God, who has greater power than the ancestors … and controls all that happens in the world' (Sawyerr, *Practice and Presence*, 47).

# Chapter 7: Non-ancestral spirits

1    See Mbiti, *African Religions*, 77. There are a number of similarities between the pneumatologies of ATR and of Judeo-Christianity. Like Limba tradition, in the Judeo-Christianity there is a strong belief in the existence of spirits [K. Ferdinando, 'Screwtape Revisited: Demonology Western, African, and Biblical', in *The Unseen World: Christian Reflections on Angels, Demons and the Heavenly Realm*, ed. A. N. S. Lane (Grand Rapids, MI: Paternoster Press & Baker Book House, 1996), 120] both good and evil (cf. Achtemeier, *HarperCollins Bible*, 236).

2    Gittins, *Mende Religion*, 53, in his work on Mende religion draws a distinction between the ancestral and non-ancestral spirits. In a footnote he states that the Mende, 'are perfectly aware of the distinction of what I call "ancestral" and "non-ancestral" spirits'. The former, are considered social, and the latter, are considered non-social.

3    Finnegan, *Survey of the Limba*, 113.

4    See Gittins, *Mende Religion*, 92–7; Mbiti, *African Religions*, 74–89; Magesa, *African Religion*, 53–7.

5    Cf. Harris and Sawyerr, *Springs of Mende Belief*, 34–53; Parrinder, *African Traditional Religion*, 43–54).

6    Cf. Evans-Pritchard, *Nuer Religion*, 28–62.

7    Ibid., 63–105.

8    Cf. Magesa, *African Religion*, 53.

9    Ferdinando, 'Screwtape Revisited', 113.

10   Harris and Sawyerr, *Springs of Mende Belief*, 1–2.

11   Cf. Parrinder, *African Traditional Religion*, 43–54; Magesa, *African Religion*, 53.

12   Cf. Ferdinando, 'Screwtape Revisited', 113.

13   Harris and Sawyerr, *Springs of Mende Belief*, 44–6, classified these spirits as 'land spirits' because they cater for the land-activities of the people.

14   In ATR, it is believed that spirits dwell in wells, springs, rivers, lakes and the sea; see Harris and Sawyerr, *Springs of Mende Belief*, 39–44; S. Jell-Bahlsen, 'The LakeGoddess Uhammiri/Ogbuide: The Female Side of the Universe in Igbo Cosmology', in *African Spirituality: Forms, Meanings and Expressions*, ed. J. K. Olupona (New York, NY: Crossroad, 2000), 38–53; K. O'Brien Wicker, 'Mami Water in African Religion and Spirituality', in *African Spirituality: Forms, Meanings and Expressions*, ed. J. K. Olupona (New York, NY: Crossroad, 2000), 198–222.

15   Cf. Magesa, *African Religion*, 53. In Sierra Leone 'a country in which natural forces often oppress at their most awesome. Religious belief is accordingly inculcated by thunder-storms, great rains and winds' (Harris and Sawyerr, *Springs of Mende Belief*, 3).

16   Finnegan, *Limba Stories*, 280, states that this spirit 'seems sometimes to be conceived of as like a snake, living in the forest' and 'sometimes as like the rainbow'. The association of *Ninkinanka* with the description of a rainbow fits well with the story that is told about him (Finnegan, *Limba Stories*, 280–3).

17   Cf. Ibid., 280.

18   Finnegan, *Survey of the Limba*, 115–6; cf. Mbiti, *African Religions*, 75; Harris and Sawyerr, *Springs of Mende Belief*, 3.

19   Cf. Ferdinando, 'Screwtape Revisited', 113.

20   See Magesa, *African Religion*, 179–89, for a discussion on the English and African usage of the word. The Limba Church condemns witches and witchcraft on the basis of Leviticus 19:26b and Deuteronomy 18:10. E. G. Parrinder, *Witchcraft: European and African* (London: Faber and Faber, 1963), 117, 122, states that the witchcraft discussed in the Bible is altogether different from anything known today and that it is therefore a mistake to use scripture to either condemn or justify witchcraft as we know it. 'The plain fact is that the Bible knows scarcely anything of true witchcraft, certainly not the New Testament, and the few injunctions found in the Old Testament refer to something else' (Parrinder, *Witchcraft*, 118).

To buttress his argument, Parrinder gives a brief study on the Hebrew words which have been translated 'witch'/ 'witchcraft' (*Witchcraft*, 120–2).

21    The belief as to which gender a witch may be varies in Africa. Like the Limba, among the Gwari, 'men and women could equally to be suspected of witchcraft' (M. F. C. Bourdillon, 'Witchcraft and Society', in *African Spirituality: Forms, Meanings and Expressions*, ed. J. K. Olupona (New York, NY: Crossroad, 2000), 186. In contrast, the Yoruba and Mende peoples believe witches are usually women (Sawyerr, *Practice and Presence*, 11). So also are the Nupe (Bourdillon, 'Witchcraft', 186). Parrinder appears not to have a clear-cut position on the issue. He states, 'witches are believed to be women, the word witch can equally well serve for men' (Parrinder, *African Traditional Religion*, 122), in other works, he has relegated witchcraft to only women [Parrinder, *Witchcraft*, 138; E. G. Parrinder, *African Mythology* (Paul Hamlyn, 1967), 92].

22    Bourdillon, 'Wichcraft', 176.

23    Sawyerr, *Practice and Presence*, 11. Because of the evil associated with witchcraft, the mystical power a witch uses to harm people can be referred to as 'evil magic' (cf. Mbiti, *African Religions*, 194--6). Magic in a nutshell is the manipulation of supernatural forces by mystical means. See Parrinder, *African Traditional Religion*, 113–220; Mbiti, *African Religions*, 193–6, for an overall discussion on magic.

24    Parrinder, *African Mythology*, 92.

25    Magesa, *African Religion*, 68.

26    Ibid.

27    Bourdillon, 'Witchcraft', 176.

28    Finnegan, *Survey of the Limba*, 119.

29    Bourdillon, 'Witchcraft', 180.

30    Ibid., 193.

31    Ibid.

32    Magesa, *African Religion*, 180.

33    Ibid.

34    Cf. Harris and Sawyerr, *Springs of Mende Belief*, 74; Bourdillon, 'Witchcraft', 176; Parrinder, *African Traditional Religion*, 118.

35    Cf. Harris and Sawyerr, *Springs of Mende Belief*, 5; Parrinder, *African Traditional Religion*, 44.

36    Among many ethnic groups in Sierra Leone, it is believed that snakes like the warmth of a pregnant woman and will wrap themselves around her leg for comfort (Harris and Sawyerr, *Springs of Mende Belief*, 5).

37    The nightly cry of an owl is considered supernatural as a manifestation of witchcraft (Harris and Sawyerr, *Springs of Mende Belief*, 5). Therefore, when an owl starts to hoot at night, people come out with sticks and metallic items and start to beat them together while using abusive and profane words against the witch who has sent the owl to come and carry out mischief.

It is said that witches do not like curses or profanity to be used against their mothers. When such words are uttered, the owl leaves and will not return for a long time.

38   The same procedure is also followed when the hooting sound of a vampire bat is heard. The sound of a vampire bat is thought to indicate that witches are sucking blood from infants (Harris and Sawyerr, *Springs of Mende Belief*, 5).

39   A gun used by witches is usually a small elongated object, sometimes with a plant or metal tube in it.

40   Cf. Harris and Sawyerr, *Springs of Mende Belief*, 74.

41   See Parrinder, *Witchcraft*, 129.

42   See Finnegan, '"Swears"', 8–26, for details on the procedure of 'swearing', types of 'swears', purpose of 'swears', postulated powers of 'swears', and control on the use of 'swears' among the Limba.

43   Harris and Sawyerr, *Springs of Mende Belief*, 75.

44   Opala and Boillot, 'Leprosy Among the Limba', 4.

45   This African method of protecting oneself and interests against malevolent spirit(s) has also been referred to by scholars as magic. Parrinder, *African Traditional Religion*, 114, refers to this act of mystical protection as 'Personal Magic' and Mbiti (*African Religions*, 193–4) sees it as 'good magic'.

46   Cf. Parrinder, *African Traditional Religion*, 114; Mbiti, *African Religions*, 193.

47   Cf. Parrinder, *African Traditional Religion*, 122; Mbiti, *African Religions*, 193.

48   A. B. T. Byaruhanga-Akiiki, 'Africa and Christianity', in *Religious Plurality in Africa: Essays in Honour of John S. Mbiti*, ed. J. K. Olupona and S. S. Nyang (Berlin and New York: Mouton De Gruyter, 1993), 192.

49   Cf. Sawyerr, *Creative Evangelism*, 107.

50   In the olden days the practice of deactivating the spirit of a witch was to dismember the corpse and bury its parts in different places. That practice has long since been discarded by the government of Sierra Leone. Other Africans as well have practices to forestall the activity of the spirit of a witch. The Temne, like the Limba once dismembered the corpses of witches, the Efik of Calabar burn the corpses, and some tribes in Nyasaland throw the corpses of witches to hyenas (Sawyerr, *Creative Evangelism*, 107).

51   Parrinder, *African Traditional Religion*, 137.

52   Cf. Ferdinando, 'Screwtape Revisited', 113.

53   Parrinder, *African Traditional Religion*, 60.

54   Ibid., 137.

55   Cf. Ibid., 137.

56   Finnegan, *Survey of the Limba*, 11.

57   Most of the people who to go perform religious rites in caves are those who have personal spirits. Because of their fearsome nature and home-like structure, caves are considered to be the home of many spirits. Offerings to personal spirits for forgiveness, thanksgiving, and prosperity are made in caves.

58   Cotton trees are believed to be the meeting places of witches. They are considered powerful spiritual centres for the agents of 'God below'. Not too long ago in Sierra Leonean politics, candidates for elections would take offerings to the bases of cotton trees for success and political prominence.

59   There are mountains exclusively for the worship of God/ancestors and there are others for the spirits.

60   There are some shrines which are only used for worshipping God and/or ancestors, while there are others for the purpose of presenting offerings and for the veneration of non-ancestral spirits. Every village/town has a sacred place which people are not allowed to enter without the approval of the priest. The only people that have the right to enter into these places freely are the priests in charge. Members of the community can only enter upon invitation. The importance of these places varies, however, some are for defence purposes, bush schooling, child bearing and others are for acquiring a better status. There are other shrines where people go to lay a curse 'swear' (th]ŋkoni) on those who have wronged them.

61   *Mami Wata* is often believed to be a naked woman with a fish tail rather than legs, and sometimes a snake often a python around her neck. The notion of *Mami Wata* as the goddess of water is common in some West African cultures. She is also known as *Mami Wota* (Jell-Bahlsen, 'The Lake Goddess', 38–53) and others call her *Mami Water* (Wicker, 'Mami Water', 98--222).

62   'In the event of misfortune it is an offending witch or spirit that is invariably sought out, which contrasts sharply with the theocentric reaction of Job or of the sufferers in the book of Psalms' (Ferdinando, 'Screwtape Revisited', 123).

# Chapter 8: Humankind

1   Mbiti, *African Religions*, 90; cf. C. Okorocha, 'The Meaning of Salvation: An African Perspective', in *Emerging Voices in Global Christian Theology*, ed. William A. Dryness (Grand Rapids, Mich: Zondervan, 1994), 73.

2   Cf. Mbiti, *African Religions*, 90.

3   Yambasu, *Dialectics*, 45.

4   From a biblical perspective, humankind is created by God (Gen. 1:26–7), formed 'from the dust of the ground' (Gen. 2:7; 3:19, 23).

5   Christians teach that because humans are uniquely created in God's image, we are placed over the rest of creation, to have dominion over and take care of it (Erickson, *Introducing Christian Doctrine*, 160; Achtemeier, *HarperCollins Bible*, 442).

6   In Yoruba religion, 'Olodumare puts his breath into the lifeless bodies which *Orisha-nla* had formed to make them living being', likewise the Akan teach that humankind consists of body and breath and are separated at death (Opoku, 'African Traditional Religion', 74–5).

The Mende believe that humankind is constituted of spirit and 'flesh, muscles, bones and all the other physical components of the human body' (Sawyerr, *God, Ancestor or Creator*, 82). In general, the Africans think that humankind is made up of 'body and soul, but the soul can have multiple contents' (Sawyerr, *Practice and Presence*, 113).

7    In the Bible, humankind is made up of soul/spirit and body/flesh (Matt. 10:28; Gen. 6:3; 2 Cor. 7:1; 1 Thess. 5:23; Col. 2:5). In the OT, the soul is the 'breath of life' that God breathed into Adam and he 'became a living being' (Gen. 2:7; cf. 46:18). The soul refers to one's life (Matt. 2:20; Mark 3:4; Luke 12:20).

8    In the story 'The Dog and the Rice' (Finnegan, *Limba Stories*, 238--9), Kanu created the Limba people, provided them with food, and taught them the techniques of farming. In several African stories, God created and put humankind in a state of paradise with all the necessities of life (Mbiti, *African Religions*, 93–4).

9    Fanthorpe, 'Locating the Politics', 18.

10   There are stories that support this belief: 'Kanu Gave Food to the Limba' (Finnegan, *Limba Stories*, 235–8), is about God's provision for the Limba; 'Kanu Gives Chiefship' (Finnegan, *Limba Stories*, 239–44) is about the institution of the Limba chieftaincy, and 'Kanu and Palm Wine' (Finnegan, *Limba Stories*, 246–7), speaks about Kanu teaching the Limba to tap palm wine.

11   In the Bible, humankind is created in the image and likeness of God. People experience the fullness of humanity only when they are in proper relationship with God (Erickson, *Introducing Christian Doctrine*, 168), and of all creation, humankind alone is capable of 'having a conscious personal relationship with the Creator and of responding to him' (Ibid., 157). In the beginning God had a cordial relationship with humankind (Gen. 2), but humankind's disobedience destroyed that fellowship and relationship (Gen. 3). This relationship was later reconciled through the atoning death of Christ.

12   Opoku, 'African Traditional Religion', 77.

13   Ibid.

14   Mbiti, *African Religions*, 90. In Judeo-Christianity, although different from God's other created beings, humans are 'not so sharply distinguished from the rest of them as to have no relationship with them', therefore, there should be harmony between humankind and the rest of the creatures of God (Erickson, *Introducing Christian Doctrine*, 160).

15   Okorocha, 'The Meaning of Salvation', 80.

16   E. M. Zuesse, 'Perseverance and Transmutation in African Traditional Religions', in *African Traditional Religions in Contemporary Society*, ed. J. K. Olupona (St. Paul, Minn: Paragon House, 1991), 178.

17   Although ecology is a wide and complex field that requires the study of organisms in their environment and the study of relationships among organisms, the various issues that are being discussed by science and religion are interrelated and both disciplines are trying to restore a common relationship between animate and inanimate existence.

18   Opoku, 'African Traditional Religion', 77.

19    The Harvard Divinity School's 'Religions of the World and Ecology' series and the World Wide Fund for Nature's 'World Religions and Ecology' series have nothing presently on ATR and ecology.

20    Opoku, 'African Traditional Religion', 78. In Judeo-Christianity, 'religious life and the earth's ecology are inextricably linked, organically related' [L. E. Sullivan, 'Preface' in *Christianity and Ecology*, ed. D. T. Hessel and R. R. Ruether (Cambridge, Mass: Harvard University Press, 2000), xi}, and environmental destruction is not only a danger' human existence, it is also 'a sin against God' [F. Rajotte with E. Breuilly, 'What is the Crisis?' in Christianity and Ecology, ed. E. Breuilly and M. Palmer (New York, NY: Orbis Books, 1992), 2]. We are God's agent in 'caring for the earth' (Achtemeier, *HarperCollins Bible*, 442).

21    Opoku, 'African Traditional Religion', 77.

# Chapter 9: Lifecycle

1    Cf. Mbiti, *African Religions*, 107.

2    Cf. Parrinder, *African Traditional Religion*, 90.

3    Mbiti, *African Religions*, 2.

4    G. C. Oosthuizen, 'The Place of Traditional Religion in Contemporary South Africa', in *African Traditional Religions in Contemporary Society*, ed. J. K. Olupona (St. Paul, Minn: Paragon House, 1991), 41.

5    Parrinder, *African Traditional Religion*, 27.

6    Mbiti, *African Religions*, 2.

7    Sawyerr, *Practice of Presence*, 10.

8    Magesa, *African Religion*, 25-26.

9    V. Mulago, 'African Traditional Religion and Christianity', in *African Traditional Religions in Contemporary Society*, ed. J. K. Olupona (St. Paul, Minn: Paragon House, 1991), 127.

10    This is similar to the Christian worldview as Erickson puts it, God 'is of value to us for what he is in himself, not merely for what he does' (*Introducing Christian Doctrine*, 83).

11    This is reminiscent of Paul's exhortation to the Romans (Rom. 8:35, 37–9).

12    This is also true of other Africans (Parrinder, *African Traditional Religion*, 91).

13    In Limba sexual ethics, 'only married women are expected to be pregnant' (NCDC, *Source Book*, 91). It is a disgrace to the family whose girl/woman is impregnated before marriage. In Freetown, the shame will be on the pregnant girl herself. Therefore, a school going Limba girl drops out of school in her early pregnancy and with the consent of her parents flees to an undisclosed place until the child is born and left with one of its grandparents or close relatives. Presently with the available forms of birth control, teenage pregnancy has dwindled considerably.

14    Magesa, *African Religion*, 83. In the Bible, conception is seen as a gift from God (Judg. 13:3; Ruth 4:13; Matt. 1:20). Children are God's gift to humankind, and it was a joyful experience

when a woman became pregnant especially after long years of waiting (Gen. 30:23; Luke 1:58).

15   A sacrifice of thanks for pregnancy and childbirth is common in Africa (Parrinder *African Traditional Religion* 91; Cuthrell-Curry, 'African-derived Religion', 459).

16   NCDC, *Source Book*, 85.

17   This is common among Africans (see Parrinder, *African Traditional Religion*, 91; Parsons, *Religion*, 36–7).

18   Parrinder, *African Traditional Religion*, 91.

19   This is also common in African societies (Parrinder, *African Traditional Religion*, 91–2; Mbiti, *African Religions*, 108–9).

20   The Mende believe that the *ngafa* (life/spirit) is from God and enters the mother's body like the Akan *kra* (a spiritual likeness of God), 'thus inspiring and giving life to her blood, that is to the foetus' (Sawyerr, *Practice and Presence*, 68).

21   Cf. Cuthrell-Curry, 'African-derived Religion', 462.

22   Mbiti, *African Religions*, 117.

23   Magesa, *African Religion*, 94; cf. Parrinder, *African Traditional Religion*, 94.

24   Cf. Finnegan, *Survey of the Limba*, 75–6.

25   Among many African cultures, 'there are closed associations which are popularly called secret societies' (Parrinder, *African Mythology*, 96). The Poro society is found in many Sierra Leonean ethnic groups, see Little, 'Role of Secret Society', 199; Parrinder, *African Traditional Religion*, 95–6; Parsons, *Religion*, 149–56; Dorjahn, 'The Initiation', 35–62. The Poro 'can be traced back for several hundred years and is related to other West African societies' (Parrinder, *African Mythology*, 96), see also (Parsons, *Religion*, 149). For various stories and myths about the origin of Poro, see (Parrinder, *African Mythology*, 96–103).

26   The Temne also call their women's secret society *Bondo* (NCDC, *Source Book*, 204). Mende (Little, 'Role of Secret Society', 200) and Kono (Parsons, *Religion*, 143) call their women's secret society *Sande*.

27   Ottenberg, 'Male and Female', 363–87, traces the similarities and differences between the organisation and rites of the male and female societies in Bafodea.

28   Ottenberg, 'Male and Female', 364.

29   Cf. Finnegan, *Survey of the Limba*, 107–8.

30   See Little, 'Role of Secret Society', 200–10; Dorjan, 'Initiation', 46–56; Parsons, *Religion*, 149, for details on the importance and significant role secret societies play in other Sierra Leonean cultures.

31   The bush is considered one of the main domains inhabited by evil forces. It is a powerful place, independent from the village or town, and that people fear to go. Witches in the bush can enter wild beasts to attack people in the vicinity. Medicinal leaves and wild plants

containing enormous powers that are used to kill and cause havoc are found in the bush. Most Limba communities have a medicine man or woman or both as head of the bush.

32    Parrinder, *African Traditional Religion*, 96.

33    The cap is seen as being more important than the gown, because of what its different parts represent.

34    With more to learn along the way, through personal observation and judgement, experience being the best teacher.

35    This practice, otherwise known as Female Genital Mutilation (FGM) is prevalent in Africa with an estimated eighty to ninety per cent of women in Sierra Leone having undergone the procedure. Public discussion of FGM in Sierra Leone is almost taboo, but some see it as a major health issue and an abuse of children's human rights. The primary objective of the procedure is to preserve female virginity by discouraging premarital sexual activity. The issue of female circumcision has generated much debate at both local and international levels. Some female African scholars are expressing their opinions against it and are in favour of its eradication 'as it reduces libido and does more harm than good', D. O. Akintunde, 'Women as Healers', in *African Women, Religion, and Health*, ed. I. A. Phiri and S. Nadar (Maryknoll, NY: Orbis Books, 2006), 163.

36    Hackett, 'Revitalization', 142.

37    Cf. Parrinder, *African Traditional Religion*, 98; Magesa, *African Religion*, 121.

38    For a discussion on *nahulu* see Finnegan, *Survey of the Limba*, 63–5.

39    Cf. NCDC, *Source Book*, 88; Finnegan, *Survey of the Limba*, 63.

40    Dorjahn, 'Marital Game', 170.

41    See Magesa, *African Religion*, 121.

42    Biblical marriage is a 'physical and spiritual union of a man and woman' (Achtemeier, *HarperCollins Bible*, 656). Usually, it was preceded by a period of engagement (Deut. 22:23; Matt. 1:18), and was normally arranged by the parents (Achtemeier, *HarperCollins Bible*, 96; De Vaux, *Ancient Israel*, 29; Packer *et al*, *Bible Almanac*, 433), or at least with the consent of the parents (Achtemeier, *HarperCollins Bible*, 96). A bride price (*mahor*), the amount of which varied depending on the demands of the girl's father (Gen. 34:12) and/or the social standing of the family (1 Sam. 18:23) was paid to the girl's father. Marriage ceremonies were almost always a very public event (Packer *et al.*, *Bible Almanac*, 435) the most important part of which was the bringing of the bride into the groom's house, in the midst of great rejoicing (Achtemeier, *HarperCollins Bible*, 656; De Vaux, *Ancient Israel*, 33–4).

43    In comparison, there are certain colognes or body sprays for men that are used to attract the attention of women.

44    Mbiti, *African Religions*, 2.

45    Cf. Finnegan, *Survey of the Limba*, 108.

46    The Hebrew calendar was centred on agriculture, and most of the major religious observances 'had an agricultural significance, for they marked the seasons of planting and harvesting'

(Packer *et al.*, *Bible Almanac*, 263). These rituals gave the farmer a feeling of personal worth and an enrichment of his faith (Packer *et al*, *Bible Almanac*, 263). In order to produce the best crop, the farmer partnered with God from planting to harvesting. The farming season began with fasting and ended with feasting and worship (e.g., Deut. 16:13–7).

47   This is true of both literate qualified applicants and unqualified or non-literate applicants.

48   Christian Limbas like the traditionalists believe that in spite of one's qualifications and experience, when applying for a job in Sierra Leone God must be consulted at the beginning of the process, and continually prayed to while on the job. At Wednesday prayer services prospective applicants ask the church to pray with them for God's blessing in their endeavours. Those who already have a job sometimes give thanks for God's provision and ask for continued prayer for job security.

49   Finnegan, *Survey of the Limba*, 36. The Israelite monarchy was instituted by God (1 Sam. 9:15–6; 10). The references to the king as 'prince' (1 Sam. 9:16; 13:14), and 'anointed one' may point to one who is designated by God. Accession to the throne was seen as a divine choice; a man is made 'king by the "grace of God", not only because God made a covenant with the dynasty of David, but because his choice was exercised at each accession' (De Vaux, *Ancient Israel*, 101). Paul exhorted the Romans that political establishments are instituted by God, and political leaders are servants of God (Rom. 13:1–6).

50   During the time of seclusion, the chief receives wisdom from the old and wise men of the society. It is also a time of deep reflection on the promises he made to his people and the responsibility that lies ahead of him. When the chief emerges out of *kantha* he is considered a new man. His old life as an ordinary citizen is gone. He wears special clothes to designate his new office and some assume a name that is preceded by the title of 'Almamy'. He is now a new man with the spiritual and physical responsibilities of his people.

51   The coronation of the King was accompanied by religious rites: the investiture with insignia (2 Kg. 11:12), the anointing (1 Sam. 9:16; 10:1; 2 Sam. 2:4; 5:3; 1 Kg. 1:39; 2 Kg. 11:12), the acclamation (1 Kg. 1:34, 39; 2 Kg. 11:12), the enthronement (1 Kg. 1:46; 2 Kg. 11:19), and the homage (1 Kg. 1:47), all have religious significance (De Vaux, *Ancient Israel*, 102–7).

52   A different word *mamo* ('thanks') is used on the third line. It carries the same meaning but is different in pronunciation from the previous word *wali* ('thanks'). This is because *mamo* is borrowed by the Thonko Limba from the Temne ethnic group.

53   The affairs of the chiefdom, section and town, in most cases do not run well in the absence of a chief. Also, the politics and lobbying that go on between the contenders and their supporters do not make the atmosphere peaceful. The choosing and installing of a chief puts an end to all political wrangling.

54   Unwise decisions and judgements by the chief affect the entire community.

55   This is analogous to the Anglican Church prayers for the welfare of the queen of England.

56   The Limba pray for rest when a good person dies. Witches and bad people are not expected to find rest and peace when they pass away.

57    Peace is a necessity at this time of great loss. Peace of mind may also mean salvation. God's salvation during times of sorrow and disappointment is essential for the survival of the community.

58    The Limba believe that God responds well to prayers said on behalf of people, especially to those said for the dead.

59    Religion and politics went side by side in Bible times. The political laws of the Israelites were based on their religious tenets. In the NT, under Roman rule, the Jews maintained their politico-religious activities through the temple establishment.

60    Mbiti, *African Religions*, 2.

61    Dr Siaka P. Stevens ruled Sierra Leone from 1968 to 1985 as Prime Minister and President respectively. Upon his retirement in 1985, he personally chose Major Gen. Joseph S. Momoh, who was head of the army and a Limba himself to succeed him. Momoh was overthrown in a military coup in 1992.

62    Hackett, 'Revitalization', 141.

63    Opala and Boillot, 'Leprosy Among the Limba', 5. For a discussion on politics and divination in the APC party, see Shaw, 'The Politician', 30–55.

64    The failed so-called counter-coup by the APC party was blamed on the false divination of an herbalist (Opala and Boillot, 'Leprosy Among the Limba', 32). This attempt to overthrow the Military government and regain power, resulted in the executions of seventeen alleged conspirators on 29 December 1992.

65    Opala and Boillot, 'Leprosy Among the Limba', 40.

66    Pouring libations at state functions is also carried out in Nigeria (Hackett, 'Revitalization', 141).

67    For a detailed study on these issues, see the works and bibliographies of P. Richards, *Fighting for the Rain Forest: War, Youth & Resources in Sierra Leone* (Oxford: James Currey, 1996), and I. Abdullah, ed., *Between Democracy and Terror: The Sierra Leone Civil War* (Dakar, Senegal: CODESRIA, 2004).

68    See P. Richards, 'Green Book Millenarians? The Sierra Leone War Within the Perspective of an Anthropology of Religion', in *Religion and African Civil Wars*, ed. N. Kastfelt (New York, NY: Palgrave Macmillan, 2005), 119–46.

69    Cf. Opala and Boillot, 'Leprosy Among the Limba', 1, 5.

70    Religion plays a vital role in Sierra Leone's judiciary system. A judge is installed after taking an oath from either the Bible or the Qur'an, and the litigants are required to swear by either the Bible or the Koran. After the annual judiciary break, the commencement of court sittings is preceded by church services in all regions of the country. These services, organised in each region by the local Anglican Church (which is considered the state church in Sierra Leone) are held to pray for the judicial system that God will bless its leaders in the dispensation of their duties.

71    A 'swear' is a curse that acts spiritually through a material object, a 'swear' is believed to be capable of consciously pursuing and discriminating culprits. It can spiritually pursue the

guilty and possibly his/her relatives also by its own divine means, and it is believed it can make no mistake. Owners of 'swears' usually give names to their 'swears' to portray there might, for example: *Th]ma fɛ/hɛ* ('eat today'); *Huth]r]* ('problem').

72    When the National Provisional Ruling Council (NPRC) military government seized power and charged many APC political appointees with the misuse of power and the misappropriation of funds, national newspapers ran stories every week of accused persons and their families visiting traditional spiritual leaders and offering expensive sacrifices to find favour in the justice system and hence escape the wrath of the military. Some of these traditional believers were not Limbas. They were, however, part of a system that encouraged traditional religion as the norm for over 20 years. See Shaw, 'The Politician', 30–55, for a discussion on politics and divination in Sierra Leone.

73    The Bible associate healing with God. In the OT, Malachi spoke about the Lord, the 'Sun of Righteousness' rising with healing in his wings (Mal. 4:2), and in a Psalm attributed to David, God is praised as the one who heals diseases (Ps. 103:3). Jesus is the 'great physician' (Matt. 8:1–4; Mark 5:1–20; Luke 13:10–13; John 9:1–7) who in his time on earth performed many healings including the woman who had been suffering from haemorrhages for 12 years, and after spending money on physicians without being cured, came to Jesus and was cured (Mark 5:25–34).

74    Cf. Finnegan, *Survey of the Limba*, 108; Mbiti, *African Religions*, 60–1.

75    Mbiti, *African Religions*, 38.

76    See Kofi Appiah-Kubi, 'Traditional African Healing System Versus Western Medicine in Southern Ghana: An Encounter', in *Religious Plurality in Africa: Essays in Honour of John S. Mbiti*, ed. J. K. Olupona and S. S. Nyang (Berlin and New York: Mouton De Gruyter, 1993), 95–107; Oosthuizen, 'Place of Traditional Religion', 47, for a discussion on traditional healing and Western medicine.

77    Opala and Boillot, 'Leprosy Among the Limba', 7.

78    Oosthuizen, 'Place of Traditional Religion', 47.

79    A medicine man or woman specialises in making medicine from special plants and leaves taken mainly from the forest to cure illnesses.

80    Cf. Shaw, 'The Politician', 32; Opala and Boillot, 'Leprosy Among the Limba', 7.

81    Opala and Boillot, 'Leprosy Among the Limba', 7.

82    In Judeo-Christianity, death is 'the end of physical and/or spiritual life' (Achtemeier, *HarperCollins Bible*, 232). Death came as a consequence of humankind's sin (Gen. 3; cf. 1 Cor 5:21–2).

83    God's death means 'natural' death (Finnegan, *Survey of the Limba*, 108; cf. Mbiti, *African Religions*, 151). In some African cultures, God created death and allows it to kill people (G. Niangoran-Bouah, 'The Talking Drum: A Traditional Instrument of Liturgy and of Mediation with the Sacred', in *African Traditional Religions in Contemporary Society*, ed. J. K. Olupona (St. Paul, Minn: Paragon House, 1991), 91.

84    Magesa, *African Religion*, 155.

85    Stories about the origin of death abound in many African cultures; see (Parrinder, *African Mythology*, 54–63). In many myths, death is the result of 'a message or item that God sent to people, but which did not reach them or was changed by the messenger on the way; or the message arrived too late: a faster messenger from God had brought another message (of loss, death)' Mbiti, *African Religions*, 61–2. In other myths, death is a 'consequence of the breakdown of communication between God and humanity caused either by an act of a human being or one of the creatures' (Magesa, *African Religion*, 156).

85    Finnegan, *Limba Stories*, 234–5.

87    Finnegan, *Survey of the Limba*, 233–5.

88    Normal funeral rites are not carried out if the deceased was a convicted witch. Special burial rites must be performed for a witch to ensure that they do not return from the grave to cause more trouble.

89    Parrinder, *African Traditional Religion*, 98.

90    W. Abimbola, 'The Place of African Traditional Religion in Contemporary Africa', in *African Traditional Religions in Contemporary Society*, ed. J. K. Olupona (St. Paul, Minn: Paragon, 1991), 55.

91    The ceremonies on the third, seventh and fortieth were borrowed from Islam (Hargrave, *African Primitive Life*, 66). Before the advent of Islam into Limba country, the Limba only had *huboka* ('cry') which took place at any time of the year when the bereaved family could afford to feed all the sympathisers.

92    See chapter five again about ancestorship.

93    R. N. Edet, 'Christianity and African Women's Rituals', in *The Will to Arise: Women, Tradition, and the Church in Africa*, ed. M. A. O. and M. R. A. Kanyoro (Eugene, Oregon: Wipf and Stock Publishers, 2005), 31.

94    L. Fanusi, 'Sexuality and Women in African Culture', in *The Will to Arise: Women, Tradition, and the Church in Africa*, ed. M. A. Oduyoye and M. R. A. Kanyoro (Eugene, Oregon: Wipf and Stock Publishers, 2005), 144.

95    M. A. Oduyoye, 'Women and Ritual in Africa,' in *The Will to Arise: Women, Tradition, and the Church in Africa*, ed. M. A. Oduyoye and M. R. A. Kanyoro (Eugene, Oregon: Wipf and Stock Publishers, 2005), 15.

96    Mbiti, *African Religions*, 159–60.

97    Ibid., 160–1.

98    Ibid., 160. In Christianity, the soul/spirit continues after death (Matt. 16:25–6), but there is no clear statement about the destiny of the body beyond the grave. In Genesis 3:19 at death the body returns to the ground from whence it came, while in Matthew 10:28 it is inferred that the body may also experience the suffering of hell, or some will be raised (1 Thess. 4:13–8).

99    Mbiti, 'God, Sin, and Salvation', 67.

# Chapter 10: Sin and salvation

1    F. M. Mbon, 'African Traditional Religion Socio-Religious Ethics and National Development: The Nigeria Case, in *African Traditional Religions in Contemporary Society*, ed. J. K. Olupona (St. Paul, Minn: Paragon, 1991), 102; Magesa, *African Religion*, 166–72. Sin to the Christian, is a 'revolt or transgression and indicating a deliberate act of defiance against God' (Achtemeier, *HarperCollins Bible*, 1026). It is 'a religious concept, because all sin is ultimately against God' (Achtemeier, *HarperCollins Bible*, 1026). Sin 'may be a matter of act, of thought, or of inner disposition or state' (Erickson, *Introducing Christian Doctrine*, 180, 196–7).

2    E. Asante, 'The Gospel in Context: An African Perspective', *Interpretation: A Journal of Bible and Theology* 55 no. 4 (2001), 361.

3    Mbiti, 'God, Sin, and Salvation', 64.

4    This tradition abounds in ATR (Sawyerr, *Practice and Presence*, 121; Mbiti, *African Religions*, 205–6).

5    Mbiti, 'God, Sin, and Salvation', 65; cf. H. J. Mugabe, 'Salvation From an African Perspective', *ERT* 23 no. 3 (1999), 240.

6    Cf. Mugabe, 'Salvation', 250.

7    Ibid., 240.

8    The Bible categorised sins also; there are sins against the supernatural: God (Exod. 20:4–7; Matt. 25:14–30; Luke 19:12–26), Jesus (Matt. 26:24), and the Holy Spirit (Matt. 12:31–2). There are sins against humankind (Exod. 20:8–17; Matt. 25:31–46; Luke 16:19–31; Matt. 23; Acts 5:1–11). There is also cultic sin (the failure to observe ritual requirements); there are political, social, and spiritual sins (e.g., envy, hate, etc); and there are intentional (Num. 15:30–1) and unintentional sins (Lev. 5).

9    Cf. Asante, 'The Gospel', 361.

10   A womaniser is known as *bakedaŋ*.

11   Mbon, 'African Traditional Relgion', 103.

12   Ibid.; Asante, 'The Gospel', 361; Sawyerr, *Practice and Presence*, 123; Magesa, *African Religion*, 172; Mbiti, *African Religions*, 202.

13   Cf. Harris, 'The Idea of God', 108; Harris and Sawyerr, *Springs of Mende Belief*, 31.

14   Just as in Limba religion, in Christianity, sin has consequences. Sin is responsible for humankind's fall from God's glory (Rom. 3:23); incurred physical death (Gen. 2:17; 3:19; Rom. 5:12; 6:23); incurred spiritual death; and destroyed humankind's relationship with God (Gen. 1:26–30; 2:7–23; Gen. 3:8; Rom. 8:7). Further, sin also affects the sinner's relationship with his/her fellow human beings (Erickson, *Introducing Christian Doctrine*, 193; K. Bediako, 'Jesus in African Culture', in *Emerging Voices in Global Christian Theology*, ed. W. Dryness (Grand Rapids, Minn: Zondervan, 1994), 102.

15   The Christian remedy for sin is entirely different from that of Limba religion. Christians believe that God first took the initiative to remedy the taint of sin by giving his son to die on the cross as the atoning sacrifice for the sin of the world (Isa. 53; Rom. 5:8–9; 1 John 2:2;

4:10). This action is described as a manifestation of God's love for humankind (John 3:16), and as a display of true love and friendship by Jesus (John 15:13; 1 John 3:16). In order to stay protected from sin, Christians must walk continuously with God and 'have fellowship with one another' (1 John 1:7). This is similar to the African concept of *sensu communis*. However, if the Christian falls, the NT has prescribed a remedy: 'If we confess our sins, he who is faithful and just will forgive us our sins and cleanse us from all unrighteousness' (1 John 1:9). In Christianity, as all sins are ultimately against God (Bediako, 'Jesus in African Culture', 102), confession to him matters as much as confession to the victim of a wrongdoing. Even if one is not forgiven by a victim, God's forgiveness is ultimately more important.

16    Mbon, 'African Traditional Religion', 103.

17    Sawyerr, *Practice and Presence*, 123.

18    This is similar to the common African saying 'God will punish you according to your deeds' (Asante, 'The Gospel', 361).

19    Mbiti, 'God, Sin, and Salvation', 64.

20    Sawyerr, *Practice and Presence*, 123.

21    Cf. Mugabe, 'Salvation', 240.

22    Okorocha, 'The Meaning', 86.

23    Mbiti, 'God, Sin, and Salvation', 67.

24    Okorocha shares a very similar story about a wealthy woman ('The Meaning', 63).

25    Ibid.

26    Ibid.

27    Mbiti, 'God, Sin, and Salvation', 67; cf. Mugabe, 'Salvation', 246.

28    Okorocha, 'The Meaning', 85.

29    Mbiti, 'God, Sin, and Salvation', 67.

30    Asante, 'The Gospel', 359.

31    Ibid., 360. According to Asante, salvation in the OT, 'is seen both in God's act of delivering Israel from Egypt and in his protection and provision for Israel as the people journeyed through the wilderness to the promised land (Deut. 6:21–3)' ('The Gospel', 357). In the NT, God and Christ are presented as Saviour, and agents of salvation. The concept of salvation is diverse; first, it is 'redemption of sin and from the dominion of Satan' ('The Gospel', 357) in order to regain fellowship with God. For the Christians, salvation can only be achieved through Jesus (Acts 4:12). It is on account of this that Christians continue to tell traditionalists and non-Christians that they are doomed to eternal destruction without Jesus. However impressive the traditionalist concept of salvation is, if they do not repent, confess, and ask Jesus for forgiveness, they will never find salvation. Traditionalists usually respond by saying: 'Jesus did not die for our sins … how Jesus could be the only mediator for every race on earth? Jesus is not part of our culture and does not know us'. The Christian concept of salvation is not, however, purely eschatological, the Greek verb *sozo* (to save) also carries the meaning 'preserve or rescue from natural dangers and afflictions', or to 'save or preserve

from eternal death' (W. Bauer, *A Greek-English Lexicon of the New Testament, and Other Early Christian Literature* (2nd English ed. trans. and aug. by W. F. Arndt, F. W. Gingrich and F. W. Danker; Chicago and London: University of Chicago Press, 1979), 798. Christian salvation, like the Limba concept, includes the 'deliverance from the evils of this life' (Ferdinando, 'Screwtape Revisited', 125). Part of Jesus mission was to preach good news to the poor, 'to proclaim release to the captives and recovery of sight to the blind, to let the oppressed go free, to proclaim the year of the Lord's favour' (Luke 4:18–9).

# Chapter 11: Sacred specialists

1    Evangelical Christians condemn sacred specialists as evil personages and workers of iniquity. They are considered to be the devil incarnate because they work under the influence of Satan to promote deception and false religion. However, like traditional priests, the Christian clergy are believed to be divinely called to lead believers in the worship of God. There are great differences between Judeo-Christianity and Limba religion. The Limba priesthood is not scripturally based, nor is it evangelically focused, and it is not for the edification of the saints for the perfection in the image of Christ. The main duty of priests in biblical times was to serve 'in the temple performing ritual functions and conducting the sacrificial services' (Achtemeier, *HarperCollins Bible*, 880). In the patriarchal period, there was no official priesthood, but like a lay priest in Limba religion, the head of the family performed sacrifices (Gen. 31:54). Christians 'transferred the role of the priest as mediator between God and humans onto Jesus whom they saw as both God and man. He became the eternal High Priest by God's appointment (Heb. 5:1–6) and supplanted the ancient sacrificial system by his own sacrifice (Heb. 7:27–8; 9:23–6' (Achtemeier, *HarperCollins Bible*, 881).

2    Limba priests, like biblical priests are believed to be called by God, and are mediators between the people and God. In both systems, the main duties of the priests are to perform ritual functions and conduct the sacrificial services.

3    Cf. Mbiti, *African Religions*, 183.

4    Cf. Parrinder, *African Traditional Religion*, 101.

5    Cf. Mbiti, *African Religions*, 184.

6    See Mbiti, *African Religions*, 183-84, for the duties of African traditional priests.

7    Cf. Parrinder, *African Traditional Religion*, 101.

8    Christians oppose divination on the basis of Deuteronomy (18:10–2). It is the strong belief of the church that all believers and practitioners of divination are doomed to hell (Lev. 20:6; Rev. 21:8; 22:15). Biblical divination like that of Limba tradition is 'an attempt to secure information …by the use of physical means, about matters and events that are currently hidden or that lie in the future' (Achtemeier, *HarperCollins Bible*, 641). Divination was not uncommon in biblical times. To 'inquire of the Lord' through an oracle was acceptable (Judg. 1:1–2; 1 Sam. 10:22). The official oracles used to 'inquire of the Lord' were the Urim and Thummim (1 Sam. 23:9–12; 30:7–8; Num. 27:21), and the casting of lots (Lev. 16:8; Num. 26:55–6; Acts 1:26). When 'the LORD did not answer him, not by dreams, or by Urim, or by prophets' (1 Sam. 28:6), King Saul resorted to necromancy by consulting the medium of Endor to bring up Samuel for him so that he could learn the outcome of the impending

war with the Philistines (1 Sam. 28:7–14). It seems that the oracular forms of Urim and Thummim and casting of lots were the only acceptable mediums for inquiry of the Lord. All other forms of divination were considered an abomination to the Lord (Deut. 18:10–12; Lev. 20:6; Ezek. 13:6–8; Rev. 21:8; 22:15).

9    Shaw, 'Gender', 287.

10    Opala and Boillot, 'Leprosy Among the Limba', 6.

11    In the Bible, divination was also the attempt to get information about hidden or future events through the use of physical objects. The oracular methods of Urim and Thummim and the casting of lots were the only acceptable mediums for enquiring of the Lord, all other forms of divination were considered an abomination to God. Although the purpose and means of divination in Limba Religion and the Bible are similar, the two systems are not exactly the same.

12    Parrinder, *African Traditional Religion*, 103.

13    Mbiti, *African Religions*, 172.

14    U. H. D. Danfulani, 'Pa Divination: Ritual Performance and Symbolism among the Ngas, Mupun, and Mwaghavul of the Jos Plateau, Nigeria', in *African Spirituality: Forms, Meanings and Expressions*, ed. J. K. Olupona (New York, NY: Crosssroad, 2000), 87.

15    Ibid.

16    Mbiti, *African Religions*, 172; cf. Oosthuizen, 'Place of Traditional Religion', 46, 48.

17    Cf. Finnegan, *Survey of the Limba*, 115.

18    Danfulani, 'Pa Divination', 87; cf. Mbiti, *African Religions*, 167.

19    See Magesa, *African Religion*, 220-34, for the methods of divination; E. M. Zuesse, 'Divination and Deity in African Religion', *History* 15 (1975), 158--68, for the forms of divination in Africa.

20    Finnegan, 'Limba Religious', 14.

21    Ibid., 15.

22    In Biriwa Limba land, *Babare wo*, specialises in catching witches by applying the juice of the *kubarɛ* tree into a the eyes of a fowl, or into a banana stem.

23    Cf. Finnegan, *Survey of the Limba*, 120.

24    Cf. Finnegan, 'Limba Religious Vocabulary', 15.

25    Opala and Boillot, 'Leprosy Among the Limba', 7.

26    Ibid., 6; cf. Shaw, 'The Politician', 32.

27    Parrinder, *African Traditional Religion*, 105.

28    Ibid.

29    Magesa, *African Religion*, 212.

30    Opala and Boillot, 'Leprosy Among the Limba', 6. For a discussion of the methods Limba
      herbalists use to treat illnesses, see ibid., 7–9.

31    Hackett, 'Revitalization', 145.

# Chapter 12: Concluding remarks

1    Sawyerr, *Practice and Presence*, 3.

2    Mbiti, *African Religions*, 9.

3    King, 'Angels and Ancestors', 24.

4    For some of the published suggested guidelines for dialogue between Christianity and ATR, see J.
     S. Mbiti, *The Crisis of Mission in Africa* (Mukono: Uganda Church Press, 1971); 'Christianity and
     African Culture', 26–40; 'Encounter of Christian Faith', 817–820; Kailing, 'A New Solution',
     489–506; T. Tienou, 'The state of the gospel in Africa', *Evangelical Missions Quarterly* 27 no. 2
     (2001), 154–62.

5    For those who will be interested, an argument for the place of ATR has been included as an
     Appendix in this study.

# Appendix

## Arguments for the place of ATR

In Sierra Leone, like in most African countries, ATR, Christianity, and Islam are the three major religious belief systems. These religions have a long history of coexistence in Sierra Leone; as in all experiences of encounter and coexistence, there have been challenges as well as benefits. People living side-by-side meet and interact personally and communally on a regular basis. They share common resources and communal benefits. The social and cultural interaction and cooperation that are involved in this dialogue of life are what compel people to fully understand the worldviews of their neighbours and seek better relationships with them. In the history of this culture of dialogue and cooperation, ATR, the host religion, which has played and continues to play a vital role in the assimilation of Christianity and Islam, seems to be marginalised and stereotyped.

In the history of inter-religious cooperation in Sierra Leone, ATR has long been marginalised. The Project for Christian-Muslim Relations in Africa (PROCMURA) was established in Sierra Leone in the early 1970s, to promote understanding and dialogue between Christians and Muslims.[1] The Inter-Religious Council of Sierra Leone (IRCSL) was formed in April 1997 as a national multi-religious organization dedicated to promoting cooperation primarily among the Christian and Muslim communities of Sierra Leone.[2] Among other things, the IRCSL strives to identify and promote principles and actions that are geared toward peace and harmony for the Sierra Leonean community.

The reasons given by some Christian and Muslim leaders, and theologians in Sierra Leone as to what is lacking in ATR that continues to prevent practitioners of Christianity and Islam from officially involving traditionalists in the socio-religious development of Sierra Leone, were based on the general missionary theology that ATR lacks the hallmarks of a true religion. One of the arguments for that is; ATR is not scriptural, unlike the Christians and Muslims who are referred to as the 'People of the Book'. In this regard, Magesa arguing for a universal recognition of ATR opposed liberal western scholars who:

> Could neither conceive nor allow that a religion dependent on oral traditions, such as African Religion is, could be regarded as an equal ... These scholars failed to consider that Judaism, for example, was an orally-based religion for many centuries before its oral story was codified in writing. The same is true

for Christianity and Islam, although for a shorter period of time. Other things being equal, orality alone cannot disqualify a religious system from qualitative greatness. In fact, the existence of written scripture must be seen as only one criterion among many.[3]

As revealed in Magesa's argument, Judaism, Christianity, and Islam were all accepted as religions before their tenets were written down. They did not attain religious status on account of their sacred writings. This raised the question of why ATR should be treated any differently. ATR theology is written on the hearts, minds, words, actions and symbols of the African people.[4] This is one of the factors responsible for the survival of African Religion; as long as those who follow ATR are alive, it will never be extinct,[5] and they are proud to discuss it, live it out, and pass it on to their children.

Each of the three religious traditions in Sierra Leone constitutes an important phenomenon and affects the future of the nation. In that respect, a programme must be developed for the constructive engagement of traditionalists, Christians, and Muslims in the emerging post-war Sierra Leone.

In the Truth and Reconciliation Commission (TRC) of Sierra Leone Act, explicit reference is made 'to the assistance from traditional and religious leaders in facilitating reconciliation'. The Commission's Final Report volume 3b; Chapter 7 paragraph 39 on the subject 'Traditional values and methods informing reconciliation' portrays the importance and indispensable contribution of African traditional values in society and public life by stating among other things that, 'the reconciliation process cannot move forward without the participation of the religious and traditional leaders'.

Therefore, neglecting or relegating ATR to an inferior position may cost Sierra Leoneans 'an essential component in the indigenous religious heritage', which constitutes 'a vital factor in the religious motivation and perception of Africans'.[6] In the spirit of justice, relations among these religious parties demand serious study. The issue of the place and inclusion of ATR in socio-religious cooperation in Africa and elsewhere is an ongoing concern among scholars. It is important at this point to briefly look at some of these works in an attempt to find relevant and helpful information for the place of ATR in the socio-religious landscape of Sierra Leone.

The work of Olupona,[7] contains essays dealing mostly with the issues and themes discussed at a conference hosted by the Council for World Religions (CWR) in Nairobi, Kenya, September 10–14, 1987 to discuss 'The Place of African Traditional Religions in Contemporary Africa'. The CWR conference was a response to the struggle and the degradation ATR continues to suffer from Islam and Christianity. It brought together scholars and religious leaders of three faith backgrounds to engage in a dialogue, in order to share ideas and discuss issues of common concern. This work is helpful in several ways, (1) it examines the constitution, structure, and significance of ATR as a dynamic changing tradition, (2) it analyses and interprets important aspects of African religion and explores its possible contributions to national development and the modernization process, and (3) it takes into consideration the impact of social change on African religion today.

Byaruhanga-Akiiki's paper, 'Africa and Christianity: Domestication of Christian values in the African church',[8] discusses some similar or parallel concepts and values between Christianity and ATR. There are valid cautionary notes when dealing with traditionalists in order to avoid the mistakes of missionary Christianity.

The recent work of Ikeogu Oke,[9] contains papers from the first International Congress of Dialogue on Civilizations, Religion and Cultures in West Africa that was held in Abuja, Nigeria, December, 2003 organised by UNESCO Inter-religious Dialogue Programme. The objective 'was to examine, through the lenses of Interreligious dialogue, such specific topics as sustainable development, situations of conflict or tension, and the HIV/AIDS pandemic'.[10] The papers proposed actions that should be considered 'if cultural and spiritual diversity is to benefit multicultural societies rather than hamper them'.[11] I will now look at these papers.

Monsignor Isizoh's paper is about the role religious leaders of Africa's three major religions – ATR, Christianity and Islam – can play to prevent or resolve conflicts.[12] 'Religious leaders' he stated, 'can get involved in resolving conflicts by acting on behalf of the marginalised and as the voice of the voiceless'.[13]

Adegbite, a Muslim scholar, presented a paper on 'The role of religious leaders in conflict resolution'.[14] He contends that religious diversity does not destroy the potency of religions. A careful look at the teachings of different religions, shows that there are many values they share in common.[15] He proposed that all practitioners 'must be taught the elements of their own religion as well as those of other faiths in their community'.[16] This would lead to a better understanding of and regard for other religions and would reduce fear.

'How to improve the relationship between Islam, Christianity and Traditional African Religion' is an essay by Prof. Abimbola.[17] He challenged the conference participants that, if they were serious about religious, ethnic and cultural harmony and peace, the topmost requirement 'is for the leadership of Islam and Christianity in Africa to accept the validity of Traditional African Religion . . . It is the stock-in-trade of the leaders of Islam and Christianity in Africa to put down Traditional African Religion, to look down on it, and not accept it as a valid religion'.[18] In his view, all the faiths of the world are valid. He pleaded with Christians and Muslims to put into practice the tolerance and respect they preach, by tolerating and respecting other religious faiths.

Prof. Ajayi's paper on 'Promoting religious tolerance and co-operation in the West African region: the example of religious plurality and tolerance among the Yoruba of south-western Nigeria',[19] discusses the example of peaceful coexistence among traditionalists, Christians, and Muslims in Yoruba land. Ajayi attributes the inter-religious tolerance and cooperation in Yoruba land to the tolerance inherited from ATR 'whose accommodation and tolerance paved the way for Islam and Christianity'.[20] There is no place, where 'tolerance and peaceful coexistence is exhibited more than in the accommodation and mutual coexistence of Traditional Religion, Islam and Christianity in Yoruba land'.[21]

In view of the long history of coexistence among the peoples of these faith traditions, and of the important role that ATR and its practitioners play in transforming the society and culture, and their impact on Christianity and Islam,[22] practitioners of these immigrant religions should make room for interfaith tolerance in Sierra Leone's socio-religious landscape.

# Notes to Appendix

1    M. B. Khanu, 'The Encounter of Islam and Christianity: A Case Study' (Diploma – Thesis, University of Hamburg, Germany, 2001), 56–7.

2    Ibid., 57–9.

3    Magesa, *African Religion*, 22.

4    Ibid., 3.

5    Mbiti, *Concepts of God*, xiv.

6    Sanneh, *West African Christianity*, 86.

7    Olupona, *African Traditional Religions*.

8    Byaruhanga-Akiiki, *Africa and Christianity*, 179–96.

9    I. Oke, ed. *Proceedings of the International Congress of Dialogue on Civilizations, Religion and Cultures in West Africa* (France: UNESCO, 2005).

10   Ibid., 27.

11   Ibid.

12   D. Isizoh, 'Managing conflicts in the African context: the role of religious leaders', in *Proceedings of the International Congress of Dialogue on Civilizations, Religion and Cultures in West Africa*, ed. I. Oke (France: UNESCO, 2005), 29–34.

13   Ibid., 33.

14   L. Adegbite, 'The role of religious leaders in conflict resolution', in *Proceedings of the International Congress of Dialogue on Civilizations, Religion and Cultures in West Africa*, ed. I. Oke (France: UNESCO, 2005), 35–6.

15   Ibid., 35.

16   Ibid., 36.

17   W. Abimbola, 'How to improve the relationship between Islam, Christianity and Traditional African Religion', in *Proceedings of the International Congress of Dialogue on Civilizations, Religion and Cultures in West Africa*, ed. I. Oke (France: UNESCO, 2005), 37–42.

18   Ibid., 37.

19   A. Ajayi, 'Promoting religious tolerance and co-operation in the West African region: the example of religious plurality and tolerance among the Yoruba of south-western Nigeria', in *Proceedings of the International Congress of Dialogue on Civilizations, Religion and Cultures in West Africa*, ed. I. Oke (France: UNESCO, 2005), 43–7.

20    Ibid., 44.

21    Ibid., 45.

22    Although Christianity and Islam are the religious traditions most Africans have converted over the century, many of these converts are influenced by ATR in their religious thoughts and expressions. They tenaciously retain elements of their traditional religious origins.

# Bibliography

Abdullah, I., ed. *Between Democracy and Terror: The Sierra Leone Civil War*. Dakar, Senegal: CODESRIA, 2004.

Abimbola, W. 'The Place of African Traditional Religion in Contemporary Africa'. In *African Traditional Religions in Contemporary Society*, edited by J. K. Olupona. St. Paul, Minn: Paragon House, 1991.

_____. 'How to Improve the Relationship Between Islam, Christianity and Traditional African Religion'. In *Proceedings of the International Congress of Dialogue on Civilizations, Religion and Cultures in West Africa*, edited by I. Oke. France: UNESCO, 2005.

Achtemeier, P. J. *HarperCollins Bible Dictionary*. New York, NY: HarperCollins Publishers, 1996.

Adegbite, L. 'The Role of Religious Leaders in Conflict Resolution'. In *Proceedings of the International Congress of Dialogue on Civilizations, Religion and Cultures in West Africa*, edited by I. Oke. France: UNESCO, 2005.

Adelowo, E-D. 'A Comparative Study of Angelology in the Bible and the Qur'an and the Concepts of Gods Many and Lords'. *Africa Theological Journal* 11 (1) 1982:151–67.

Ajayi, A. 'Promoting Religious Tolerance and Co-operation in the West African Region: The Example of Religious Plurality and Tolerance Among the Yoruba of South-western Nigeria'. In *Proceedings of the International Congress of Dialogue on Civilizations, Religion and Cultures in West Africa*, edited by I. Oke. France: UNESCO, 2005.

Akintunde, D. O. 'Women as Healers'. In *African Women, Religion, and Health*, edited by I. A. Phiri and S. Nadar. Maryknoll, NY: Orbis Books, 2006.

Alharazim, S. D. 'The Origin and Progress of Islam in Sierra Leone'. *Sierra Leone Studies* (21) 1930:13–26.

Alie, J. A. D. *A New History of Sierra Leone*. London: Macmillan, 1990.

Appiah-Kubi, K. 'Traditional African Healing System Versus Western Medicine in Southern Ghana: An Encounter'. In *Religious Plurality in Africa: Essays in Honour of John S. Mbiti*, edited by J. K. Olupona and S. S. Nyang. Berlin and New York: Mouton De Gruyter, 1993.

Asante, E. 'The Gospel in Context: An African Perspective'. *Interpretation: A Journal of Bible and Theology* 55 (4) 2001:355–66.

Awolalu, J. O. *Yoruba Beliefs and Sacrificial Rites*. London: Longman, 1979.

_____. 'The Encounter Between African Traditional Religion and Other Religions in Nigeria'. In *African Traditional Religions in Contemporary Society*, edited by J. K. Olupona. St. Paul, Minn: Paragon House, 1991.

Banton, M. P. *West African City: A Study of Tribal Life in Freetown*. Oxford: Oxford University Press, 1957.

Bauer, W. *A Greek-English Lexicon of the New Testament, and Other Early Christian Literature*. 2nd English ed. trans. and aug. by W. F. Arndt, F. W. Gingrich and F. W. Danker. Chicago and London: University of Chicago Press, 1979.

Bediako, K. 'Jesus in African Culture'. In *Emerging Voices in Global Christian Theology*, edited by W. A. Dryness. Grand Rapids, Mich: Zondervan, 1994.

Bourdillon, M. F. C. 'Witchcraft and Society'. In *African Spirituality: Forms, Meanings and Expressions*, edited by J. K. Olupona. New York, NY: Crossroad, 2000.

Byaruhanga-Akiiki, A. B. T. 'Africa and Christianity'. In *Religious Plurality in Africa: Essays in Honour of John S. Mbiti*, edited by J. K. Olupona and S. S. Nyang. Berlin and New York: Mouton De Gruyter, 1993.

Conteh, K. J. *A Short History of the National Pentecostal Limba Church: 1948–2001*. Freetown: Nabstech, 2002.

Cuthrell-Curry, M. 'African-Derived Religion in the African-American Community in the United States'. In *African Spirituality: Forms, Meanings and Expressions*, edited by J. K. Olupona. New York, NY: Crosssroad, 2000.

Danfulani, U. H. D. 'Pa Divination: Ritual Performance and Symbolism Among the Ngas, Mupun, and Mwaghavul of the Jos Plateau, Nigeria'. In *African Spirituality: Forms, Meanings and Expressions*, edited by J. K. Olupona. New York, NY: Crosssroad, 2000.

Davidson, J. 'The Doctrine of God in the Life of the Ngɔmbe, Congo'. In *African Ideas of God: A Symposium*, edited by E. W. Smith. London: Edinburgh House Press, 1966.

De Vaux, R. *Ancient Israel: Its Life and Institution*. Grand Rapids, Mich: Eerdsman, 1997.

Dorjahn, V. R. 'The Initiation and Training of Temne Poro Members'. In *African Religious Groups and Beliefs*, edited by S. Ottenberg. Folklore Institute, 1982.

———. 'Changes in Temnes Polygamy'. *Ethnology* 27 1988:367–390.

———. 'The Marital Game, Divorce and Divorce Frequency Among the Temne of Sierra Leone'. *Anthropological Quarterly* 63 (4) 1990:169–182.

Downes, R. M. *Tiv Religion*. Ibadan: Ibadan University Press, 1971.

Dymond, G. W. 'The Idea of God in Ovamboland, South-West Africa'. In *African Ideas of God: A Symposium*, edited by E. W. Smith. London: Edinburgh House Press, 1966.

Edet, R. N. 'Christianity and African Women's Rituals'. In *The Will to Arise: Women, Tradition, and the Church in Africa*, edited by M A. Oduyoye and M. R. A. Kanyoro. Eugene, Oregon: Wipf and Stock Publishers, 2005.

Eitel, K. E. 'Contextualization: Contrasting African Voices'. *Criswell Theological Review* 2 (2) 1988:323–4.

Erickson, M. J. *Introducing Christian Doctrine*. Grand Rapids, Mich: Baker Book, 1992.

Evans-Pritchard, E.E. *Nuer Religion*. Oxford: Clarendon Press, 1956.

Fanthorpe, R. 'Locating the Politics of a Sierra Leonean Chiefdom'. *Africa* 68 (4) 1998a:558–84.

_____. 'Limba "Deep Rural" Strategies'. *Journal of African History* 39 (1) 1998b:15–38.

Fanusi, L. 'Sexuality and Women in African Culture'. In *The Will to Arise: Women, Tradition, and the Church in Africa*, edited by M. A. Oduyoye and M. R. A. Kanyoro. Eugene, Oregon: Wipf and Stock Publishers, 2005.

Fashole-Luke, E. W. 'Ancestor Veneration and the Communion of Saints'. In *New Testament Christianity for Africa and the World: Essays in Honour of Harry Sawyerr*, edited by M. E. Glasswell and E. W. Fashole-Luke. London: SPCK, 1974.

_____. 'Introduction'. In *Christianity in Independent Africa*, edited by E. W. Fashole-Luke, R. Gray, A. Hastings and G. Tasie. London: Rex Collins, 1978.

Ferdinando, K. 'Screwtape Revisited: Demonology Western, African, and Biblical'. In *The Unseen World: Christian Reflections on Angels, Demons and the Heavenly Realm*, edited by A. N. S. Lane. Grand Rapids, Mich: Paternoster Press & Baker Book House, 1996.

Finnegan, R. H. 'Limba Religious Vocabulary'. *Sierra Leone Language Review* (2) 1963:11–5.

_____. '"Swears" Among the Limba'. *The Sierra Leone Bulletin of Religion* 6 (1) 1964:8–26.

_____. *Survey of the Limba People of Northern Sierra Leone*. London: Her Majesty Stationery Office, 1965.

_____. *Limba Stories and Story Telling*. Oxford: Clarendon, 1967.

_____. 'How to Do Things With Words: Performative Utterances Among the Limba of Sierra Leone'. *Man* 4 (4) 1969:537–51.

_____. 'Speech, Language and Non-literacy: The Limba of Sierra Leone'. In *Literacy and Orality: Studies in the Technology of Communication*. Oxford: Blackwell, 1988.

Fisher, H. 'Ahmadiyya in Sierra Leone'. *Sierra Leone Bulletin of Religion* 2 (1) 1960:1–10.

Fyfe, C. *A Short History of Sierra Leone*. London: Longman, 1979.

Fyle, C. M. *Alimamy Suluku of Sierra Leone, c. 1820–1906: The Dynamics of Political Leadership in Pre-Colonial Sierra Leone*. London: Evans, 1979.

_____. *The History of Sierra Leone: A Concise Introduction*. London: Evans, 1981.

Gittins, A. J. *Mende Religion: Aspects of Belief and Thought in Sierra Leone*. Steyler Verlag – Wort Und Werk, Nettenal, 1987.

Hackett, R. I. J. 'Revitalization in African Traditional Religion'. In *African Traditional Religions in Contemporary Society*, edited by J. K. Olupona. St. Paul, Minn: Paragon House, 1991.

Hargrave, C. G. *African Primitive Life: As I Saw It in Sierra Leone British West Africa*. Wilmington NC: Wilmington Printing Co., 1944.

Harris, W. T. 'The Idea of God Among the Mende'. In *African Ideas of God: A Symposium*, edited by E. W. Smith. London: Edinburgh House Press, 1966.

Harris, W. T. and Sawyerr, H. *The Springs of Mende Belief and Conduct*. Freetown: Sierra Leone University Press, 1968.

Hart, W. A. 'Woodcarving of the Limba of Sierra Leone'. *African Arts* 23 1989:44–53.

Hollenweger, W. J. 'Foreword'. In *Religious Plurality in Africa: Essays in Honour of John S. Mbiti*, edited by J. K. Olupona and S. S. Nyang. Berlin and New York: Mouton De Gruyter, 1993.

Hopgood, C. R. 'Concepts of God Amongst the Tonga of Northern Rhodesia (Zambia)'. In *African Ideas of God: A Symposium*, edited by E. W. Smith. London: Edinburgh House Press, 1966.

Houtman, C. *Exodus*. Vol. 1. Kampen: KOK Publishing House, 1993.

Idowu, E. B. *African Traditional Religion: A Definition*. London: SCM Press, 1973.

_____. *African Traditional Religion: A Problem of Definition*. London: SCM Press, 1977.

Ikenga-Metuh, E. *God and Man in African Religion*. London: Geoffrey Chapman, 1981.

Isizoh, D. 'Managing Conflicts in the African Context: The Role of Religious Leaders'. In *Proceedings of the International Congress of Dialogue on Civilizations, Religion and Cultures in West Africa*, edited by I. Oke. France: UNESCO, 2005.

Jell-Bahlsen, S. 'The Lake Goddess Uhammiri/Ogbuide: The Female Side of the Universe in Igbo Cosmology'. In *African Spirituality: Forms, Meanings and Expressions*, edited by J. K. Olupona. New York, NY: Crossroad, 2000.

Junod, H. A. *The Life of A South African Tribe*. Vol. 2. London: Macmillan, 1927.

Kailing, J. B. 1994. 'A New Solution to the African Christian Problem'. *Missiology: An International Review* 22 (4):489–506.

Kalu, O. U. 'Ancestral Spirituality and Society in Africa'. In *African Spirituality: Forms, Meanings and Expressions*, edited by J. K. Olupona. New York, NY: Crossroad, 2000.

Kandeh, J. D. 'Politicization of Ethnic Identities in Sierra Leone'. *African Studies Review* 35 (1) 1992:81–99.

Kastfelt, N., ed. *Religion and African Civil Wars*. New York, NY: Palgrave Macmillan, 2005.

Khanu, M. B. 'The Encounter of Islam and Christianity: A Case Study'. Diploma thesis, University of Hamburg, 2001.

King, F. J. 'Angels and Ancestors: A Basis for Christology'. *Mission Studies* 11 (1) 1994:10–26.

Little, K. L. 'The Role of the Secret Society in Cultural Specialization'. *American Anthropologist* 51 1949:199–212.

Lockyer, H. *All the Angels in the Bible: A Complete Exploration of the Nature and Ministry of Angels*. Peabody, Mass: Hendrickson Publishers, 1995.

Lucas, J. O. *The Religion of the Yorubas*. Lagos: CMS Bookshop, 1948.

Magesa, L. *African Religion: The Moral Traditions of Abundant Life*. Maryknoll, NY: Orbis Books, 1997.

Mbiti, J. S. *Concepts of God in Africa*. London: SPCK 1970.

_____. *The Crisis of Mission in Africa*. Mukono: Uganda Church Press, 1971.

_____. 'Christianity and African Culture'. *Journal of Theology for Southern Africa* 1 1977:26–40.

_____. 'Encounter of Christian Faith and African Religion'. *Christian Century* 97 (1) 1980:817–20.

_____. *Bible and Theology in African Christianity*. Nairobi: Oxford University Press, 1986.

_____. *African Religions and Philosophy*. London: Heinemann, 1989a.

_____. 'God, Sin, and Salvation in African Religion'. *Journal of the International Theological Centre* 16 (1) 1989b:59–68.

Mbon, F. M. 'African Traditional Socio-Religious Ethics and National Development: The Nigeria Case'. In *African Traditional Religions in Contemporary Society*, edited by J. K. Olupona. St. Paul, Minn: Paragon House, 1991.

McCulloch, M. *Peoples of Sierra Leone*. London: I.A.I, 1950.

Migeod, F. W. H. *The Languages of West Africa*. London: Gregg International, 1971.

Mugabe, H. J. 'Salvation From an African Perspective'. *ERT* 23 (3) 1999:238–47.

Mulago, V. 'African Traditional Religion and Christianity'. In *African Traditional Religions in Contemporary Society*, edited by J. K. Olupona. St. Paul, Minn: Paragon House, 1991.

Nadel, S. F. *Nupe Religion*. London: Routledge & Kegan Paul Ltd, 1954.

National Curriculum Development Centre. *Source Book for four Sierra Leonean Languages*. Freetown: Print Sundry and Stationers, 1993.

Niangoran-Bouah, G. 'The Talking Drum: A Traditional Instrument of Liturgy and of Mediation with the Sacred'. In *African Traditional Religions in Contemporary Society*, edited by J. Olupona. St. Paul, Minn: Paragon House, 1991.

Nyamiti, C. *African Traditional Religion and the Christian God*. Spearhead Eldoret, Kenya: Gaba Publications, n.d.

Oduyoye, M. A. 'Women and Ritual in Africa'. In *The Will to Arise: Women, Tradition, and the Church in Africa*, edited by M. A. Oduyoye and M. R. A. Kanyoro. Eugene, Oregon: Wipf and Stock Publishers, 2005.

Oke, I. *Proceedings of the International Congress of Dialogue on Civilizations, Religion and Cultures in West Africa*. France: UNESCO, 2005.

Okorocha, C. 'The Meaning of Salvation: An African Perspective'. In *Emerging Voices in Global Christian Theology*, edited by W. A. Dryness. Grand Rapids, Mich: Zondervan, 1994.

Olson, G. *Church Growth in Sierra Leone*. Grand Rapids, Mich: W. B. Eerdmans, 1969.

Olupona, J. K, ed. 'Introduction'. In *African Traditional Religions in Contemporary Society*, edited by J. K. Olupona. St. Paul, Minn: Paragon House, 1991.

Oosthuizen, G. C. 'The place of Traditional Religion in Contemporary South Africa'. In *African Traditional Religions in Contemporary Society*, edited by J. K. Olupona. St. Paul, Minn: Paragon House, 1991.

Opala, J. and F. Boillot. 'Leprosy Among the Limba: Illness and Healing in the Context of World View'. *Social Science and Medicine* 42 (1) 1996:3–19.

Opoku, K. A. 'African Traditional Religion: An Enduring Heritage'. In *Religious Plurality in Africa: Essays in Honour of John S. Mbiti*, edited by J. K. Olupona and S. S. Nyang. Berlin and New York: Mouton De Gruyter, 1993.

Ottenberg, S. 'Artistic and Sex Roles in a Limba Chiefdom'. In *Female and Male in West Africa*, edited by C. Oppong. London: George Allan, 1983.

_____. 'Two New Religions, One Analytic Frame'. *Cahiers d'Etudes Africaines* 24 (4) 1984:437–54.

_____. 'Religion and Ethnicity in the Arts of A Limba Chiefdom'. *Africa* 58 (4) 1988a:437–65.

_____. 'The Bride Comes to the Groom: Ritual and Drama in Limba Wedding'. *The Drama Review* 32 1988b:42–64.

_____. 'The Dancing Bride: Art and Indigenous Psychology in Limba Weddings'. *Man* 24 1989:57–78.

_____. 'One Face of a Culture: Two Musical Ensembles in a Limba Chiefdom Sierra Leone', edited by R. Antoine, *Carrefour de Cultures: Melanges Offerts a Jacqueline Leiner*. Tubingen: Gunter Narr Verlag, 1993.

_____. 'Male & Female Secret Societies Among the Bafodea Limba of Northern Sierra Leone'. In *Religion in Africa: Experience and Expressions*, edited by T. D. Blakeley, W. E. A. van Beek and D. Thomson. London: Heinemann, 1994.

_____. *Seeing With Music: The Lives of Three Blind African Musicians*. Seattle: University of Washington Press, 1996.

_____. 'Stories and Storytelling: The Limba'. In *African Folklore: An Encyclopedia*, edited by P. M. Peek and K. Yankah. London: Routledge, 2004.

Packer, J. I, Tenney, M. C., White, W. Jr., eds. *The Bible Almanac*. Nashville: Thomas Nelson Publishers, 1980.

Parrat, J. *Reinventing Christianity: African Theology Today*. Grand Rapids, Mich: Eerdmans, 1995.

Parrinder, E. G. *African Traditional Religion*. London: Sheldon, 1962.

_____. *Witchcraft: European and African*. London: Faber and Faber, 1963.

_____. 'Theistic Beliefs of the Yoruba and Ewe Peoples of West Africa'. In *African Ideas of God: A Symposium*, edited by E. W. Smith. London: Edinburgh House Press, 1966.

_____. *African Mythology*. London: Paul Hamlyn, 1967.

_____. *Africa's Three Religions*. London: Sheldon, 1969.

Parsons, R. T. *Religion in an African Society*. Leiden: E.J. Brill, 1964.

_____. 'The Idea of God Among the Kono of Sierra Leone'. In *African Ideas of God: A Symposium*, edited by E. W. Smith. London: Edinburgh House Press, 1966.

Plog, F. and Bates, D. G. *Cultural Anthropology*. 2nd ed. New York, NY: Alfred A. Knopf, 1980.

Rajotte, F. with E. Breuilly. 'What Is the Crisis?' In *Christianity and Ecology*, edited by E. Breuilly and M. Palmer. New York, NY: Cassell Publishers, 1992.

Richards, P. *Fighting for the Rain Forest: War, Youth & Resources in Sierra Leone*. Oxford: James Currey, 1996.

_____. 'Green Book Millenarians? The Sierra Leone War Within the Perspective of an Anthropology of Religion'. In *Religion and African Civil Wars*, edited by N. Kastfelt. New York, NY: Palgrave Macmillan, 2005

Sanneh, L. *West African Christianity: The Religious Impact*. Maryknoll, New York: Orbis Books, 1983.

_____. *Piety and Power: Muslim and Christians in West Africa*. Maryknoll, New York: Orbis Books, 1996.

_____. 'A Resurgent Church in a Troubled Continent: Review Essay of Bengt Sundkler's *History of the Church in Africa*'. *International Bulletin* 25 (3) 2001:113–15.

Sawyerr, H. 'Ancestor Worship II: The Rationale'. *The Sierra Leone Bulletin of Religion* 8 (2) 1966:33–9.

_____. *Creative Evangelism: Towards a New Christian Encounter With Africa*. London: Butterworth, 1968.

_____. *God, Ancestor or Creator: Aspects of Traditional Belief in Ghana, Nigeria and Sierra Leone*. Harlow: Longmans, 1970.

_____. *The Practice of Presence: Shorter Writings of Harry Sawyerr*. Grand Rapids, Mich: Eerdmans, 1996.

Schreiter, R. J. *Constructing Local Theologies*. Maryknoll, NY: Orbis Books, 1985.

Setiloane, G. M. 'Traditional World-View of the Sotho-Tswana'. In *Christianity in Independent Africa*, edited by E. W. Fashole-Luke, R. Gray, A. Hastings and G. Tasie. London: Rex Collings, 1978.

_____. *African Theology: An Introduction*. Cape Town and Johannesburg: Blackshaws (Pty) Ltd, 1986.

Shaw, R. 'Gender and the Structuring of Reality in Temne Divination: An Interactive Study'. *Africa* 55 (3) 1985:286–303.

_____. 'The Politician and the Diviner: Divination and the Consumption of Power in Sierra Leone'. *Journal of Religion in Africa* 26 (1) 1996:30–55.

Skinner, D. E. 'Mande Settlement and the Development of Islamic Institutions in Sierra Leone'. *The International Journal of African Historical Studies* XI (1) 1978:57–8.

Smith, E. W., ed. 'The Whole Subject in Perspective'. In *African Ideas of God: A Symposium*. London: Edinburgh House Press, 1966.

Stevenson, R. C. 'The Doctrine of God in the Nuba Mountains'. In *African Ideas of God: A Symposium*, edited by E. W. Smith. London: Edinburgh House Press, 1966.

Sullivan, L. E. 'Preface'. In *Christianity and Ecology*, edited by D. T. Hessel and R. R. Ruether. Cambridge, Mass: Harvard University Press, 2000.

Sunberg, C. *Conversion and Contextual Conceptions of Christ: A Missiological Study Among Young Converts in Brazzaville, Republic of Congo*. Lund, Sweden: Team Offset and Media, 2000.

Taylor, J. V. *The Primal Vision: Christian Presence Amid African Religion*. London: SCM Press, 1963.

Tienou, T. 'The State of the Gospel in Africa'. *Evangelical Missions Quarterly* 27 (2) 2001:154–62.

Turay, A. 'Missionary Work and African Society: James Booth in Tonko Limba'. *African Research Bulletin* 7 (2) 1977:36–54.

Westermann, D. *Languages of West Africa*. London: Oxford Press, 1952.

Wicker, K O'Brien. 'Mami Water in African Religion and Spirituality'. In *African Spirituality: Forms, Meanings and Expressions*, edited by J. K. Olupona. New York, NY: Crossroad, 2000.

Wyse, A. *The Krio of Sierra Leone: An Interpretive History*. London: C. Hurst & Co., 1989.

Yambasu, S. J. *Dialectics of Evangelization: A Critical Examination of Methodist Evangelization of the Mende People in Sierra Leone*. Accra, Ghana: AOG Literature Centre, 2002.

Zuesse, E. M. 'Divination and Deity in African Religion'. *History of Religion* 15 1975:158–82.

_____. 'Perseverance and Transmutation in African Traditional Religions'. In *African Traditional Religions in Contemporary Society*, edited by J. K. Olupona. St. Paul, Minn: Paragon House, 1991.

# Index